Building Analytics Teams

Harnessing analytics and artificial intelligence
for business improvement

John K. Thompson

BIRMINGHAM - MUMBAI

Building Analytics Teams

Producer: Dominic Shakeshaft
Acquisition Editor – Peer Reviews: Suresh Jain
Content Development Editor: James Robinson-Prior
Technical Editor: Saby D'silva
Project Editor: Tom Jacob
Copy Editor: Safis Editing
Proofreader: Safis Editing
Indexer: Rekha Nair
Presentation Designer: Sandip Tadge

First published: June 2020

Production reference: 1260620

Published by Packt Publishing Ltd.
Livery Place
35 Livery Street
Birmingham B3 2PB, UK.

ISBN 978-1-80020-316-7

www.packt.com

Pack<t>

packt.com

Subscribe to our online digital library for full access to over 7,000 books and videos, as well as industry leading tools to help you plan your personal development and advance your career. For more information, please visit our website.

Why subscribe?

- Spend less time learning and more time coding with practical eBooks and Videos from over 4,000 industry professionals
- Learn better with Skill Plans built especially for you
- Get a free eBook or video every month
- Fully searchable for easy access to vital information
- Copy and paste, print, and bookmark content

Did you know that Packt offers eBook versions of every book published, with PDF and ePub files available? You can upgrade to the eBook version at www.Packt.com and as a print book customer, you are entitled to a discount on the eBook copy. Get in touch with us at customercare@packtpub.com for more details.

At www.Packt.com, you can also read a collection of free technical articles, sign up for a range of free newsletters, and receive exclusive discounts and offers on Packt books and eBooks.

In Praise of

Thomas H. Davenport, Distinguished Professor, Babson College and Research Fellow, MIT Initiative on the Digital Economy, author of *Competing on Analytics* and *The AI Advantage*:

"Much has been made of the data scientist as the hero of analytics and AI, but John Thompson reminds us in this book that the key unit of analytical performance is the diverse and integrated team. Successful analytics require a multifaceted set of tasks in a well-managed process, and Thompson knows how to make it work. His deep experience comes through on every page."

Judith Hurwitz, President and CEO, Hurwitz & Associates:

"John's deep expertise and real-world experience adds depth to this excellent book. The focus on best practices is an essential to the success of leaders in advanced analytics."

Bill Schmarzo, Chief Innovation Officer, Hitachi Ventara:

"]ohn's new book is designed to prepare business executives for the hard and grueling job of building an analytics-centric organization. As I would expect, John does not pull his punches as his book details the processes and even more importantly, the analytic mindset that must be transformed in order to exploit the customer, product, and operational value buried in an organization's data. John's book is the most detailed, real-world "roadmap" I've read for organizations that want to become analytics-driven. But, as John points out so well, this will not be an easy journey and requires a management team with the fortitude to see it through. But for those organizations who can follow the roadmap and see the transformation through to the end, great fortune awaits!"

Kirk Borne, Principal Data Scientist, Data Science Fellow, and Executive Advisor at Booz Allen Hamilton:

"If you are reading this now, that means you are living through the most dynamic period of innovation and technological revolution in history. This 4th industrial revolution is triggered by, fueled by, and sustained by massive flows of data. Data flows into, across, and out of organizations worldwide at the speed of light, that is, at the speed of hyperconnected people, processes, and products, capturing their behaviors, contexts, influences, and outcomes. This intensely needed book by John Thompson helps executives and managers set up analytics teams for business value creation, operational effectiveness, and mission success. The fundamental requirement on these analytics teams is to assist and maintain the forward progress of business at the lightning speed of data. The various components of data-intensive operational business systems are covered tactically and strategically in this book: analytics culture, advanced analytics project management, team dynamics, and right-sized artificial intelligence deployments. Competitive advantage is now a moving target and insufficient for survival; dynamic market leadership is essential. With this book, executive leaders and analytics teams will be guided to develop sustained, strategic, and even revolutionary advantage from massive data flows through advanced analytics and AI centers of excellence."

Foreword

Over the past couple of decades, analytics, for the most part, has evolved from groups of report writers somewhat resembling "typing pools" from days gone by to an assortment of organizational and operating models requiring a wide range of technical and business skills. Few have been witness to, or incited, these advancements more than John Thompson.

But at the same time, in *Building Analytics Teams: Harnessing analytics and artificial intelligence for business improvement*, you can sense John's palpable impatience at how so many enterprises continue to take old-school approaches to analytics, or latch onto the latest technology trends with nary a thought given to the necessary introduction of organizational change and team-based approaches. This is where this book differs from others you may have read... or skimmed hoping to find the answers.

As John's and my hometown legend Michael Jordan once quipped, "There's no I in TEAM, but there is in WIN." Analytics has become a team sport, and such teams require strong leadership to win at it. And just as any player on any winning team will tell you, the organization is bigger than just the players. It starts at the top and goes down to the support personnel. With this mindset, John shares his decades of experience, not just in building high-functioning analytics teams, but also in bringing along the entire organization, from the top down.

Moreover, the book thankfully skips past the banality of building basic **business intelligence** (**BI**) solutions and focuses exclusively on advanced analytics such as data science and **artificial intelligence** (**AI**). As those of us who have been in the business long enough have come to realize, pretty pie charts, beautiful bar charts, and dashing dashboards rarely move the needle on the business.

Over the past several years, I personally have compiled a compendium of over 500 real-world examples of high-value and innovative analytics. Only a handful of these stories were the result of some simplistic hindsight-oriented analytics. Instead, for the most part they involved teams of data curators or "wranglers," data integration professionals, statisticians or data scientists, and visualization experts with an unrelenting passion and unwavering executive support—in pursuit of proving hypotheses, performing root-cause diagnostics, predicting customer and market behavior, and prescribing strategic and operational actions.

Sure, these kinds of projects had an IT component, but they were not IT projects by any means. And if you had any doubt before reading this book as to whether analytics projects belong in the IT department or not, John makes it abundantly clear that they do not. Indeed, it is this straddling of the domains of data, technology, and business that makes analytics projects particularly challenging, and difficult to get right. Especially the contemporary tug-of-war between the traditional and emerging roles of the Chief Information Officer (CIO), Chief Data Officer (CDO), and Chief Analytics Officer (CAO) can create all sorts of unproductive drama. And the often-speculative nature of analytics, that is, hypothesis generation and testing and retesting, can render even the most seasoned leader scrambling for ways to justify projects up-front. Then there's the issue of actually implementing the results. "Mr. Iknowbetter" and "Ms. Thatsnothowwevealwaysdoneit" always seem to appear at the moment when it's time to start applying the new analytics insights.

Organizations are rife with disparate assortments of personas, which for the novice manager can seem to present roadblocks for analytics projects. Yet John shares not only how to understand these personas, but how to harness them inside and outside the immediate analytics team. While "diversity" and "inclusion" may be the HR buzzwords du jour, John goes beyond the bromide to explain precisely how individuals from different personal and professional backgrounds can coalesce into high-functioning and innovative analytics teams—including, as he notes, hiring bright young people without preconceived notions of what cannot be done. Additionally, the book details different approaches to team operating models such as "factory," "artisanal," and "hybrid" models, and the pros and cons of each, along with sound advice on creating and managing an analytics **center of excellence** (COE).

While reading this book, I found myself sorrowful for the thousands of analytics leaders who have struggled over the years without this kind of experiential wisdom at their fingertips. At the same time, I'm excited for today's and tomorrow's analytics leaders who, upon reading this book, will surely become the "I" in "WIN" for their organizations.

Douglas B. Laney

Principal, Data & Analytics Strategy, Caserta

Contributors

About the author

John K. Thompson is an international technology executive with over 30 years of experience in the business intelligence and advanced analytics fields. Currently, John is responsible for the global Advanced Analytics and Artificial Intelligence team and efforts at CSL Behring.

Prior to CSL, John was an executive partner at Gartner, where he was a management consultant for market-leading companies in the areas of digital transformation, data monetization, and advanced analytics. Before Gartner, John was responsible for the advanced analytics business unit of the Dell Software Group.

John is coauthor of the bestselling book *Analytics: How to Win with Intelligence*, which debuted on Amazon as the #1 new book in Analytics in 2017. *Analytics: How to Win with Intelligence* is a book that guides non-technical executives through the journey of building an analytics team, funding initiatives, and driving change in business operations through data and applied analytical applications.

John's technology expertise includes all aspects of advanced analytics and information management, including descriptive, predictive, and prescriptive analytics; artificial intelligence; analytical applications; deep learning; cognitive computing; big data; data warehousing; business intelligence systems; and high-performance computing.

One of John's primary areas of focus and interest is creating innovative technologies to increase the value derived by organizations around the world.

John has built start-up organizations from the ground up and he has reengineered business units of Fortune 500 firms to enable them to reach their full potential. He has directly managed and run sales, marketing, consulting, support, and product development organizations.

He is a technology leader with expertise and experience spanning all operational areas, with a focus on strategy, product innovation, growth, and efficient execution.

John holds a Bachelor of Science degree in Computer Science from Ferris State University and an MBA in Marketing from DePaul University.

Acknowledgments

- To my wife, Jennifer; as she knows, I would have never written one book, let alone multiple books, without her encouragement, guidance, and support. She knows before I do what I need to do and should do, and even more importantly, she moves me to the realization without letting me know that she was the one who helped me arrive there. She is kind, gentle, fiercely intelligent, and the most caring person I have ever known. Thank you, Jennifer, for over 25 years of love and support. Here's to 25 more!

- To my daughter, Kathryn, who shows me the beautiful confluence of her deep intelligence and incredible creativity each day. I am continually impressed by your insights, energy, and wide range of interests, talent, and verve. I enjoy our conversations and time together immensely. Thank you for your love and support.

- To my son, Zachary; your steadfast determination and unwavering efforts in moving forward the things in your life that you set your mind on is impressive to me. I look to you for inspiration when my motivation starts to flag. You are fun, witty, and a great joy to be around and with. Thank you for your love and support.

- To Tom Davenport; I have no doubt that you agreeing to write the foreword for my previous book, *Analytics: How to Win with Intelligence*, played a significant role in its success. Thank you for agreeing to contribute to my initial foray into becoming an author, and thank you for all the conversations and meetings we have had, which have inspired me to put my thoughts forward on how analytical projects, technologies, and teams should be built, managed, and grown to achieve measurable and substantial change in the world. Thank you.

- To my best friend of over 40 years, Joseph Pistrui; we have had some incredible times and great fun. Thank you for being there through thick and thin. Your perspectives, ideas, and guidance have been invaluable to me personally and professionally. Your steadfast attitude and insights have moderated some of my more radical ideas and adventures. Thank you for your gentle guidance and insights. Thanks, buddy.

- Special thanks to John Whittaker for contributing his time, experience, and insights as a peer reviewer. John's unique perspective enriched and improved the book during the editing process. Thanks, John.

About the reviewer

John Whittaker is a business leader, entrepreneur, and subject matter expert on leveraging emerging technology. His experience includes leadership of software, technology, and information management businesses at world-class organizations such as Dell, Quest Software, and Persistent Systems. Additionally, he has participated in building successful information security, e-commerce, and data analytics-driven products businesses from start-up through mergers, acquisitions, and IPO. John graduated with high honors from Biola University with a Bachelor of Science in Organizational Leadership and earned an MBA at Chapman University's Argyros School of Business and Economics in Southern California. John currently resides in Austin, TX, with his wife of 28 years, Rachel, and has two adult children, Alison and Matthew, and a son in law, Sean Summers, who live in California.

Acknowledgement and special thanks to John Thompson for the opportunity to have participated in his creative process for this book and for being a great friend, leader, and collaborator. Additional thanks and acknowledgement to the impressive partners, bosses, mentors, and leaders who gave me an incredible opportunity to learn and grow professionally with their guidance and example (in reverse chronological order): Chris O'Conner, Anand Deshpande, Sandeep Kalra, Mritunjay Singh, Tom Kendra, Michael Dell, John Swainson, Matt Wolken, Steve Dickson, Tim Leyden, Jon Sullivan, Mario Leone, John Taylor, Chris Andreozzi, Ron Fikert, Maria Cirino, Roger Eld, Jeff Basford, Pete Ellis, Ray Pollum, and Gene Lu.

Prologue

While writing this book, the COVID-19 pandemic has emerged and has been spreading across the world. It is a global phenomenon that has infected hundreds of thousands of people, killed thousands, and has wiped trillions of US dollars from the markets around the world. This is a health crisis of epic proportions. The scale of the human tragedy is difficult to comprehend, and many lives will be ended, and multiples of that number will be irrevocably altered. My thoughts and condolences go out to all who have lost a loved one, friend, colleague, or acquaintance.

I wish I could be assured that this is a once-in-a-lifetime event, but I am confident that it is not; the analyst in me says that it will not be the last pandemic that I experience in my lifetime. I am not one to be a pessimist or a Cassandra, but I would feel remiss if I attempted to lead anyone down the path of believing that these types of events will not happen again in the foreseeable future.

I will not spend much time on the failures of leadership in multiple countries, the US included, but I do want to point out that data and analytics has a positive, predictive, and preventative role to play in this unfolding human drama and in future health events.

Timely, accurate, and widely available data on infections, propagation, treatments, supplies, climate, recovery, human demographics, temperature readings, quarantines, self-isolation, government-mandated actions, and more is required to enable anyone who has the skills and interest to produce insights that can help stop the spread, understand the behavior of people before and after infection, and communicate to the public in a timely and informed manner.

The world needs all types of related and non-related data captured, stored, annotated, and made available to individuals, academics, researchers, corporations, and governments. We also need the aforementioned analytics professionals to share and publish their findings quickly and globally.

Data, speed, and transparency are our allies in this battle and all future challenges that face humanity. The behaviors that will not serve our higher good are keeping data to ourselves or our individual companies, not publishing findings that illuminate an element of the pandemic or the unfolding situation, not converting to the production of materiel that can help fight the virus or other future foes, and not being proactive and taking steps that seem like they might be an overreach at the time. There are other behaviors that we must avoid, but I am not trying to be exhaustive, merely illustrative.

What should we as analytics professionals and organizations be doing? We should be sharing our data, expertise, and analytical capabilities. We should be looking for a way to help locally, regionally, nationally, and globally. We need to be forward and outward looking to help our families, friends, and all of humanity in any way we can. This too shall pass, but it will not be the last time. Data and analytics can and will help, but not without our proactive and engaged effort. Let's be a community that is a force for good, for the development of insights, and for the proactive and swift end to suffering. We as an analytics community have the tools; now we need to show the will to be engaged.

TABLE OF CONTENTS

Chapter 3: Managing and Growing an Analytics Team . . . . ·93

Chapter 4: Leadership for Analytics Teams 125

Preface

This book is for senior managers and executives who are contemplating hiring, or have already made the commitment to hire and manage a team of individuals with the purpose of designing, building and implementing applications and systems based on advanced analytics and artificial intelligence.

Who this book is for

This book is intended for senior executives, senior and junior managers, and those who are working as part of a team that is accountable for designing, building and delivering business success through advanced analytics and artificial intelligence systems and applications. Having at least 5 to 10 years of experience in driving your organization to a higher level of efficiency will help you to fully understand the material covered.

What this book covers

Chapter 1, An Overview of Successful and High-Performing Analytics Teams, sets the stage and describes the fundamental organization and principles involved in building and managing an analytics team.

Chapter 2, Building an Analytics Team, discusses and describes who to hire, how to construct and manage a team, and the building blocks of beginning analytic operations.

Chapter 3, Managing and Growing an Analytics Team, begins the discussion of engagement with other parts of the organization. The chapter delves into engaging functional managers, creating internal interest and beginning the cadence of building analytical applications.

Chapter 4, Leadership for Analytics Teams, outlines how to lead an analytics team and how to represent analytics leadership to the organization.

Chapter 5, Managing Executive Expectations, provides an overview of and guidance on how to engage with C-level executives to gain their support, buy-in, and funding for analytics teams, projects, and a corporate wide analytics engagement and process.

Chapter 6, Ensuring Engagement with Business Professionals, describes the best way to engage with functional business leaders and managers to gain their support and to ensure that they guide their teams to engage in the analytics process.

Chapter 7, Selecting Winning Projects, outlines the process of selecting projects and the optimal method of building a portfolio of projects for each team member and the team as a whole.

Chapter 8, Operationalizing Analytics – How to Move from Projects to Production, outlines the pitfalls and problems associated with moving from a project mode into a production cycle. The chapter describes how to move through and past the challenges in a successful manner.

Chapter 9, Managing the New Analytical Ecosystem, discusses how to manage the organization and the analytics team in a manner that enables the team to continue to innovate while supporting the growing body of analytical applications and models that are built and deployed.

Chapter 10, The Future of Analytics – What Will We See Next?, outlines what we can expect to see in analytics in the coming years.

To get the most out of this book

- This book can be read as a guide to establishing and building an analytics function and has been written as if the reader would read the book from beginning to end to learn about the particular requirements of building an analytics team.

- The book can also be used as a reference guide that can be put on the shelf and referred to over time as challenges and obstacles present themselves.

- The book is most valuable and useful to people who are:
    - ○ planning to start the process of building a new analytics function in a corporation
    - ○ evolving an existing analytics function from one structural and operational type to another.

Download the color images

We also provide a PDF file that has color images of the screenshots/diagrams used in this book. You can download it here: `https://static.packt-cdn.com/downloads/9781800203167_ColorImages.pdf`.

Conventions used

Bold: Indicates a new term or an important word.

Get in touch

Feedback from our readers is always welcome.

General feedback: If you have questions about any aspect of this book, mention the book title in the subject of your message and email us at `customercare@packtpub.com`.

Errata: Although we have taken every care to ensure the accuracy of our content, mistakes do happen. If you have found a mistake in this book we would be grateful if you would report this to us. Please visit, www.packtpub.com/support/errata, selecting your book, clicking on the Errata Submission Form link, and entering the details.

Piracy: If you come across any illegal copies of our works in any form on the Internet, we would be grateful if you would provide us with the location address or website name. Please contact us at copyright@packt.com with a link to the material.

If you are interested in becoming an author: If there is a topic that you have expertise in and you are interested in either writing or contributing to a book, please visit authors.packtpub.com.

Reviews

Please leave a review. Once you have read and used this book, why not leave a review on the site that you purchased it from? Potential readers can then see and use your unbiased opinion to make purchase decisions, we at Packt can understand what you think about our products, and our authors can see your feedback on their book. Thank you!

For more information about Packt, please visit packt.com.

INTRODUCTION

This book is intended for senior managers and executives who are contemplating or have made the commitment to hire and manage a team of individuals with the stated purpose of designing, building, and implementing applications and systems based on advanced analytics and artificial intelligence. If you believe that this objective can be accomplished in a year or less and can be achieved cheaply, do not buy this book. You should stop reading, cancel your current plans, and save your money.

Making a commitment to drive your organization to a higher level of effectiveness and efficiency is what you are doing. Just as if you were deciding to build a state-of-the-art factory or if you and your team were entering into a completely new market or geographic region of the world – if you do not have a multiyear view, then you should seriously reconsider undertaking this journey.

In this introductory section, we will walk through the process of succeeding in the analytics journey from beginning to end. We will assume that you are just starting to consider building a team, selecting projects, succeeding and failing at those projects, learning from those failures, moving from a development and test mode environment to a production mode environment, evolving from manual or traditional digital processes to data-driven, analytically enriched processes that improve with time, and undertaking the related and resulting organizational change management initiatives that are required to actualize the value realization that you planned for when you started this journey; and, of course, managing the executive expectations of the scale of investment, the scope of change, the speed at which the return on investment will be realized, and the realities associated with becoming an analytically driven organization. This set of steps comprises the "macro" process of an organization becoming analytically driven.

Becoming data and analytically driven

One of the mindset changes as well as the organizational process changes that is required to be successful in this journey is that by becoming a data and analytically driven organization, you at some point realize that the organizational change you seek is never "done." This process is evergreen and ever changing.

Along with the "macro" process of organizational and mindset change, there is a "micro" process of evolving and changing in response to the needs, wants, and desires of customers, patients, the market, the environment, suppliers, investors, stakeholders, and competitors. From the perspective of the middle of the processes as described, these processes at the execution level are usually described, organized, and discussed as projects. The larger overall process is typically made up of projects that focus on a specific objective or goals, but the overall process is dynamic and ever changing. If you, your leadership, and your organization want to be part of this continual evolution, then your organization, data operations, and analytical models and processes need to be set up and organized in a way that accounts for and reacts to the constant collection of relevant data inputs, updates and tests the models being developed and deployed, monitors execution and performance, and refreshes the analytical contents and models at the appropriate time and cycle.

One of the pitfalls that most organizations fall prey to is to think that the projects are the process – they are not. The projects are the execution mechanism. The projects are important for organization, management, funding, tracking, and reporting, but the projects are the trees. The forest is the organizational commitment to being analytically driven, the desire to continually improve, the interest in being open to new data and the evolution of the market, services, competition, consumers, patients, and stakeholders. The forest is the strategy to be a market leader. Do not lose sight of the forest for the trees.

An analytical mindset

For those readers who are analytics professionals, let's draw an analogy. Advanced analytics models are trained on data. The data represents the world or the subject area at the time that the data was collected. Once the model is trained and that model is accurately "predicting" *the* characteristics of the subject area as represented by the training data, the model is "locked." By locking the model, we end the training phase and we move the model into production.

The model ingests and examines data in the operational world and predicts the information that we are interested in. But we all know that the world changes and so does the data that is the byproduct of those activities. The models must be updated or retrained using current data to ensure that the models are generating predictions based on data that is as close to the current state of the world as possible. We "unlock" the model and train it again using new data. The model now predicts based on the new frame of information. The model continues to track the evolution of changes in the operational world through these cycles of training and production through its operational life cycle.

People are like analytical models, but sadly, the great majority of people lock their mental models and rarely, selectively, or not at all do they open those mental models to update their views to align with the new reality of the world. This is one of the primary reasons why people are called "out of touch" or clueless.

Let's, as a group, keep in mind that the world and all the phenomena in it evolve and change. Just because we were exposed to a set of norms, technologies, cultural constructs, and other conditioning when we were growing up, that does not mean that we cannot retrain our models to include new norms and activities. We do not need to throw away the old, but we can include the new and have a richer view, a more inclusive view of the world. Let's unlock and retrain our mental models frequently.

Thank you for indulging that brief detour. Let's now return to discussing and describing the "macro" process, or having an analytics strategy.

The essence of being analytically and data-driven is to be dynamic and guided by empirical evidence and measurable factors. Some of the most successful companies are organized and operate in this manner and have done so for years, but now the speed and pace of change have made this way of operating an imperative rather than a nice-to-have for firms that want to be at the top of their league tables.

Building an analytics team and an environment for collaboration

You will need to hire a leader. You will need to empower and fund that leader to hire and lead a team. I refer to this team as the **Advanced Analytics and Artificial Intelligence Center of Excellence** (**AA&AI COE**). The COE leader and team will need to learn the broader organization and to build a network of collaborators, sponsors, and allies. This new network, which we will refer to as the **Community of Practice**, or **COP**, will span the entire organization and global operations. If your organization numbers in the thousands, the AA&AI COE will be less than 50 staff members within the first two years and the COP will be a few hundred in number.

The most recent COP that I built took approximately a year to reach critical mass and was made up of between 400 and 500 staff members spanning the globe, including every operational department in the company. I stopped counting after the first 14 months, but, in the first year, I held over 600 introductory meetings. To be clear, I did not meet with 600 hundred people, no, I met with well over 1,500 people – I had 600 meetings and some of the meetings were with 20 to 50 people.

I traveled to every continent and spent much of my time on the road and in discussions with executives, managers, and people who should be involved.

The primary objectives of those meetings were to:

- Communicate and convince executives, senior managers, managers, and individual contributors that they should collaborate with the AA&AI COE team and the other staff members in the COP

- Communicate that the AA&AI COE team was established to help them understand and develop analytics to drive their operations forward in the manner that they dictate

- Empower their staff members to join the COP and to join projects in conjunction with the AA&AI COE staff to develop analytical applications, models, and new ways of reaching higher levels of effectiveness and efficiency

- Let them know that we were not there to judge their ideas and current state of operating, but to help them see how data and analytics will help them reach and exceed their operating goals

- Improve employee engagement and remove the tedious parts of staff members' duties to enable those staff members to focus on the more creative aspects of their work that leverages their experience and expertise

Collaborators in the analytics journey

Let's define the taxonomy and naming of the collaborators that we will discuss and describe in the book and work with on our analytics journey. I will be referring to executives as sponsors, because they typically set the direction and control funding and staffing for their organization.

Also, I will be referring to managers as stakeholders, as they typically own the headcount that is needed to collaborate with the AA&AI COE staff. And finally, I will be referring to the staff members of the operational departments as subject matter experts. The AA&AI COE leadership, data scientists, data engineers, data visualization experts, and others cannot be successful without the full-throated support of sponsors, stakeholders, and subject matter experts. A transparent and trust-based relationship between all parties is crucial to our joint success.

I have explained in keynote speeches, fireside chats, articles, white papers, meetings, books, and more that AA&AI will change jobs, and in the process eliminate certain jobs and job content, but the process is to take the robotic work out of a given job and enable people to focus on higher-value work and tasks. Our objective is not to take jobs away from people and give those jobs to robots. It is to make work more engaging and fulfilling for people.

The new AA&AI COE and the COP network will need resources and funding. The executive leadership of the organization will need to publicly support the related data and analytics initiatives.

Selecting successful projects

At this point in the process, the analytics leadership and the AA&AI COE team can begin to discuss and select an operational area or areas to partner with to begin to evaluate options for analysis and possible operational improvement. The AA&AI COE will discuss the potential areas for improvement with the operational or line-of-business executives and teams. The discussion and selection of areas for examination and improvement through data and analytics sounds like it should be straightforward and encounter little to no contention in the process, but even in the most apolitical organizations, this is not the case.

Organizational dynamics

Executives and senior managers will span the range of behaviors, from exuberant and public support to actively attempting to block projects and progress.

Building the AA&AI function and capability in an organization will be seen by some as an opportunity to grab more budget or funding and to create a larger organization or empire. You, as the executive sponsoring or building this new capability, need to be aware of this dynamic and ready to evaluate the motivations and abilities of these managers. It is entirely possible that these existing managers may understand data and analytics and have the experience, expertise, and knowledge of how to be successful in the macro and micro processes described earlier in this introduction. If that is the case and you believe in them, then the organization has a head start in the process, but if they do not have the requisite experience and knowledge, and they think that the success that they have had in other, possibly only tangentially related, areas or projects will propel them to success in this venture, then your efforts will have a tumultuous start.

The premise of this book is that undertaking the journey to build an organization or organizational function/capability to be analytically and data-driven is unique and different in many respects. In my personal experience, it has been proven to be the case numerous times. Handing this process to people who have little to no direct experience is a mistake and it will prove to be so nearly 100% of the time. One of my animating and driving factors for writing this book is to help you avoid this fate and failure the first time, not the second or third time.

If this is truly the first time that an organization is engaging in building systems and applications based on advanced analytics and artificial intelligence, then the number of potential areas for improvement will be numerous.

There will be no shortage of opportunities to improve the business and realize significant returns that exceed most of the existing investment returns in the corporate project portfolio.

In this environment, one of the challenges will be to convince the executives and managers that the initial returns being calculated and communicated are real and can be realized. In this case, the hype is true. Systems and applications based on AA&AI will change all aspects of work and operations, if companies have the fortitude to hire and engage AA&AI teams, to let the new AA&AI COE team members engage with sponsors, stakeholders, and subject matter experts in the existing operational areas and lines of business, and the organization has the breadth of vision to know that being analytically and data-driven means changing how the firm operates in all aspects of the organization. If these conditions are true and exist in earnest, you are truly lucky and should set to work immediately. The stars have aligned, and your journey will, mostly, be smooth as you set off on your path.

If you are fortunate, and I have been fortunate in most of the organizations I have engaged with, you will have one or two, or maybe a handful, of executives and senior managers that will step forward and jump into the analytics process with full commitment. They will tell their teams that the AA&AI COE is to be considered part of their team and that they want to attack vexing problems and not to change only at the margin of operations, but that they want to change operations at the core. They want to use data and analytics as a competitive tool to best the competition.

These are the people who will be promoted in 18 to 24 months based on the risk they took with you and your team. I am happy to say that over the past 3 decades, my teams have helped multiple people move up in their careers. Those sponsors have gone out on a limb for us and we have delivered for them, their teams, their organizations, and, in some cases, their higher aspirations.

You will be supported by the sponsors and pioneers that we just mentioned, while you will be opposed by the naysayers, Luddites, and those that want to abscond with your funding and team. After you, your AA&AI team, and the pioneers and their teams deliver groundbreaking functionality, operational improvements, and significant returns in the first year to 18 months, a portion of the opposition will convert to supporters. These are the people who jump on the bandwagon or get in front of the parade once success is guaranteed. Welcome them for the time being; if the tide turns in the future, they will turn against you in a heartbeat. They are not allies, but can be useful when the time is right. The naysayers and Luddites will always oppose you, your team, and your agenda. Be polite, be kind, and roll over them with success.

To close the discussion of organizational dynamics and politics, if the organization numbers in the thousands, spans the globe, and is committed to improving through the use of data and analytics, your team of a handful of people cannot deliver on every possible area of improvement. There are two areas of augmentation of your capabilities that you should support and actively promote.

Competitive advantage or simply staying competitive

First, you should consider outsourcing certain projects to competent, capable, and proven third parties. The projects to be considered are those that others in your industry have completed and are now considered tables stakes to be competitive at the new level of efficiency and effectiveness that the industry operates at or that the market, customers, suppliers, and patients demand. Projects like inventory management, supply chain efficiency, or designing servicing maps for optimal territory coverage by a sales team – these are projects that have been successfully executed across numerous industries with well-known and published success stories.

Find an experienced third party with a long track record of success and outsource the project. Of course, you need competent team members to manage the project, but you do not need analytical professionals to manage this relationship and process. To be clear, you cannot wash your hands of the project either. The project will need oversight and analytical validation, which you and your team will need to provide, but daily supervision is not required on your part.

Second, you should support the operational areas that want to invest in business intelligence, descriptive statistics, and small-scale predictive analytics. Your team cannot do it all, but your team can help these functional areas hire the right staff members, undertake initial projects, and consult on predictive and prescriptive applications in the future. Helping the organization build a broader and deeper capability is part of your responsibility and it will build a network of supportive team members who aspire to grow in their skills and abilities and may be good candidates to join the AA&AI COE in the future. It can only help your cause and ease your journey to build an ecosystem of talent that the organization pays for and nurtures that could become the future talent for your team.

The core collaboration/innovation cycle

Once sponsors have committed their teams to the process of improvement through data and analytics, and candidate areas for improvement have been selected, then the AA&AI COE team and the functional team (that is, the sponsors, stakeholders, and subject matter experts) can begin to analyze the operational area, the processes, the data, the organizational resistance to change, and the feasibility that the required data exists today and in a historical form. The AA&AI COE team can explain to the functional team the analyses that will be experimented with and undertaken and the analytical pipeline and models that will be developed.

The functional team will need to understand the process changes, the new mode of operating, and the resulting changes to their personnel needs and daily functions.

After a common understanding of the area to be analyzed and improved through data and analytics has been developed, the functional team and the AA&AI COE team can begin to gather data, build pilot environments, and discern whether the hypothesis developed to this point in the process is possible and probable. There is a non-trivial chance at this point in the process that the hypothesis will be proven to be incorrect and/or the data required will not be available in the quantities and historical depth needed to build reliable models. There are several reasons why the pilot could prove that this path will not drive measurable or significant business value or not be technically feasible.

Let's assume, for the sake of our discussion, that the pilot project delivers measurable results and it appears that a robust analytical model (or models) and a revised and improved operational process that includes the analytical pipeline and model(s) can be designed and implemented. In addition to the data being available, we have the legal and ethical right to use the data for the stated purposes, the functional team and leadership remain in their roles, and the senior and executive leadership remain committed to the effort. In short, all the organizational contextual factors remain constant or at least supportive of the effort we are undertaking.

With the pilot project complete, the probability of a prototype being technically successful is reasonably possible, the organization remains committed, and funding continues, now the AA&AI COE team can begin to collaborate with the functional team to build a full-scale prototype system or application to prove that the system will work as designed and deliver reliable analytical results to the operational team members who will use the production output to change decisions and reach a higher level of productivity, efficiency, and effectiveness.

Once the prototype has been built and tested, then it is time to begin to talk about how to implement the next iteration of the data flows, analytical models, governance systems, process changes, and end user interaction systems to realize the benefit of all the work that has been completed to date. It is very difficult to state this next fact, and even harder for most readers to believe it, but this is where most efforts fail. We will explore the numerous reasons why many analytic projects fail at this point later in our discussion in *Chapter 8, Operationalizing Analytics – How to Move from Projects to Production.*

Let's assume that the process does not fail, so now is the time to build data feeds for production systems, prepare the routine and regular processes to move from analytical modeling in test environments to inserting and refreshing analytical models in production systems, and prepare functional teams to understand the changes that will be required from them to support the newly modified production processes.

Focusing on self-renewing processes, not projects – an example

Perhaps a concrete example can ground our discussion to make it clearer and more understandable where we stand in the overall process and the pitfalls that face the combined analytical and functional teams.

Let's use the example of retail store site selection. Before the widespread use of data and analytics, organizations had site selection teams that performed research on the proposed region, markets, and neighborhoods; visited prospective locations; scouted sites; and spent time talking with local business people, local governing bodies, landlords, real estate agents, brokers, and others. They compiled briefing books on the various options and made presentations to management regarding their process and the locations that the site selection team felt were the best bets. This process could take weeks to months to possibly years.

Why is this traditional process not optimal and why does this type of process drive urgency in a dangerous way?

Most of the data collected in this type of process is static and refers to a particular point in time. Revising the supporting analyses can take weeks or months due to the need to go back to source systems and people. There is a sense of urgency in the process, which is a good thing, but in many of these cases, the sense of urgency is because the analysis, the possible target location, and the conditions of the analysis have an expiration date.

What do I mean by an expiration date? Much of the work executed was executed as a project. The datasets were gathered at a point in time; the conversations were all relevant to the day, and maybe the weeks, in which they took place; and the prospective location may be of interest to numerous buyers for multiple purposes. The relevancy and timeliness of the data and the analyses derived from the data begins to age and deteriorate in value the day it is complete. The main objective of the project is to select a site. The selection needs to be made relatively quickly or the work that was done will become out of date or stale. If too much time has elapsed, the data gathering, creation of the analyses, and the evaluation of the potential sites will need to be done again to ensure that the conditions as understood are still valid. Urgency for the sake of ensuring that the conditions remain as outlined in a report is not a good reason to move quickly.

What does the new process look like when augmented with data and analytics?

The overall process for the most part remains the same from a structural perspective. The site selection teams perform research on the proposed region, markets, and neighborhoods, visit locations and scout sites, and spend time talking with local businesspeople, local governing bodies, landlords, real estate agents, brokers, and others.

But the differences are as follows:

- The new store site selection application is built to automatically receive updated data from all relevant sources when those sources are updated. All data is always up to date and ready to use without additional effort from the AA&AI COE team or the functional team.

- The first activity that a site selection team undertakes is to run a model that analyzes all relevant data on current income, demographics, unemployment, similar store sales for the competition and for industry comparators, same-store sales in the organization's current operations, and any other relevant factors that the company has decided have an impact on the success of new locations. The site selection team will run this model for the entirety of the target country, not just the local area for the potential new store.

- The application provides the ability to simulate and optimize the entire network of stores and considers cannibalization of the company's existing stores by new stores, competitive market entry, and store closings. The effect of competitive and own network activity, such as pricing changes, marketing campaigns, changes in operating hours, and more can easily and quickly be modeled and examined.

The site selection team is now examining strategic store network considerations rather than trying to decide where to put a store. The cycle of iteration given the new application has a span of minutes rather than days or weeks. The site selection team can consider thousands of scenarios before they present a single plan.

Simulations and optimization work literally has no limits. The team can run millions or billions of scenarios if they choose to. This is how an **artificial intelligence** (**AI**) model or environment learns how to win at games like chess or Go, and in the new world of online multiplayer games, an AI application runs billions of games or simulations of games to determine how to win. This application for selecting a site is no different.

The site selection team, armed with the simulated optimal plan, will present to senior or executive management their recommendations. Now, if the team is truly confident, and they should be, and the senior or executive management is interested and engaged, and they should be, the meeting should not be a static presentation. The meeting should start with a presentation of the optimal plan but should evolve into an open discussion where varying objectives are proffered, discussed, and run through the site selection application in real time.

Senior management and executives will have contrasting and possibly conflicting views of what "optimal" means to them as individuals and to their functional areas of the company. The site selection team, supported by the AA&AI team, should be able to sit with the senior managers and executives and model the varying scenarios described by the attendees, and the application should run in real time so that results are presented in seconds. This iterative and interactive process enables the group to explore ideas and scenarios and optimize for the objectives that are most important to the operating results of the company in that moment.

What is different between the two processes? Previously, the site selection team was picking a site. After the collaboration with the AA&AI COE team, the site selection team models overall network changes at the store and program levels for the company.

The site selection team can now consider direct and indirect competition, including ancillary market factors such as shipping, unemployment rates, and income levels, along with other macro-economic factors. The site selection team can run billions of scenarios and execute real-time collaboration with senior and executive management to optimize the overall objectives of the company. Together, they can model the entire network to examine the impact of changing the operational plan to determine where to expand the store network before making any physical or operational changes. Only a small change...

That is the overall process you are considering, or possibly have undertaken, or maybe taken a swing at and are recalibrating your efforts. It doesn't matter which of those conditions are true – this book is a guide for you. A guide to help you understand best practices, to learn about pitfalls, and to shortcut your way to success.

This process has been executed exceptionally well by some and incredibly poorly by others. In some cases, the same person or team has done both! I have done both.

Summary

I hope that after reading this introduction, your interest has been sparked and that you are intrigued about how to execute and drive the analytics process forward in your profession and in your organization. The process will not be quick, it will not be easy, and in some parts of the process, you will not enjoy it, but it won't be dull, it won't be boring, and you will always be learning. If you are a lifelong learner, and the chances are good that if you have read this far you are, a career in analytics is one of the most fulfilling careers you can choose.

People continually ask me something along the lines of, "Analytics is such a hot and current field, how did you find yourself in it so many years ago?" My response is typically something like, "I am a lifelong learner. I live to learn new things. Not just things about data and analytics, but I do love learning about those topics too. I love to learn about everything – ethics, physics, math, credit risk evaluation, failure rates of PC hardware, human behavior while in distress, pricing dynamics, volunteering rates, retail merchandising mix modelling, and more." I go on to ask, "What other career can you be working on a credit risk evaluation application in the morning and discussing the optimal flow of oil through a plant that manufactures mayonnaise in the afternoon?" Most of the people I am interacting with say something along the lines of "None that I know of." And they are right; no other profession feeds lifelong learning and curiosity like analytics.

For those who are insatiably curious about our world, the universe, all aspects of human behavior, and more, analytics is the place to be. Welcome to the journey. I hope that you find this book useful, valuable, and fun to read.

I look forward to interacting with you soon at an event, online, or over the telephone.

All the best,

John

AN OVERVIEW OF SUCCESSFUL AND HIGH-PERFORMING ANALYTICS TEAMS

"Say something once, why say it again?"

—David Byrne

Introduction

Given that we are just starting our journey together to explore the topic of this book—*the building, managing, and ongoing success of high-performing advanced analytics teams*—let's ensure that we are on the same page. Let's take a moment to set the stage, to synchronize our understanding of what we will be examining and discussing in this book.

My primary motivations in writing this book are to:

- Serve fledgling and experienced front line managers in the field of advanced analytics by helping them avoid mistakes of the past and to assist them in taking the appropriate paths to building sustainable and synergistic teams that can and will engage productively in the exciting process of building these new levels of machine intelligence, and

- Help senior managers and executives understand the investments needed, the timelines required, the problems that can be addressed, and the value to be derived from including talented teams and appropriate managers and management in their organizations.

Throughout this book, we will be talking about teams involved in building advanced analytics and artificial intelligence systems. These are systems that learn and improve over time. We are not talking about static business intelligence applications, dashboards, or reports that outline, visualize, or describe the past. No matter how often a dashboard is refreshed, even a real-time interactive dashboard is still a representation of the past.

Throughout our dialog and this book, the terms *advanced analytics* and *artificial intelligence* will be used interchangeably. For clarity, advanced analytics is a broader term encompassing the practice and use of statistics, machine learning, simulation, and optimization. Artificial intelligence refers to machine learning and other analytical approaches that learn from data over time.

In this book, our discussion of advanced analytics systems will encompass analytical applications, individual models, ensembles of models, systems, platforms, and cloud, on-premises, and hybrid environments.

Our discussion will also outline analytical applications, models, and environments that are built on and utilize the following analytical techniques: descriptive statistics, Bayesian approaches, mathematical principles and theories, **artificial intelligence (AI)**, **machine learning (ML)**, simulation, and optimization. Our discussion of advanced analytics will be as broad as possible.

Don't worry—this is a non-technical treatment of the topics. We will not delve into the finer points of ML or any of the subject areas listed here. If you are interested in the technical details of any of these fields, there are numerous consultants, experts, pundits, academic papers, presentations, conferences, symposia, books, and classes that you can engage with to enrich and deepen your technical knowledge. There are too many organizations and events to list or refer you to, but for a solid overview, you might want to start your line of inquiry by using online learning platforms like Coursera, Udacity, or Udemy. Given that those platforms are aggregators from some of the premier universities from across the United States and around the world, you will find much of what you seek from a technical perspective on those platforms.

A few words about what we will not be discussing or what advanced analytics and AI is not. We will not be exploring the topic of sentient machines or artificial general intelligence. These areas of development and topics are interesting to me, and many people, but they are more in the realm of science fiction at this point. We will be focused on the topics of building an analytics function in your organization and how to build and manage a high-performance team. Advanced analytics applications are focused on describing, predicting, prescribing, simulating, or optimizing the immediate present or the future. Artificial intelligence systems are dynamic; they are like a rocket in that they are always off course, but continually course correcting. The teams that build these systems know this.

They know that they are building living and live systems. They know that they must consider a staggeringly wide range of scenarios. They know that the systems that they build can dramatically improve business operations and, in the end, the results of those operations.

Let's start to examine in detail the factors and forces that are affecting advanced analytics in the general market, looking at jobs created, technological evolution, level of success achieved, public perception of the value of advanced analytics, government regulations, and more.

The future of jobs and AI

The impact AI will have upon employment is a widespread topic of discussion in the popular, technical, and industry press and among employers, employees, and thought leaders.

The question I am asked in almost every internal and external presentation that is attended by more than a handful of people is something like, "How many and what type of jobs will be eliminated by AI?"

The first few times I was asked this question, I brushed it off with a brief answer, assuming that it was a passing curiosity by the person asking the question and there was no real concern or emotion behind the inquiry. I was wrong in that regard.

This question is on the minds of many people and it is weighing on people as a real concern. In the past year, I have been asked the same or similar questions in presentations and discussions in Australia, United Kingdom, Germany, Switzerland, and the United States.

Rather than continuing to brush aside the question, I have started answering the question with one of the many studies that has proven, again and again, that AI and related technologies and systems are net job creators in the short and long term. Let's examine a few of those recent studies.

AI is an engine of job creation

One of the relevant studies is from the World Economic Forum's Center for the New Economy and Society, *The Future of Jobs Report, 2018*. The report includes research and findings that illuminate and explain the detailed job changes that are expected to be seen, country by country, on a global basis. The report suggests that the new jobs created will be significantly larger in number than those eliminated, and those new jobs will be higher paying and have a more secure future.

"A 2018 report from the World Economic Forum (WEF) even suggested that, while we may displace 75 million jobs globally by 2022, we'll create a net positive of 133 million new ones. The WEF believes — with the current data in mind — that robots and algorithms will improve the productivity of existing jobs and create several new ones in the future. Perhaps future workers won't get a job — they'll create their own. No amount of angry hand waving or puerile legislation can stop this. We cannot even begin to fathom some of the otherworldly technologies and new career fields that'll one day arise." [1]

I have experienced this exact dynamic in the workplace. In one instance, people were hired to execute a rather dull and rote process in the finance department to move data from one system to another. The people hired were young, smart, eager, and willing to learn. They discovered that the organization had licensed **robotic process automation** (**RPA**) software.

The young staff members took it upon themselves to learn the software and become proficient in automating the repetitive processes, thereby eliminating the jobs that they were hired to do. Did they lose their jobs? Yes. Did the company recognize their initiative and talent? Yes. What do they do now? They automate manual processes across the company.

Now, the company has fewer openings, and no-entry level staff members to execute manual data movement, but the firm now has a number of open positions around the world for entry-level staff members to build automated data movement processes in RPA software. Previously, the data entry roles were lower paying, dead end jobs with few to no development paths or planned ways to move up in the organization. Now, the jobs are entry-level analyst roles with higher pay and a planned path to a better job and an explicit development plan.

I am aware that the previous example is not an AI case, but many organizations cannot grasp the leap to AI without taking an easier first step in an area like process automation.

As a manager or executive who is interested in and wants to drive change, you must be aware of the ability of your organization to understand, enact, fund, and assimilate change. You may want the organization to begin operating like a top tier firm in relation to advanced analytics and AI, but the organization may be run by fast followers, laggards, or even worse, luddites.

Keep in mind and look closely at the people who are the senior executives in the firm; how did they get to their positions and how long have they been in the firm? More than likely, they will be the gating factor in how quickly the organization changes and how the organization changes.

I am betting that once you take a close look at these people, you may want to recalibrate your ambitions regarding the timeline to achieve success with AI and related technologies.

Many jobs will never be changed by AI

Numerous people ask me if there are any jobs that will not be automated out of existence by AI. Rather than asking this question, I think it is more insightful and helpful to ask, "Why are there so many jobs today that have not been automated away?"

The essence of the problem can be found in Polanyi's Paradox. Michael Polanyi, a British-Hungarian philosopher, stated, given that *"We can know more than we can tell, we shouldn't assume that technology can replicate the function of human knowledge itself."* [2]

We humans operate on and with a substantial amount of tacit knowledge that we have a very difficult time expressing to other people. One of the core elements of automating a task or replacing a person with AI is that we need to understand and describe what the job entails at a sufficiently detailed level, in order to replicate the job with automation tools and/or with AI. Without this ability, we cannot automate the task and we certainly cannot expect AI to undertake the work. One timely example can be summed up as, just because a computer can know everything there is to know about a car, doesn't mean it can drive it.

In late 2019, Rob May posited a related idea. In reality, advanced analytics will create whole new industries, or at least subsegments of industries, where people who can afford the services will seek out human curated goods and services that have a high degree of creativity and customization. These services and goods will be sought after because they contain an element of elegance or personalization that is only possible through the involvement of human thought, expression, and craftsmanship. [3]

Regarding the jobs created in the aforementioned category, there will not be a significant number of jobs that will move the employment numbers in any one country, and there is no hard data to back up this claim, but I do believe that May is correct in his core assertion. AI will not create deeply personal experiences.

AI will predict outcomes and it will make operations more effective and efficient, but it will not deepen most, if any, experiences for people. The lesson to learn from this example is that there are a number of market segments that will be created for industrious people. With these, they will serve firms and individuals in ways that are made more valuable by being in opposition to the mass change created by AI.

These types of jobs and businesses will be small, but the prestige and expense of engaging with these firms will be extremely high. These firms and offerings will be the opposite of Amazon, Walmart, and other firms that operate high-velocity, low-margin businesses. The offerings from these companies will be deeply personal, highly connected, coveted, limited, and very expensive.

If AI will create more jobs, let's prepare for those jobs

In my view, the bottom line on employment is that AI will create and enrich jobs in a net positive manner on all accounts. In some cases, maybe not the job you have today but there will be lots more jobs available because of AI.

AI will drive change in the job market. Foundationally, the changes will be that the rote and robotic elements of jobs will be automated away, and those elements will be accomplished through software and hardware. A relevant and salient aspect of automation and the enablement of systems through advanced analytics is that humans and machines are good at different sets of tasks. Jobs will lose the robotic and mechanistic elements of work and they will gain, or become more focused on, the elements that people are good at, tasks like creative thinking, writing, presenting, and collaborating.

Gartner, the technology and analyst firm, maintains that:

"AI Will Create 2.3 Million Jobs in 2020, While Eliminating 1.8 Million. The number of jobs affected by AI will vary by industry; through 2019, healthcare, the public sector, and education will see continuously growing job demand while manufacturing will be hit the hardest.

*Starting in 2020, AI-related job creation will cross into
positive territory, reaching two million net-new jobs in
2025. In 2021, AI augmentation will generate $2.9 trillion
in business value and recover 6.2 billion hours of worker
productivity." [4]*

Jobs will evolve and AI will drive that evolution

My experience with job evolution is a personal one. I started out
working for my father as an automotive mechanic. I moved on to
working on farms and eventually, I ended up running mills, drill
presses, and lathes in factories that fed the automotive and defense
industries in rural Michigan. As a teen, I saw that jobs were being
eliminated and families were in distress as the old manufacturing
base in Michigan was contracting. It is unlikely if you are reading
this book that you or your children are working in these types of
jobs, but the changing dynamic of work that we are discussing in
this book is the same dynamic that I was faced with when I was
18 years old.

We need to be aware that when economists conclude there
is no evidence of overall job losses that can be directly attributed
to any one technology or market evolution, including AI, they are
talking at a global, macroeconomic level. Of course, the effects
of AI and automation will differ from region to region and from
country to country.

Sean Fleming, Chief Economist of the World Bank, remarked
that:

*"This has been mostly as a result of the use of robotics
and automation in the manufacturing sector, which has
displaced large numbers of workers. In some cases, those
former manufacturing workers have found employment in
the service sector.*

But there are also pockets of left-behind communities in parts of the developed world, where several generations of families are adjusting to life without work." [5]

At the macro level, there will be more jobs and better jobs for workers and employees, but let's not gloss over the fact that real change will occur, and is underway. A recent study found that a growing proportion of manufacturing jobs now require a college degree:

"More than 40% of manufacturing workers have a college degree today, according to a Wall Street Journal analysis of workforce data. That's up from 22% in 1991. If growth continues at the same pace, college-educated manufacturing workers will overtake the number of workers with a high school degree or less within the next few years, the Journal found." [6]

People around the world need to be aware that change is constant, and it has been this way for generations. It is hard to look forward and determine the jobs that will be in demand in 20 to 40 years. Yes, I did mean 20 to 40 years. If you are reading this book, it is highly probable that you will not be working in 20 to 40 years, but your children and perhaps their children and the staff members that you are mentoring will be working. You want to be able to help them, to counsel them on where the future is heading, and this will be in relation to employment and a fulfilling and engaged career.

Looking decades out into the future is challenging for some and invigorating for others. I vividly remember telling my mother that I was quitting my solid and reliable job as an automotive mechanic at a local Ford dealership to attend college, to study a new field called computer science. Her response was, "You are ruining your life." It was hard for her to look out into the future.

Luckily for me, I ignored her advice and counsel. Now, my son, who recently graduated with a degree in computer science, and our daughter, who is studying data science and user experience design, joke, "Those computers, I think that there is a future in working with them." Each time we say it, we laugh and smile knowingly.

AI and data serve us, not the other way around

Another dynamic to keep in mind, at least in the United States, is that the social safety net is not in place to take care of everyone's economic needs in full. For the most part, people in the United States will have to work longer and, in many cases, they will not have the traditional or historical retirement at the end of a fixed number of working years. Finding work that is intellectually stimulating, engaging, and that will not be automated away or redesigned to eliminate human involvement will continue to present an enormous challenge for everyone.

Remember the old saying, find something that you love to do, and you will never work a day in your life. Hackneyed, but there is a kernel of truth in that statement. If you enjoy or love what you do, you will engage in it almost effortlessly, it will not tire you out, you will do it for longer, and you will have the zeal to evolve the role to fit the needs of the market today and in the future. When I think of my work and profession through this lens, I can see being involved in the market and industry for another 20 to 40 years, and still being passionate about my work and contribution.

I worked at IBM in the 1990s. My manager was Dave Carlquist. Dave was, and is, smart and driven, and possesses substantial emotional intelligence, far more than I have or will ever have. Years later, I was waiting to board a flight in Chicago's O'Hare airport. We were all standing there looking at our phones, and I looked up, and Dave was standing next to me. I smiled and poked him with my elbow.

Dave looked up and we laughed and started to catch up on the events of the intervening ~15 years. We were about to board the plane and Dave said to me, "You know, when you were going on and on about how data and analytics were going to be the lifeblood of all organizations, I thought that you were out of your mind." I smiled and said, "Not out of my mind, just early to the party."

These societal, economic, and technological factors and trends point out that the following are useful premises to keep in mind:

1. Human creativity will not be taken over by AI; in fact, just the opposite will be true. Human creativity will be more valued and valuable in the future.

2. Collaboration between people cannot be automated away. Again, just the opposite will be true. Technology will facilitate better collaboration, but the essence of effective collaboration will become more valued and valuable.

3. Communication skills in all forms will become crucial and more valuable.

4. **User experience (UX)** design and construction, the interface between technology and people, will become more important. The UX will become paramount in the engagement of people with systems, applications, and platforms.

5. Advanced analytics and AI developers will be in high demand.

6. AI will make simple, transactional interactions more efficient, but will do little to enrich sophisticated, nuanced interactions.

7. The technology roadblocks that we face today, and some of the very recent past, like the efficiency of machine learning models to be effectively trained, computing capacity, natural language processing, quantum computing, and a wide array of other issues, will be solved in the near future.

Change is constant – aim as far as you can see

The farm job that I had when I was 16 doesn't exist anymore, but there are farmers and farm workers who are working each day to bring food to the market. Farming is a widely varied industry. From artisanal, organic family farms to large corporate organizations running farming operations, farming still exists, but for some, it is not the farming that their grandparents were engaged in, and for some people, that is a loss, but not an inevitable outcome.

Find what you are passionate about, look far into the future, find the intersection of the two, or the multiple relevant intersections of trends and evolving markets that you care about, and work toward them. Listen to everyone who wants to give you advice, even if you'll ignore most of it. You will find your path and you can help others find theirs.

Employment is a very personal experience. There will continue to be the need for employees, managers, executives, entrepreneurs, innovators, and solo agents. Look decades out into the future. Think about what excites you, what the essence of the value is that you bring today and how you might want to bring even more value in the coming weeks, months, years, and decades to come. Continue to learn, engage, and guide people forward, and you will have a long and exciting career.

Let's turn our attention to the future and where opportunity lies for broad sections of the population and general workforce.

The future is long – there is much work to be done

Being deeply involved in the evolution of data, analytics, and learning systems for over 30 years, I never seriously believed, and do not believe, that AI systems will outright replace most humans in the realm of work.

The idea that people will be replaced by software across a wide range of industries in a short time period—causing despair, depression, and loss of motivation and engagement across societies—will not happen. There are people across the world who are prone to fearmongering and have an interest in furthering the dialog at the extreme end of the spectrum. Software that provides process automation and enables predictions will not replace entire industries in the short term.

In my first book, *Analytics: How to Win with Intelligence*, I wrote:

> *"It has taken 50 years to completely automate transactional systems. It has also taken about 50 years to build out the first layer of information management systems, and we have not completed that ecosystem yet.*

> *Looking 10 to 15 years in the future, we foresee having very sophisticated and automated modeling, data preparation, and model management systems. During that time, we will also continue evolving the math and analytical techniques used. For such systems, we have typically approached horizontal problems first – marketing effectiveness, customer loyalty, manufacturing quality, cyber security, and so on. It will take another 20 to 30 years to perfect these systems.*

> *Somewhere in that time window, we will start to build vertical applications for specific industries, such as automotive, healthcare, pharmaceutical, energy, security, and telecommunications. This will be a long, complex process.*

> *Thus, in total, we foresee between 90 to 120 years' worth of work before we complete our analytics journey. Obviously, we have much to do, but thankfully the work has been both interesting and engaging." [7]*

Given the difficulty we have seen in the market for self-driving cars and related technologies, I stand by my prediction that we will not see widespread deployment of AI-based platforms that will cause significant job transformation and reformulation until 2150.

If you were counting on the creation, provision, and delivery of universal basic income due to losing your job to an AI system, you will be very disappointed. Best to keep your skills sharp and keep going to work each day. For nearly every advanced analytic system that my teams and I have built, we have worked with the subject matter experts and their teams after the implementation, and the employees are happier and are focused on higher-value work. Moreover, the humans often take credit for the better decisions being made that are either completely the work of the analytical model, or substantially supported by the output of the applications and/or models. No one ever complains about being on target more often through the augmented workflow of the human/AI collaboration. And the AI system never asks for credit, so it works out well for all involved.

In my personal experience, there is a significant amount of mundane and boring work to be automated away, and a corresponding amount of critical thinking and higher-level decisions to be made every day. These higher-level decisions remain in the remit of human cognition.

Learn and leap

"The lessons of technological innovation remind us that progress always entails thinking the unthinkable and then doing things that were previously impossible," Tim O'Reilly, the founder and CEO of O'Reilly Media, says in chapter 15 of his most recent book, *WTF?: What's the Future and Why It's Up to Us*. That's why he's optimistic that technology will augment, not replace, jobs. But, he says, "learning will be an essential next step with each leap forward in augmentation." [8]

In their new book, *Augmented Intelligence: The Business Power of Human–Machine Collaboration,* authors Judith Hurwitz, Henry Morris, Candy Sidner, and Dan Kirsch define augmented intelligence in this way:

> *"...beyond artificial intelligence, there is augmented intelligence, which can significantly transform how we can leverage knowledge, artificial intelligence (especially machine learning), and various tools that support advanced analytics. So, what is augmented intelligence? Augmented intelligence is an approach that uses tools from artificial intelligence to perform well-defined tasks, such as those that are part of decision making. But for augmented intelligence, the human works in collaboration with the machines. Humans need to evaluate the results of automated tasks, make decisions in non-routine situations, and also assess if and when the data must be changed due to changing business needs and demands." [9]*

We are on an evolutionary journey in developing and deploying artificial intelligence systems. A few facts will help set the stage as to the global effort in developing systems with advanced analytics and AI:

> *"According to Evans Data Corporation, there were 23 million software developers in 2018, this number is expected to reach 26.4 million by the end of 2019 and 27.7 million by 2023. 29% of developers worldwide were using some form of AI or ML as of 2018 and an additional 5.8 million are expected to start using AI or ML within the next 6 months." [10]*

The number of people who are developing these systems may seem like an overwhelming army of people toiling away, in every company imaginable, to automate away every job possible. This is not the case. While there are a significant number of developers working with AI and the number is growing, the majority of those developers are just beginning to experiment with AI-based technologies. And while AI and advanced analytics as a general topic garners an outsized amount of coverage from the press and pundits, we are in the early stages of a long journey.

Let's recap the main points discussed up to this point. AI will have an effect on jobs—it will actually, in all likelihood, create more jobs than it eliminates, but we need to be aware that these new jobs will be different and require higher-level skills than the jobs that are replaced. AI will augment and extend existing jobs. The idea that AI will eliminate jobs is overblown; in most cases, AI will remove the mundane aspects of work and allow people to focus on elements of work that call on more creative and subjective skills. Jobs have been evolving since the creation of work. AI is just another factor in that continuing evolution. AI is different and it has the potential to drive wide-ranging changes, but it is just another factor in the evolution of work.

To bring this process of job evolution into sharper focus, let's outline a recent example. One of my teams built a forecasting application, which we will discuss in greater depth in *Chapter 8, Operationalizing Analytics – How to Move from Projects to Production*. In relation to the operational staff who were employed to update and run the previous version of the forecast in a spreadsheet-based system, all of them were rendered unnecessary by the new forecasting application. Did all those 30+ people lose their jobs? No, they did not. Rather than having the staff manually obtain data, clean data, and load the data into a spreadsheet, the employees were retrained to be business analysts.

They went from being spreadsheet managers to analysts. Their job composition changed from 80% data management to 75% business analytics. Their new jobs are harder to learn, but pay more, are more secure, and provide for more job advancement and mobility. Now, the challenge is for the employer to retain them, given their newly acquired analytics skills. This is a much better place for the employees to be in from a career perspective, and the employees are more valuable to the employers. Everyone wins.

Now that we have discussed the potential impacts of AI upon jobs, and how those jobs can evolve into more secure and fulfilling jobs, let's consider another area where AI could bring major changes: the global education system.

AI in the education system

Over a decade ago, I was asked by the university where I did my undergraduate degree to review their new curriculum for teaching students the skills needed to be a business analyst. My input centered on the fact that there were no courses to impart communications skills and emphasize teamwork in the program. Reviewing the current course catalog, it appears that the suggestions I offered were added and remain in the program, and now, Ferris State University offers a program referred to as Data Analytics. [11]

I have spoken with administrators and staff members at the University of Illinois, Oklahoma State University, and the University of Michigan about data science, teaching data science, and preparing students for the changing world of data, data science, advanced analytics, and artificial intelligence. Clearly, my sample is small and limited to the university staff that I have been able to meet and talk with personally. What I have seen and observed is that teaching data science is being done most effectively and creatively outside the colleges of engineering. Engineering, unfortunately, has, in general, been slow to respond to the opportunities provided by AI.

The old...

The engineering curriculums are time tested and proven to produce graduates who excel in the disciplines required to be a successful engineer in the chosen field of study; fields like chemical engineering, civil engineering, mechanical engineering, electrical engineering, and many more. However, to be successful at the global, societal, national, and company levels, we need more qualified professionals than all the engineering schools in the world could produce each year.

Michael Webb of Stanford University, when talking about the need for universities to broaden their ability to produce well prepared graduates who can work in the fields of advanced analytics and data science, remarked:

> *"New technologies create winners and losers in the labor market. They change relative demands for occupations, even as they improve productivity and standards of living. Understanding these distributional consequences is important for many purposes. For example, it allows policymakers to design appropriate education and skills policies, and helps individuals make good choices about what careers to pursue."* [12]

The US and global educational system changes slowly, but it does shift according to the market. I have been working with New Trier High School for over a decade. Working as part of the advisory board, in collaboration with Jason Boumstein, we have reviewed and brought in courses related to engineering and artificial intelligence.

Tom Finholt, Dean and Professor of Information, School of Information, at the University of Michigan, has taken what was a program focused on library science and transformed the offering into a curriculum that focuses on teaching, training, and preparing students to be leaders in the fields of data science, UX design, and more.

Tom has moved the program away from the previous paradigm, that is, of forcing left-brained students to memorize and execute technical strictures and structures in a rigid and driven manner.

I experienced the old style of teaching in my undergraduate and graduate programs. It does not work for large segments of the student population. I remember sitting in my Introduction to Assembly Programming class as a freshman. My professor said something similar to, "This class will be hard; 50% of you will not be here after the midterm. If you are a computer science major, you will need to take this class as many times as needed to pass in order to remain in the computer science program." No comforting sentiments in that speech.

...and the new

Dean Finholt and his team have created a program and approach that is more inclusive and diverse in how it attracts, evaluates, accepts, and educates tomorrow's leaders in data science. I am very excited to see how this new approach increases the number and quality of people entering the fields of data engineering, data science, advanced analytics, and related fields of work.

One of the more accessible methods for people of all levels of interest is online learning. The School of Information at the University of Michigan is using Coursera to broaden their reach. The course—*Programming for Everybody (Getting Started with Python)*—has enrolled nearly 950,000 students and has garnered over 73,000 reviews with an aggregate score of 4.8 out of 5. The instructor, Charles Severance (also known as Dr. Chuck), was tasked with creating an introductory course for people who were creative, open, and possess the ability to learn in a non-traditional manner. [13]

I do not see much interest from the colleges of engineering in augmenting or changing how they are teaching students to be data scientists. As I said, my sample is very small and quite limited, but I do see a significant amount of innovation and change in business schools, newly created colleges like the School of Information at the University of Michigan, and other schools and universities to attract new types of students in new and innovative ways.

If we continue to believe that the only way to provide society with the talent and skills needed in the future is to push people through rigid, and in some cases, outdated curriculums while sitting in lecture halls listening to graduate students, we will not deliver for the students, our communities, and the world in general.

The main points that I would like you to take away from this section is that our education system needs to evolve, and whether you are an adult returning to school, a high school student preparing to attend university, a parent of a student about to attend, or in the midst of attending university, you need to look closely at the educational offerings and curriculum of the school or program you or your child will be attending.

The old ways of teaching what are considered traditionally technical skills and imparting a body of knowledge, in some cases, are outmoded. This means they will not work for the broad audience that society needs to attend and graduate from university, with the skills needed to be successful in data science and advanced analytics.

The education system is changing, but as you or your child are entering that system, you need to be aware of what the current offerings are and how they can prepare you or your child for the realities of today and the future.

We have discussed how the educational system of today needs to change to serve a broader audience in the future. Let's now turn our attention to how people who are drawn to analytics and analytical thinking are unique, and how we can best support our colleagues, coworkers, and employees in our journey to deliver value to our companies and societies through data and analytics.

We are different

Over the past 37 years, as an observer of human behavior, I have learned a great deal about the people who are drawn to, and are good at, developing advanced analytics systems and environments.

Different in a good way

In the past five years, I have had firsthand experience of the failures I have discussed up close in companies as diverse as biopharmaceuticals, computer hardware/software, and research and consulting services. This is a widespread and ubiquitous problem.

I refer to myself, and the teams that I build and manage, as being "special snowflakes." I say this because it is evocative of the truth. In addition to being truthful, I say it because the differences we exhibit and embody are a very positive aspect of our personalities and the value that we deliver. The rest of the organization needs to know that these teams and individuals are different, and that difference can be, and is a source of power, change, and competitive advantage. These differences are not to be managed out or reduced; they are to be understood, nurtured, and employed for the greater good.

Each individual that I have hired over the years who has turned out to be a brilliant developer, programmer, data scientist, business analyst, system engineer, data engineer, or data architect has been an unusual or unique person.

The ugly duckling

I first encountered this dynamic over a decade ago. I was running the operations of a UK-based company. We had a staff member that did not get along well with the team, and not just one or two other people, but the entire staff in the location that he worked in. He was multiple levels down in the organization from my position, but it had been raised to my attention that the organization as a whole would prefer to, in British parlance, make this position and person redundant. To put it in the American vernacular, the team wanted him fired.

I met with him. We talked a few times and I realized that we had an emerging need in an area where this person had been taking night classes. He possessed early stage skills, a strong desire, and it appeared that he had an aptitude for the work that we needed to have done.

Working from home was not very common at the time, but his commute was inordinately long, and it was not productive to have him in the office. I proposed that he start to work from home, and that he begin, as a side project, to build what the company would need in the coming weeks and months, but not to tell anyone.

By this time, he had been transferred to me as a direct report. He and I agreed that he would continue with his existing duties, to see if he could and would be productive working from home, and we would collaborate on the side project.

He did not need to collaborate closely with anyone on his regular duties. He had to receive work, execute his work, and return the completed work to the team that delivered the input materials to him. He executed this work efficiently, effectively, and flawlessly. Also, he worked in the same mode with me on the side project.

When removed from the office and having his communication reduced to email and a few phone calls, his productivity soared. The idiosyncrasies that were the cause of the interpersonal difficulties were not an issue any longer.

One of the problems was that he would fall asleep at his desk in the office. People were put off by this and attributed it to him being lazy. As it turns out, he did his best work at night. I told him that I did not care if he worked all night and slept some of the day; as long as his work throughput, quality, and responsiveness were good, I had no issues with his schedule.

When the side project was complete, I presented it to the management team and included the staff members who were the most vocal proponents of this person being dismissed. The reviews were uniformly positive and unanimous that the work was good and that the group would be very happy to have this application, and platform, represent the brand and company in the market. The belief in the room was that this work was accomplished by an outsourced third party. When I announced that it was built by the staff member from his new side project while he worked at home, the reaction was a muted agreement that keeping him on staff and engaged was the right course of action.

After a couple years of this arrangement, he resigned. He had developed a small, one-man consultancy, offering his services to companies in the US, UK, and Europe. He worked from his house and was making significantly more money and seemed the happiest I had ever seen him. He went from being despised and derided to being a successful employee and eventually an entrepreneur.

He sent me an email a few years ago thanking me for seeing what others had not: his passion, skill, dedication, and drive to be a contributing member of the team. He was an outcast. He did not know how to ask for an environment that would allow him to flourish. And rather than looking for a way for him to be successful, the rest of the organization went about shunning him and making him feel incapable and unprofessional for how he looked and behaved.

This wasn't the only brilliant individual I've encountered during my time working in the world of business and analytics.

A diamond in the rough

I inherited a brilliant analyst when I took over a business unit of a large technology company. This person came to me after my first all-company meeting. In that meeting, I told the entire global operation that anyone could come to my office at any time to discuss any topic. I also explained that I came into the office early and usually caught up on email, communications, and projects before other team members arrived, but that I was open to having impromptu conversations at that time.

This person came in and explained that he had started out as a social worker, helping people through challenging situations in their lives. A few years before this conversation, he decided that he wanted to pursue a master's degree in social work. As part of his studies, he was required to take a class in introductory statistics. It turned out that he was a natural at math and statistics. He was unaware of this gift and talent. He explained that he had lived in the town where the company maintained its headquarters and that he had never travelled very far, but that he wanted to travel as much as possible.

I smiled and said, "Be careful what you ask for, we may able to give it to you."

Over the next year, this young man proved to be an invaluable staff member, due to the fact that he listened carefully to clients in all industries and of all levels of seniority and expertise, from senior executives to data scientists and business analysts who were both prospects and clients. He could translate what they described and needed into not only system specifications, but working prototypes quickly, easily, and accurately. He was amazing at his job. We had him on a plane each week, and he loved it. He travelled to Japan, Western and Eastern Europe, Canada, Mexico, and more.

His unique combination of empathy, math acumen, verbal, written, and presentation communication skills, comfort with uncertainty, lack of ego, and pure joy in helping people made him exceptionally successful. Of course, all of this comes with a unique set of personal needs and personality traits, but those idiosyncrasies made him who he is. He continues to be a valued employee, a reliable person, and a contributing member of the team and his community.

Ideal traits

In both the preceding vignettes, the majority of managers would not have seen the synthesis of skills and traits as being diamonds in the rough. When they both came to me, they had been sidelined and pigeonholed as a "type" of person. That was wrong, and it was a disservice to both and the value that they could and did bring to the respective companies and clients.

For the most part, individuals who are adept at building analytical environments possess or exhibit the following characteristics:

- Optimistic yet skeptical

- Intensely curious

- Mostly introverted

- Logical

- A combination of left and right brain orientation at the same time

- Intelligent

- Self-critical

- Prone to perfection

- Social, but reserved

- In some cases, they appear to exhibit a lack of focus or possibly too much focus

Managing a high-performing analytics team is a unique endeavor. Such teams need solid guidance, but, in general, do not react well to micromanagement.

Management by a non-practitioner or novice typically ends in failure. Managing a team that is building advanced analytics environments is not the same as managing a typical information technology project. Many firms fail in the organizational design phase of building an analytics team. Organizations and managers often fail to realize that managing a group of analytics professionals is more similar to managing a group of creative professionals than it is to managing a group of programmers. We will talk more about this in *Chapter 2, Building an Analytics Team*.

A common mistake

The great majority of non-technical people, and I include corporate executives in this category, think and believe that a technical resource is the same regardless of whether they are developing transactional systems (for example, **Enterprise Resource Planning** (**ERP**), **Customer Relationship Management** (**CRM**), and so on), business intelligence, dashboards, or artificial intelligence applications.

Executives, across a wide range of industries, tend to think and act as if any technical resource is interchangeable with any other. And part of this problem stems from the fact that they see technical people as resources. They do not understand, and for the most part, do not try to understand, the nuances of the various differences between the skillsets, motivations, and intrinsic interests of individuals who possess technical talent. This mindset and view is patently false, and it is one that causes companies around the world to waste millions, if not billions, of dollars each year.

A partial cause of this situation is that the technology function is a relatively new addition to the corporate structure. Think of accounting, manufacturing, sales, and distribution.

These functions have been in organizational structures for millennia. No competent executive would say that we can take a top performing sales professional and put them in accounting. It sounds ludicrous to even say it.

But, given that the technology function has been part of the corporate environment for less than 80 years, we hear nonsensical statements like, "We can take the developers who created the CRM system and have them build the artificial intelligence system for predictive maintenance." This is a ridiculous idea that is bound to fail, but I have had senior executives, across several industries, say this exact thing to me and believe this is a reasonable statement or question. They truly believe that they know what they are talking about.

Part of this lack of understanding comes from the fact that senior executives know that the technology function is relatively new, and it is different, but they do not want to know how or why it is different. They are willing to delve into the intricacies of international tax policy or transfer pricing, but ask them to dive into the details of how an artificial intelligence system will revolutionize manufacturing or supply chain operations, and that topic is not worth the intellectual energy to understand at a deep and functional level. That is for the "technical people."

This problem is not limited to a lack of understanding of the composition of project teams, but also a lack of the skills, experience, and expertise needed to manage teams that are tasked with building advanced analytics systems. Again, senior management sees a person who has managed the implementation of an enterprise system like a business intelligence environment and/or application, and they assign them to build a self-healing supply chain management platform. A grave error.

Obscured vision

These mistaken beliefs and the decisions made about hiring, organizing, and undertaking advanced analytics projects dooms a substantial percentage of efforts to fail before those projects have even started. And the disappointing fact is that the executives who have made these mistakes have no idea that they have set the project on the road to failure, even before any funds have been spent or a single person hired. And at the end of the failed projects, those executives will lay the blame at the feet of the technology, or the technical team or the outsourcing partner or all of them, but little to no cause for failure will be attributed to their lack of leadership or understanding of what was to be undertaken or accomplished.

I see this today in companies that has decided to place advanced analytics teams in the individual functional and operational areas around the world. The idea sounds rational, and the approach appears to be justified, and it can be, but it takes a deep understanding of the business and the analytical applications and technologies that will be applied. There are precious few people in this organization that understand the triumvirate of business requirements, technical skills, and solution development/application. What has happened in this specific instance is that managers have hired people who professed to have, but in reality, do not possess the technical and business skills to competently approach the solution development process. The disconnect between the business operators, the newly hired data scientists and analysts, and the hiring managers have delivered almost no results in the set timeframe.

When leaders and managers allow this kind of rudderless environment to be built or to develop, data scientists resign and move on.

The hiring managers are confused as to why they couldn't manage these projects, just like they did other, seemingly similar, projects, and the executives grumble that the teams did not deliver the promised return. A powerful mix of failure, frustration, and resentment ensues.

It is difficult to see the problems clearly from the individual perspectives of the players involved, but when you take a view with a bit of distance, it is easy to see that the projects undertaken in this approach had a very small chance of succeeding.

Given that we have outlined where we can see pitfalls in the strategic direction set for analytics teams and groups, let's examine the optimal organizational structure and where the analytics function and team should fit into the overall company.

The original sin

Senior management decides that they need to enter the race to build applications that contain artificial intelligence (whatever that means to them).

They decide that since most of the discussion that they observe in the management journals, technology press, and the media in general has a flavor of technology or comes from a geographic region known for technology, they will put the advanced analytics team under the technology function managed by the **Chief Information Officer (CIO)**, **Chief Technology Officer (CTO)**, or worse, under the **Chief Financial Officer (CFO)**. Senior management has taken the first step to failing.

Let's take the case of placing the advanced analytics team in the technology department, or under the CIO, first. It may take a year or 18 months, but the advanced analytics and artificial intelligence team will fall prey to the information technology mindset.

Advanced analytics projects are not the same as information technology projects. Installing an instance of Salesforce is relatively easy and a well-known and generally linear process.

Advanced analytics projects are not, for the most part, linear. They are iterative, marked by exhilarating successes, and punctuated by dead ends, missteps, and disproved theories. Most information technology professionals, while intelligent and mildly curious, do not have the interest or fortitude for the iterative or recursive nature of advanced analytics projects.

Also, information technology professionals typically do not have the skillset to develop artificial intelligence applications. Staff members in information technology functions have evolved over the past 30 to 40 years, from developing bespoke systems to installing systems, managing customizations, and configurations. Information technology professionals are more oriented to vendor and project management than they are to core development. There is no judgment in that statement; it is a proven fact.

The information technology function is a support function—a cost center, not a creative function—that lives by project plans and has a reticence or visceral fear of failure or being late or over budget. Information technology teams have been treated like a support function for the last 30 to 40 years, and the teams that work in the information technology department act accordingly.

Advanced analytics teams, at least high-performing analytics teams, are seeking to solve one or a series of challenging problems. The pursuit of the solution is the goal, not adherence to a budget number or delivery according to a preset date. The optimal solution, the source of competitive advantage, is the objective.

Placing the advanced analytics team under the accountability of the CTO is better than under the CIO if the CTO has an innovation charter within their remit. As an example, the CTO's remit may include finding ways to productize unique data generated by operations.

This would likely be an area that the CTO would have an interest in driving, while also having the connections and political capital to enact it successfully. One of the downsides would be getting the CTO team to engage with the functional areas that the CTO is unfamiliar with, like IT operations, sales, marketing, HR, finance, facilities, and so on. The CTO will typically be tasked with creating new approaches to existing challenges. If this is the case, then it is possible that the AI team will have a fruitful run as part of this functional organization, but success is not guaranteed.

Drawing the reporting lines of the advanced analytics team under the organization of the CFO is worse than putting the team under the CIO. At least under the CIO there is a distant history of technologists building and deploying solutions. Under the CFO, the entire mindset is process orientation and cost containment. Not exactly the wide-ranging, creative mindset needed to develop novel solutions to drive competitive step change in an organization and industry.

Again, it may take a year or 18 months, but the advanced analytics and artificial intelligence team will fall prey to the finance organization mindset. The finance team is a very focused group, and they should be. They need to manage the financial flow, systems, and reporting that make the company operate efficiently and effectively. As the finance team gets squeezed to do more with the same staffing or less, they will look for relief. They will look to cut heads in the advanced analytics team to hire more people to run the day-to-day processes of finance and accounting.

The objective and goals of the advanced analytics team and group will rarely, if ever, align with the corporate goals and objectives of the finance team. And you know what happens when there is a misalignment of goals and objectives with the management above any team: that team gets their headcount and budget cut or held at a level that does not enable expansion.

We have discussed where not to put the analytics leader and the advanced analytics team, so now, let's outline the optimal place in the organization for the analytics function.

The right home

As I have said, the most successful advanced analytics teams are creative groups staffed with talented, motivated, curious people who can convert business discussions with subject matter experts into analytical applications and solutions that can drive operational change on a daily basis. The analytical teams that realize the most success have wide-ranging mandates to drive practical and pragmatic change resulting in competitive advantage.

Where in the organization are the senior executives whose mandates encompass this arena?

The best organizational home for the advanced analytics team is reporting directly to either the **Chief Operating Officer (COO)** or the **Chief Executive Officer (CEO)**.

If a COO exists, it would be rare to see this group under the CEO, unless the CEO is younger, ambitious, and engaged. Recently, there have been a handful of **Chief Analytics Officer (CAO)** appointments reporting to the CEO. This is typically a move to illustrate where the CEO wants to place emphasis. It will be interesting to see how long this type of reporting relationship remains in place, before evolving into a new form and structure.

Working directly for the CEO can work, and it is one of the optimal reporting structures for the CAO and the advanced analytics teams, but it is often difficult to gain time with the CEO to ensure alignment and focus. To be clear, reporting to the CEO is the best direct reporting relationship the CAO can, and would, want to have, and if the CEO prioritizes the relationship with the CAO and publicly funds and supports the mission of the advanced analytics team, then this is the best possible organizational structure.

Having the CAO report to the COO is the next best reporting structure to have in place. The COO has the corporate functions under their control, and can direct the functions to collaborate with the CAO and the advanced analytics team to examine processes, data, and more to drive innovation and change.

Continuing down the senior management structure, the third best place for the CAO to report is to the Executive Vice President of Business Development and Strategy. This role typically owns mergers and acquisitions, strategy, and corporate development. Therefore, the mission to drive innovation typically resides in this group. Given the amount of change that the CAO and the advanced analytics team will drive, they need to be reporting to a corporate change agent with the organizational power to direct the functional groups to engage and collaborate.

We've discussed the implications of having a CAO and an advanced analytics team, and we have talked about appropriate environments in which such a team and leadership might thrive. This brings us to the final section of this chapter. As we conclude our exploration of the operating context for, and overview of, analytical teams, we need to discuss the topic of ethics.

Ethics

I considered writing a book on the implications, needs, and requirements of ethics in analytics, but I decided against completing that project. Why? First, there are several very good books that have been published on the topic. Second, ethics should be part of our mindset in everything that we do. Given that belief, I felt that it was better to imbue this book, and every book that I will write in the future, with a subtext of ethics. All through the content of this book, I will discuss and call out how ethics impact and inform choices, and how to consider the ethics of the decisions being made.

Society, as a whole, is concerned about the implications of advanced analytics and artificial intelligence. Given what has happened with social media and the bad actors involved in those platforms, there is replace with: grounds for concern which drives the need for consideration that all innovations have the potential to be deployed and employed for unethical purposes.

Researchers, experts, pundits, company executives, government ministers, legislators, and others have written and spoken at length about the potential value and operational downsides of governmental interventions like the **General Data Protection Regulation (GDPR)** enacted by the **European Union (EU)** and the **California Consumer Privacy Act (CCPA)**. One fact is for certain: we have passed the point where self-regulation by companies is an acceptable approach to constraining corporate policy and behavior in the use of data, advanced analytics, and artificial intelligence.

Governments are stepping in and will continue to step in. If building a business on a fair business proposition and providing value to customers, consumers, partners, and society is not enough of a guideline for corporate executive and managers, there will be more guidelines and regulations forthcoming from multiple jurisdictions.

Let's proceed under the premise that everything we do and all the choices we make in relation to data and analytics have the best interest of the consumer, customer, patient, and all involved in mind. Let's also keep in mind that the further we stray from this core premise, the more likely it is that we will cause harm to our business, reputation, and the wellbeing and peace of mind of our customers, patients, and broader society.

The further afield we take our efforts away from being ethically aligned, the harder the fall will be when the correction comes from either internal or external forces. Be assured that we will be forced to explain our actions and efforts at some point in the very near future.

Transparency, ethical actions, and honesty will be our guiding principles.

Summary

In this chapter we have started our journey of understanding the market and organizational context in which high-performing analytics teams live and operate.

We have touched on the perception, reality, value, and concerns surrounding AI and its implications for jobs and careers, which are mainly positive in the long term and disruptive for some in the short term.

We have discussed how analytics professionals are not your typical employees and should be evaluated from a results perspective, and not on the basis of their supposed interpersonal failings or challenges. This aspect of hiring and managing high-performance analytics professionals will be replace with: thwarted in the current work environment of hyper political correctness, but should also be helped by the move to incorporate diversity and inclusion in our organizations.

We touched on the optimal and less than optimal organizational structures that should and shouldn't be used to house and grow an advanced analytics team and its functionality, and we wrapped up by touching on the all-important topic of ethics.

We have set the stage for our wide-ranging discussion of how to be successful as an analytics leader. Thank you for coming on this journey with me.

Now, let's move on to discussing the topic of how to hire and build a high-performing analytics team.

Chapter 1 footnotes

1. *Will robots steal our jobs?*, August 20, 2019, Mike Colagrossi, `https://www.weforum.org/agenda/2019/08/the-robots-are-coming-but-take-a-breath`

2. Polyani's Paradox, `https://en.wikipedia.org/wiki/Polanyi%E2%80%99s_paradox`

3. Rob May's thoughts on startups, angel investing, and becoming a venture capitalist, `http://coconutheadsets.com/`

4. *Gartner Says By 2020, Artificial Intelligence Will Create More Jobs Than It Eliminates*, December 13, 2017, Rob van der Meulen & Christy Pettey, `https://www.gartner.com/en/newsroom/press-releases/2017-12-13-gartner-says-by-2020-artificial-intelligence-will-create-more-jobs-than-it-eliminates`

5. *Robots aren't stealing all our jobs, says the World Bank's chief economist*, January 11, 2019, Sean Fleming, `https://www.weforum.org/agenda/2019/01/robots-aren-t-wiping-out-jobs-yet-according-to-the-world-bank-s-chief-economist/`

6. *You Probably Need a College Degree to Get a Factory Job Now*, December 10, 2019, Kaitlin Mulhere, `https://money.com/manufacturing-jobs-college-degree/`

7. *Analytics: How to Win With Intelligence*, January 7, 2017, John K Thompson & Shawn Rogers, `https://www.packtpub.com/data/analytics-how-to-win-with-intelligence`

8. *WTF?: What's the Future and Why It's Up to Us*, October 10, 2017, Tim O'Reilly, `https://www.amazon.com/WTF-Whats-Future-Why-Its/dp/0062565710`

9. *Augmented Intelligence: The Business Power of Human–Machine Collaboration 1st Edition*, November 1, 2019, Judith Hurwitz, Henry Morris, Candace Sidner, Daniel Kirsch, `https://www.amazon.com/Augmented-Intelligence-Business-Human-Machine-Collaboration-dp-0367184893/dp/0367184893/ref=mt_hardcover?_encoding=UTF8&me=&qid=`

10. *How many software developers are in the US and in the world in 2019?*, December 27, 2019, `https://www.daxx.com/blog/development-trends/number-software-developers-world`

11. Ferris State University, Course Catalog, `http://catalog.ferris.edu/programs`

12. *The Impact of Artificial Intelligence on the Labor Market*, Michael Webb, Stanford University, November 2019, `https://web.stanford.edu/~mww/webb_jmp.pdf`

13. *Programming for Everybody (Getting Started with Python)*, University of Michigan, Coursera, `https://www.coursera.org/learn/python`, Dr. Charles Russell Severance, `https//www.coursera.org/instructor/drchuck` and `https://www.dr-chuck.com/`

CHAPTER 2

BUILDING AN ANALYTICS TEAM

*"Those who cannot remember the past are condemned
to repeat it."*

—George Santayana

Creating a highly functional and successful **advanced analytics** and
artificial intelligence (AI) team is a unique and nuanced endeavor.
On the face of it, the process of building an analytics team may not
seem to be different from building any other functional or technical
team, but this is where problems typically start.

In this chapter, we will discuss the organizational context in
which you and your new team will be operating, and, as part of the
discussion, we will outline the characteristics of the communication
and collaboration interface between the analytics team and the
functional/operational teams. Also, we will examine hiring in non-
traditional populations that you should consider when building
a high-performance analytics team.

We will examine the possibility that young professionals can play a unique and valuable role in taking calculated risks and accelerating your innovation agenda. And, finally, we will conclude the chapter with a discussion examining the possible operating models for your analytics team, the implications of each model, and how to evolve the team over time given organizational objectives, budget considerations, and other relevant constraints.

Organizational context and consideration

One of the primary considerations to keep in mind is that the context in which the advanced analytics and AI team operates is different than operational teams. Operational and functional teams, like finance and manufacturing, work in their defined domains and rarely deviate from their cyclical processes. Analytics teams work across the entire organization, interfacing with all levels of the company with a focus on discovery and innovation.

The interface between the advanced analytics and AI team and the other groups and teams is one that needs and deserves more attention than it currently receives. The advanced analytics and AI team is focused on disruption, creativity, and innovation. This is an activity that is marked by success and discovery, followed by setbacks and retrenchment. Functional areas are characterized by smooth, predictable process flows, and well-established processes that move forward along an established path at an established pace. When interfacing the work of the advanced analytics group with that of a functional group, the communication and planning of how these two teams will interface and collaborate is critical. Any time there is a creative, iterative, innovative, and unpredictable process feeding into a smooth, well planned, and reasonably static process, there are opportunities for miscommunication, misunderstandings, missed deadlines, and unplanned results.

In *Chapter 8, Operationalizing Analytics – How to Move from Projects to Production,* we will look more deeply into this topic and describe how best to optimize the collaboration and communication between the analytics and operational teams.

A high functioning analytics team acts more like a management consulting group or an internal consultancy than a functional team. This is where teams can and will experience natural friction and sources of contention. In addition to the mismatch in the cycle times, process types, and the kind of work executed, analytics teams are typically not known for being the most tactful and deft in their handling of sensitive topics and subjects. And when the analytics team is discovering new ways of executing processes or interpreting models and results, there are real and substantial areas for misunderstandings to arise. These are challenges that are not widely known or understood, but they will occur, and they can and should be anticipated and considered in the team-building phase of the process.

Another consideration is that while the advanced analytics and AI team utilizes data and technology to accomplish its goals and objectives, the analytics team is not a technology team. The functional teams may perceive the advanced analytics and AI team as an extension of the information technology team and that is a limiting view and a source of future problems. Typically, those issues and problems are in the perceptions of the functional teams and their leadership. The problems manifest themselves in inappropriate requests and the delegation of tasks that are not a good use of the analytical team's time and resources. Many of these requests are to build simple reports and dashboards or to acquire or pull data from internal and external systems. The leadership of the analytics team needs to be clear that the analytics team is not an adjunct or extension of the business intelligence team or reporting group and these types of requests are better served by other individuals and teams.

The leadership of the analytics team needs to direct the functional team members and managers to the appropriate contacts in the company to service these requests.

Advanced analytics and AI teams are drivers of deep examination and change. Analytics is a transformational process. Analytics is typically the first step in a transformational process. Problems typically arise when the advanced analytics team finds new and novel ways of doing business from a process perspective or finds data proving that the existing operational processes and activities are not in alignment with the most productive or efficient way to operate.

One of the results of advanced analytics teams engaging with functional teams is requirements for change in the functional organization. The projects executed by analytics teams in conjunction with functional teams are containers for longer-term digital transformation and change. The immediate projects kick off a requirement for process change or, at the very least, an examination of the need for change.

The functional teams and their management leaders may see and be enthusiastic about the immediate projects, but they may not be ready for the larger transformation that is discovered, and possibly required, at the conclusion of the project at hand. The challenge in this situation is that the advanced analytics team needs to be ready to communicate and manage not only the immediate project but the communication of the possible paths of change for the functional team. Technical skills, building PowerPoint slides, and discussing the validity of the analytical methods will not enable the advanced analytics team to manage these larger and more complicated organizational change processes.

The advanced analytics and AI team members you are seeking are more than experts in advanced analytics; you are seeking staff members who are agents of change and can act as guides to the broader organization about how to undertake changes at a scale and scope that the organization can understand and undertake without experiencing traumatic disruption.

These are broader considerations to keep in mind as we begin to consider the type of advanced analytics and AI teams we can afford and want to hire. There are many team structures and constructs that we can use to begin our journey and understanding some of the most pertinent organizational considerations will help us get off on the right foot. Now that we have set some of the organizational context, let's move back to our discussion of building the team.

We all know, and should follow, many of the well-known rules, structures, and norms of building a new team. It is clear that we should begin with ethical, sensible, and legal team-building foundations such as pay equity, clear reporting lines, defined roles, a flat hierarchy, and more, but there are also many elements of building a high-performing, highly collaborative analytics team that, in some cases, appear paradoxical. In this chapter, we will delve into the more unique aspects of building an advanced analytics and AI team.

We will examine what we have learned from our career and what we know we will continue to leverage in our team-building efforts. We'll also look at what we should discontinue doing because it does not serve our greater goals in constructing what we hope will be a dream team. There will also be new things introduced in this chapter that you can try in your ongoing search for improvement in building your team.

New innovative minds

Experience and expertise are wonderful attributes and, in many cases, are a requirement for individual and team success. Your team needs staff members who have both experience and expertise, but you also need bright, young sparks who do not know what has been done before, and therefore, do not place limitations on their thinking and approaches to challenges that most experienced staff members would consider impossible to solve.

Hiring smart young staff members can be a good check on confirmation bias, which we commonly see in staff that have been in an organization for a considerable number of years.

Early in my career, I was asked to join a team at a client site. It was a good client with interesting challenges in a growing industry. The firm was one of the leading **Consumer Packaged Goods (CPG)** companies in the world. The team leader from my company was quite poor; she only wanted people on her team who parroted back her thoughts and slavishly followed her directions. For the most part, the team did just that and toed the line she set out each day. She exhibited a strong project manager mindset. She wanted the trains to run on time, no projects were to deviate from their project charters, all projects should be delivered on time, and all projects were to be reviewed and approved by her.

After being at the client site for about a month, I was approached by a leader in the client organization and asked to listen to an idea for a new way to solve a long-standing, vexing challenge. I listened carefully and asked a few questions to ensure that I understood exactly what the client wanted and needed. After the office grew quiet, I spent the night building what had been described and discussed. The next day, I demonstrated the newly built application for the client team. The consensus was that this was a vast improvement over what had been the state of the art up to that point. The application was fast, accurate, and utilized source data and intermediate results from 17 internal and external databases. Previously, no one had considered approaching the challenge in this manner because the brand management and information technology teams involved to date thought it was impossible to do.

This was my first "impossible" project. Some of the primary reasons why the project was a success were:

1. I had no idea of the current state of the art for this type of application in the CPG industry.

2. I had access to all the information and databases needed to build the application.

3. I was given a complete overview of the business problem by a senior functional leader who owned the problem and wanted a solution as soon as possible.

4. I acted without asking for approval to spend my time on the "project."

5. I worked through the night building, what seemed to me, the most efficient application to solve the challenge.

The team leader from our firm was not happy and asked that I be removed from the team. I was surprised, but in hindsight, her reaction could have been predicted. Her metrics for success centered on project delivery dates and adherence to agreed project charters, and control of the team. The innovation that was delivered was spontaneous and unplanned and, while the client was very happy, and continued to employ the application for years, she was very upset that the project did not flow through her.

I went on to be assigned several "impossible" projects across the CPG industry in the US and UK. My managers knew that I enjoyed difficult technical challenges and the clients were impressed with the novel approaches and solutions that were developed and delivered competitive advantage to them.

Young, talented staff members view challenges from new and varied perspectives. They use new thinking, new technologies, and see prospective solutions in new and unique ways. Unleash their creative and innovative spirits and you will see solutions that you had not dreamed of before.

This is another area where leadership from the analytics team is important. You will be asking young, talented, and creative analytics team members to work with functional team members and leaders.

The young staff members need support to ensure that they understand the challenge completely, communicate thoroughly, and do not over commit to delivering more than they can in too short a time frame. Analytics leadership needs to set the expectations with the functional team and leadership about timing, the type of results they can expect, and if this is a project that will produce a singular outcome to derive insights or a set of models that will require implementation by inserting those models into existing processes. One-time insights are easy to understand and work with. Production-based models require processes, workflows, and procedural changes, which may be harder to understand and take more time to plan for and implement.

Internships and co-op programs

One approach to gaining access to young, intelligent, and pre-screened talent is to work with select undergraduate and graduate-level universities to hire undergraduate and graduate-level students on internships and co-op programs. This approach enables the students to work on varied and challenging real-world problems and situations, and you and your team have an opportunity to "interview" these prospective employees over multiple months.

An important aspect of this approach is to assign the interns and co-op participants work that is important to the business and that has the possibility to change the way business is executed. Giving the students "busy" work is a waste of everyone's time and energy. You must be ready for you and your team members to mentor and manage the young team members. You must also be ready for projects to fail, but to learn from those failures, and you must be ready for projects to succeed and that those successes will demand and require that company to change to take advantage of new innovations, insights, and processes.

An important consideration is that younger staff members will have less experience in certain areas such as written and verbal communication skills and stakeholder management. If your efforts to drive innovation are to reap the maximum benefit, you will be putting these young, untested interns in collaboration with subject matter experts and business sponsors in functional areas of the company. The combination of the intern's technical expertise and enthusiasm coupled with the deep functional knowledge of the subject matter experts is a potent and desirable combination that can, and will, lead to breakthrough developments, but you will need to teach the young staff members how to interface with the more senior functional staff members in a manner that is appropriate for the project and overall business environment.

Over the years, I have provided detailed feedback to all the universities that I collaborate with, and have collaborated with, that their students need more training and skills in communication, collaboration, and the softer skills needed in the workplace. The university curriculums are changing, but we will need to further these skills in our recent graduates. Be ready to mentor and manage young team members in order to minimize, and possibly avoid, gaffes and faux pas on their part.

Internships and co-ops are a great way to bring new talent into your organization. If you can initiate, develop, and scale this type of program, you can hire the majority of your new staff members through this program. I suggest that you make this type of hiring a priority. I have employed this approach successfully and recommend that you consider it as well.

Diversity and inclusion

Your team will benefit from diversity in all aspects that you can amalgamate. Diversity in age, gender, organizational level, geographic origin, socioeconomic means, faith (and lack thereof), educational background, sexual orientation, neurodiversity, circadian rhythms, and more will make your team more effective and valuable.

Advanced analytics and AI teams are made up of a wide range of personalities, from the introverted to the highly extroverted, from the careful and thoughtful to the impulsive and innovative. Analytics teams benefit greatly from the varied perspectives that a wide spectrum of individuals bring to the collaborative environment.

Perhaps you have seen teams where the leader hires mostly people that think, act, and look like themselves. In extreme cases, this is called conative cloning and it can lead to myopic thinking and a narrow focus when approaching challenges and the resulting solutions. If you think of hiring as a continuum, on one end of the spectrum you have a group that is a conative clone of the leader. Groupthink is common and no one challenges the direction set by the leader for the strategy of the group or the approach taken for each project. This is not the optimal approach for any group. On the other end of the spectrum, you have a team that is so diverse that they cannot communicate or understand each other to such an extreme that little to no collaboration can take place. This is not desirable either. As with most things in life, somewhere in the middle of this continuum is where you want to operate.

It helps to have guidelines in hiring. We need to be careful and cognizant that our guidelines do not become dogma and that we do not fall foul of our original goal of building an effective, cohesive, collaborative group that can work internally as project teams in numerous configurations among the team members, but also a team that connects easily and collaborates with all functional areas and levels of the company and with external partners of all types.

One area of diversity that is not typically discussed because it is unique to advanced analytics and AI teams is the diversity of knowledge in analytical approaches. The team is better served from having individuals who are experts, but experts in various analytical approaches. The team needs experts in natural language processing for text-based applications, neural networks for image processing, deep learning for a wide range of predictive applications, decision trees for problems with a large number of relevant variables to be considered, and emerging fields like video and audio processing.

The team needs a varied collection of experts who can lead projects that require the aforementioned specialized analytical techniques; experts who can and will lead the initial projects requiring these techniques. The experts will mentor the other team members in learning the technologies, techniques, and other considerations of building solutions for the class of problem being addressed. The experts act as teachers and mentors for the other team members to become proficient, if not experts, in the technique being used for the immediate project, and on the next project, a different expert provides the same opportunity for the other team members to learn from them and broaden their technical portfolio of skills. This dynamic is important for the analytics team to grow in their collaboration skills as a team and for individuals to grow in technical proficiency.

Of course, all team members need to be experts in basic mathematics, and it is useful and helpful if they are well educated and competent in basic and advanced statistics and probability theories. These are the foundational technical skills that we would expect from an intern or co-op student joining the team for an interim assignment and we would certainly expect this level of competency from anyone that we might consider bringing on to the team as a full-time team member.

The advanced analytics and AI team needs to have a foundational operating premise that they are all valued and respected members of the team and that they all have valid views that can be freely expressed in a positive manner to improve any project that they are involved in or to review a colleague or sub-team. It is expected that everyone respects all other team members personally and professionally and that our differences are a source of strength that provides our team with a broader and deeper view than any other team in the organization or that of our partner organizations.

One of the founding goals of the group is to start out with a diverse team and to grow in a manner that includes as much diversity across as many aspects as conceivable and practically possible.

Neurodiversity

Starting from childhood, I have seen and experienced a substantial range of human behavior over the course of my life. The United States has had a convoluted and complex journey when considering the best path of engagement and treatment for people who exhibit degrees of mental health.

It is important that you and your team are aware that the inclusion of neurodiversity is desired and has been, informally, part of the consideration of the assembly and management of development teams and advanced analytics teams for decades.

Neurodiversity is the new and current label for people who exhibit a wide range of mental health conditions and syndromes. Most of us are aware of Asperger's syndrome, Down's syndrome, and a number of other conditions that we now describe and label as neurodiversity.

Leading companies like Dell, EY (Ernst & Young), Microsoft, and SAP have well-established neurodiversity hiring and management programs. Companies need to establish and understand their objectives and goals when making a commitment to expanding their talent pools to include neurodivergent employees:

> *"At Dell, we believe that everyone has unique strengths and skills to contribute in the workplace. We strive to create an environment that is inclusive and accessible for all. As neurodiversity is a broad category, we decided to first focus on an effort for those on the autism spectrum, rethinking the traditional interview process and removing barriers that may limit an individual from fully showcasing their true abilities and potential." [1]*

Dell Technologies launched a pilot Autism Hiring Program in Hopkinton, Massachusetts, that included a 2-week skills assessment for intern selection, followed by a 12-week summer internship for the selected adults with **Autism Spectrum Disorder (ASD)**. By the end of the pilot, several interns were hired as full-time employees, and the program was expanded and brought to Dell Technologies' headquarters at Round Rock, Texas:

> *"We've seen tremendous talent come in through this program—talent that would otherwise be overlooked if we were not actively recruiting in these non-traditional ways," says Lou Candiello, Senior Manager of Diversity Talent Acquisition at Dell Technologies. "We have filled critical positions across cybersecurity, data analytics, software engineering, artificial intelligence, and more with truly gifted and neurodiverse talent." [2]*

The talent pool of people who are considered neurodiverse is large and growing:

> *"About half a million people on the autism spectrum will legally become adults over the next decade, meaning a large majority will have the potential to enter and contribute to the future workforce. As an organization committed to bringing diverse perspectives to the table, investing in hiring and training adults with autism is not only the right thing to do, it makes clear business sense. This group has incredible strengths: strong attention to detail, commitment to quality and consistency, creative and "out-of-the-box" thinking and lower turnover rates." [3]*

Hiring in this area brings special requirements and you will need to ensure that leadership understands and supports the inclusion of a wider range of employees than would be typical. You will need to collaborate closely with the Human Resources department to ensure that you and your team are operating within the guidelines for hiring and managing a team that is outside the norms for the organization. Also, the initiative needs to be a long-term, strategic program that is supported and funded over multiple years:

> *"Dell's executives say that their recruitment efforts are part of a long-term strategy to diversify its workforce, and that the company won't abandon them just because the unemployment rate ticks back up." [4]*

Hiring neurodiverse talent is beneficial for the company, team, and the employees. It is important that these types of programs are designed, developed, and deployed in expanding economic cycles. These programs and the gains established by them are fragile overall, but the changes can be life-changing for individuals:

> *"For workers hired during the good times, the benefits can be enduring. Economic research has found that once people are drawn into the labor force, they tend to stay in it. That may be especially true for workers with disabilities or other barriers to employment who thrive once given a job — but who struggle to get that chance in all but the strongest job markets." [5]*

You must be mindful to ensure that you are hiring people who are capable of functioning in a team environment and working over a period of years in collaborative situations. The variety of people that you will bring together will require consideration of the physical environment, the team dynamic, the workload assigned, and more.

At a high level, this is not tremendously different than any other team, but the team members you hire will, in many cases, exhibit heightened sensitivities to light, sound, interruptions, and other considerations that may not be designed into the traditional physical environment to ensure a harmonious and productive setting.

Diversity of thought, action, and ideas are good and positive attributes, but we are talking about hiring people who may need additional consideration and accommodation in their team and work environment. Accommodation is expected, but you must be able to distinguish between those individuals that simply need an accommodation like noise-canceling headphones or larger monitors to be productive and those that cannot and will not be able to function in even a well-designed workspace.

Keep this in mind: special consideration and accommodation, yes; special treatment, no.

Disciplinary action

Hiring and firing team members remains part of the management of any team. I have had employees confront me and express dismay that I was dismissing a staff member. The law requires many things of managers and corporations. When someone breaks the law or flouts company policy, they do not get a free pass just because they belong to a diversity category. When things go wrong, there are consequences; this does not change because we are hiring a wider range of people. As a manager, you must treat all employees, across all classes and categories of staff members, the same and that includes disciplinary action.

Performance management, merit, and incentive bonuses, and all aspects of personnel management still exist and must be executed with the advanced analytics and AI team.

There are aspects of human behavior that cannot be tolerated, and need to be avoided, or reacted to when they occur. If these aspects cannot be avoided or managed in a professional manner, action must be taken to protect the overall staff and the organization. People who exhibit aggressive behavior, those who are not respectful of others, those who will not listen and collaborate to build upon the offerings and ideas of others, and those that cannot perform their duties even when accommodations have been made and consideration given to their needs must be subject to disciplinary action up to and including dismissal.

Delaying disciplinary action is always an error in judgment. If you feel the need to take disciplinary action in relation to an employee, then you should contact the Human Resources department immediately and move forward. By delaying action, you are putting yourself in jeopardy.

I encountered a situation where an employee was not performing their duties. In this case, the employee was falling behind in deliverables, withdrawing from the group, and acting in a divisive manner. I chose to speak with them directly and explain that they were not fitting in with the team and that the exhibited performance did not meet with the expectations that we had agreed to when this staff member joined the team over a year ago. This employee knew that we were moving toward dismissal and decided to go to Human Resources to file a formal complaint. The reason for the complaint was to forestall the dismissal; there was no factual basis for the complaint. When the complaint was fully investigated, the claim was found to have no merit. However, the employee stalled the dismissal long enough to find another job outside the company. The objective had been accomplished from the employee's perspective. Had I approached the Human Resources department first to start the disciplinary process, rather than being open, honest, and transparent with the employee, the firm would have been protected from this baseless allegation.

Always act in a collaborative manner with the aligned functional groups in the organization, but never delay, when deciding on how to proceed with disciplinary action.

Labor market dynamics

As of late 2019, the United States is experiencing one of the longest economic expansions on record. The current unemployment rate in the United States is below 3%. Hiring practices have needed to evolve to ensure that employers can continue to find employees. Of course, this will change as the economic cycle ebbs and flows, but at this time we have an opportunity to bring in talented, skilled, and committed employees who may have been sidelined due to disabilities, personal situations, or other unfortunate life events:

> *"With the national unemployment rate now flirting with a 50-year low, companies are increasingly looking outside the traditional labor force for workers. They are offering flexible hours and work-from-home options to attract stay-at-home parents, full-time students, and recent retirees. They are making new accommodations to open jobs to people with disabilities. They are dropping educational requirements, waiving criminal background checks, and offering training to prospective workers who lack necessary skills." [6]*

Let's make the most of this opportunity to improve the lives of as many people as possible.

During the writing of this book however, the world has experienced the COVID-19 pandemic. Please refer to the *Prologue* of the book for commentary on how the pandemic impacts analytics teams.

A fit to be found

When I heard the phrase "fit to be found" a few years ago, I thought that this was absolutely ridiculous and the idea held no truth, but upon reflection and numerous opportunities to revisit the idea, I firmly believe that this concept is true. For each person, there is a perfect job or role and for each role or job, there is a perfect person to fill that role.

For each person that you have on your staff – or possibly this applies to you and your current role, every day that someone remains in a job that they despise, dislike, or do not want to do, they are keeping that job or role from the person who would absolutely love to be doing it on a daily basis. And for each day someone is in a job that they do not enjoy, they are not in the perfect job for them. I have stood up in front of multiple companies, divisions of Fortune 500 firms, and teams that I have led and outlined this premise.

I follow the explanation of the premise outlined above with the following offer: if you are in a role that you do not like, speak up. I, and the management team, will not hold this against you. We will work with you to find a role that you like and possibly love, either in the department, division, or company or outside the company. I want people to enjoy and love their work. If the job isn't working for you, then it isn't working for the company.

This is a rare and unique position and proposition. I have lost employees because they wanted out of the company and we helped them to leave, but I have gained many more engaged, happy, and loyal employees because of this position and policy. It works. Give it a try with your analytics teams.

Evolved leadership is a requirement for success

On my multi-decade journey of driving innovation in and through analytics, not just at the technological level, but at the practical, day-to-day level, I have been constantly reminded of the critical need for company leadership teams to understand, support, and sponsor corporate efforts in managing data as a strategic asset and creating analytics to drive transformation. Every organization that undertakes this transformational effort requires engaged and informed leadership that understands and views this as a long-term, strategic, organizational change management process.

"We need to become a focused medicines company that's powered by data science and digital technologies," [7] said Vas Narasimhan, CEO of Novartis AG, in an interview with the *Wall Street Journal* in February 2018. For every CEO that thinks like Mr. Narasimhan, there are multiple CEOs who have little to no idea what data and analytics can do for their company.

I recently was in a meeting with a C-level executive in a life sciences company that exclaimed that he could build and drive analytics and a company transformation with a handful of interns and that investing in analytics was not required. If this position is the same or similar to the position espoused by the executives in the company you work in, either find another job in the firm if you want to remain in the company or find a job in another company if you want to remain working in analytics.

Without public C-level support, sponsorship, and funding, you and your team are wasting your time. I refer to this view as the caveman mentality. The caveman approach to business is diametrically opposed to advanced analytics and the two will repel each other and success. You cannot club your way to success; nuance and subtlety are needed.

Continual learning and data literacy at the organizational level

Advanced analytics and AI teams can do great work and deliver impressive models, but if the front-line workforce is not trained, upskilled, and directed to implement and use the new processes, models, and insights, then it is all for naught:

> *"As AI tools become easier to use, AI use cases proliferate, and as AI projects are deployed, cross-functional teams are being pulled into AI projects. Data literacy will be required from employees outside traditional data teams— in fact, Gartner expects that 80% of organizations will start to roll out internal data literacy initiatives to upskill their workforce by 2020." [8]*

> *"In Gartner's third annual chief data officer survey, respondents said that the second most significant roadblock to progress with data and analytics is poor data literacy, rooted in ineffective communication across a wide range of increasingly diverse stakeholders. Data and analytics leaders must learn to treat information as a second language and data literacy as a core element of digital transformation." [9]*

In a previous role, our team built and delivered an analytical model to a functional business unit. The application was delivered in multiple phases; each phase took from 3 to 5 months. Each phase delivered stand-alone functionality that was intended to be used immediately by the business analysts. During the first year, the analytics team was receiving questions about the applications and requests for additional and improved functionality. Also, we received continual positive feedback about the application and the value that it delivered.

When the business team was asked to present the application to new management, the team admitted that they dabbled with the application, but never used it to actually change how they managed the relevant processes or made decisions based on the insights produced by the descriptive, predictive, and prescriptive models in the application.

The analytics team was surprised to say the least and the new management team questioned the value of the entire effort. In the end, the new management dictated that the new application be an integral part of the new process and that the team employ the insights as part of the revised decision-making process.

Organizational change can be hard, and, in most cases, it needs to be mandated to ensure that staff members follow through to leverage innovations and developments.

In *Chapter 10, The Future of Analytics - What Will We See Next?*, we expand upon the concept of and need for data and algorithmic literacy, innovation, and the widespread use of a broader set of analytic approaches. A small percentage of innovative companies are exploiting data and analytics to the fullest and those companies are utilizing a narrow set of algorithms and technologies. We will all be better served by expanding the implementation of data and analytics in a manner that will engender trust and bring analytics into the mainstream of technology and everyday use.

Defining a high-performing analytical team

What does it mean to have a high-performing advanced analytics and AI team?

It means that the team is staffed with the highest-caliber team members that you can attract, afford, and retain. The team is cohesive and collaborative and willing to review the projects of each other and sub-teams. The team members are willing to work together for the greater good of the whole team.

The advanced analytics and AI team members connect professionally with executive and senior managers across the entire company. When the analytics team interacts with senior managers and executives, the staff members outside the advanced analytics team have a positive and assured reaction to the team members. The advanced analytics team members work in a collaborative manner with the subject matter experts and each group respects the other and builds trust across the teams.

The advanced analytics team presents initial results with confidence and receives feedback and input from internal and external parties to improve data quality, model results, and the fit of the applications built for use by end users and business analysts and other data scientists outside the advanced analytics and AI team. Projects are scoped, described, undertaken, and completed and the groups move on to execute subsequent projects with enthusiasm and engagement.

When these foundational team dynamics are in place and improving over time, you have achieved the establishment of a high-functioning advanced analytics capability for your team and organization.

The general data science process

Data science projects have a general process that the majority of well-run projects follow. Let's outline the overall data science approach to a project to ensure that we have a shared understanding of the approach. The structure of the team is irrelevant to this process. Any data science team will execute a project process for most data science-related projects that are similar to the following list of steps:

1. Project ideation

2. Engagement with project sponsors and subject matter experts

3. Project charter initiation

4. Project charter refinement

5. Project management

6. Convening team meetings

7. Obtaining internal and external data

8. Testing various analytical techniques

9. Building analytical models

10. Designing the user interface (UI) and user experience (UX)

11. Presenting interim results

12. Discussing the level of success or failure in the modeling process

13. Planning for the testing of models and applications in the user workflows and daily processes

14. Planning for the production implementation of models and applications

15. Presenting the models and applications to end users

16. Receiving and acting upon suggested changes to the data, models, and applications from users, sponsors, and subject matter experts

17. Turning the final products over to the information technology team to integrate into the technology architecture

18. Turning over the final products to the end users for use in their daily workflows

19. Setting up the rhythm of communication for the on-going maintenance of models and applications

20. Beginning the next phase of work on the models or applications or moving on to the next project

The recommended process flow above works well for data science projects that are managed in the traditional waterfall project management methodology, but the process also works well in the agile project management methodology. Recently, we have been managing projects with the agile approach and the results have been reliable and repeatable. Either approach works well. My experience has been that the project management methodology used depends more on the training of the project management team and the culture of the company rather than any factor related to a data science project.

Team architecture/structure options

In my mind, most concepts exist on a continuum. Building a successful advanced analytics and AI team is typified by two approaches that inhabit the two poles of the relevant continuum – Artisanal or Factory:

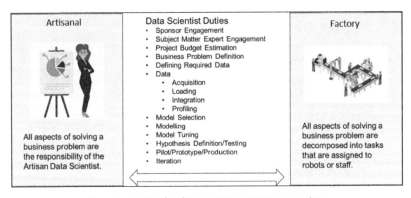

Figure 2.1: Artisanal and Factory team structure comparison

The Artisanal team architecture/structure

Let's start with the Artisanal approach.

The Artisanal approach is where the data scientists are the owners, managers, experts, and driving force behind their projects.

The data scientists design and execute every step of the process. The data scientists engage with the project sponsors, the subject matter experts, internal and external consultants, syndicated data providers, and any other individual or group that has a role to play in the project.

Data scientists capable of executing and managing the artisanal approach possess exemplary communication skills, are open to listening to a wide range of stakeholders, can work with internal and external parties, are knowledgeable about a wide range of analytical techniques, are probably experts in one or two analytical approaches, have the ability to understand the immediate next steps as well as the long-term project goals and objectives, and can translate the technical objectives of the project into business goals and financial returns.

Data scientists who can execute this model successfully are the most skilled data scientists that you can find and hire.

When does it make sense to take the Artisanal approach to building your analytics team?

1. **Cost**: While individual data scientists will cost more (you will need to pay top market rates for these staff members), the aggregate cost of the entire staff will be less than in the Factory model.

2. **Focus**: We are still assuming that you are just committing to building a team and launching the corporate analytics initiative. The organization is, in all likelihood, not ready to undertake more than a handful of advanced analytics and AI projects. And the projects that you will undertake are probably high profile and very important. Hence, you want to start with a small number of highly qualified projects that line up with the technical expertise of the data scientists that you will be hiring.

3. **Hiring**: It will be easier for you to find 3 to 5 highly qualified and talented data scientists rather than trying to hire 15 to 30 people who have narrow and specific skills that fit into the data science process outlined above.

4. **Team cohesion and dynamics**: Hiring a few rock stars and treating them right and molding them into a team is easier and more fun than hiring a large number of people focused on more mechanical work.

5. **Executive buy-in**: When highly qualified data scientists complete their work and present the projects and related business impact to project sponsors and senior executives, you will have greater executive buy-in and an easier time obtaining new and additional funding for team expansion.

6. **Word of mouth**: When the initial project succeeds, the subject matter experts will talk to subject matter experts in other areas of the company. Those subject matter experts will talk to their managers who in turn will seek you out to discuss how they can sponsor projects with your team.

7. **Team marketing**: After the success of the initial projects, you will have stories to tell of business improvement and transformation. Nothing increases your chances of future success like past success.

8. **Personal reputation**: Your personal effectiveness and the organizational awareness of the impacts of your team and your individual efforts will raise your profile and provide you with access to new opportunities.

The Factory team architecture/structure

Now let's move to the opposite end of the continuum or spectrum and discuss the Factory approach to building an advanced analytics and AI team.

The Factory approach draws its name from the mass production approach to a process-oriented endeavor. Envision a factory where there are stations and personnel who occupy those stations performing a singular task. Imagine an automotive factory where one team puts in the engine and transmission assembly and another person puts on a tire. The Factory approach to data science is similar to that of the automotive assembly process.

In the Factory model, the work process is broken down into single-focus, repeatable steps, and the process is staffed with people appropriate to execute those steps as part of the larger data science process. You may structure the team in several ways.

One possibility would be to structure the work process in the following manner:

1. Data acquisition

2. Data cleaning and integration

3. Feature engineering

4. Model building

5. Model validation

6. Project management

7. Stakeholder (sponsor and subject matter expert) management

8. Project-to-production management

9. Ongoing model and application upgrades and maintenance

The Factory process relies on a larger number of people who are executing smaller, specialized steps in the overall process.

When does it make sense to take the Factory approach to building your analytics team?

1. **Cost**: While the individual staff members will cost much less, the aggregate cost of the entire staff will be more than in the Artisanal model, but to be fair, the team will be much larger and have a substantially larger aggregate team capability and throughput. The cost in this approach is greater in aggregate, but the Factory approach enables a model and foundation for scaling the corporate capability and functionality.

2. **Focus**: We are still assuming that you are just committing to building a team and launching the corporate analytics initiative. If you are fortunate enough, executive management may have made a significant, public commitment to going full throttle into analytics. In that case, the organization has already committed to undertaking substantial and well-funded advanced analytics and AI projects. The projects will be high profile and very important. You want to take direction from executive and senior management as to where to start from a project perspective, and that will determine who you hire first.

3. **Hiring**: Hiring is easier in that the team members do not need to be multifaceted data science or analytics professionals, but you do need to hire more people than in the Artisanal approach. A suggested approach is to design your data science approach and look to hire one person for each station or step of the process to start. Optimally, it would be best if you could hire leaders for each station or step in the process, but in some cases, you will need to start with entry-level talent to have a functioning end-to-end process.

4. **Executive buy-in**: As the leader of the advanced analytics and AI team and effort, you will be presenting the projects and related business impact to project sponsors and senior executives. Hiring will take longer than in the Artisanal approach and therefore you will need to manage executive expectations of when the initial projects will deliver operational results.

5. **Word of mouth**: When the initial project succeeds, the subject matter experts will talk to subject matter experts in other areas of the company. Those subject matter experts will talk to their managers who in turn will seek you out to discuss how they can sponsor projects with your team.

6. **Team marketing**: After the success of the initial projects, you will have stories to tell of business improvement and transformation. Nothing increases your chances of future success like past success.

7. **Personal reputation**: Your personal effectiveness and the organizational awareness of the impacts of your team and your individual efforts will raise your profile and provide you with access to new opportunities.

The Hybrid team architecture/structures

We have outlined the two ends of the spectrum for hiring an advanced analytics and AI team. I recommend that you select one and execute toward building a functional, high-performing team. The objective of reaching a high-performing team can be achieved from either starting point with the same probability of success.

What happens now? A few things can happen. You can maintain the Artisanal or Factory model that was the starting point of this journey, but more than likely, the team will begin to evolve. You can let the team morph and change on its own, but it is smarter and better for the team if you manage the evolution.

The midpoint of the continuum that we have discussed is the Hybrid model. Of course, your team can skew toward the Artisanal or the Factory model, and in both cases, that is fine, and you will have a functioning team and operation. You should determine how the team evolves.

Do you want the Factory model to move toward the other end of the spectrum where you augment the existing Factory type operation with Artisanal data scientists? This can work very well. You can have the Factory operation undertake the work to support the data scientists – work such as data acquisition, data integration, structuring visualizations, and building infrastructure and security elements required to support complete applications.

Conversely, you can move in the reverse or opposite direction and build a Factory operation in addition to your existing Artisanal team.

Typically, the Artisanal team will be working on high-value applications that will have a substantial impact on business operations. These high-value applications can be considered proprietary intellectual property and you may want to engage the legal team to protect them via patent applications.

In addition to these high-value applications, there will be applications that you should build and implement that ensure that your firm and operations maintain competitiveness and cost-effectiveness. These analytical applications vary based on the industry and market that the firm operates and competes in, but some examples that are relevant to multiple industries and markets are supply chain simulation, pricing optimization, dynamic delivery route determination, and many others. These applications can be built and deployed by the Factory elements of your operation and team or outsourced to third-party consultants. The consulting effort would be managed by the Factory operation of the team.

With a Hybrid model, you can achieve the creation and deployment of innovative intellectual property that can change the competitive profile of the company and you can build applications that keep your firm at the leading edge of operational effectiveness and efficiency. The Artisanal group can drive innovation, and change, through the deployment of highly valued patentable applications that put and keep the firm on the leading edge of any industry. The Factory group can build, deploy, and maintain analytical applications that achieve and maintain operational efficiency across global operations at scale.

I have built and evolved analytics teams starting at each end of the spectrum. My preferred method is to start with an Artisanal team and evolve toward a Hybrid model. Starting with the Artisanal model has a number of benefits to you, the analytics team, and the company as a whole. The first benefit is that starting with an Artisanal team enables you and the analytics team to connect with C-Level and senior executives on mission-critical problems. The second benefit is that you and the analytics team can act like a SWAT team, moving quickly to understand the problem, moving through modeling the problem, and offering solutions and insights in a matter of weeks or days rather than months or years. The early success can be followed up by taking on larger, more complex problems, which will require a larger team, which marks the start of the evolution toward the Hybrid model. This approach works very well, and I recommend it highly.

The implications of proprietary versus open source tools

Over the past 20 years, there has been a significant change in technology that enables teams and individuals to design, develop, and deploy analytical applications. The change has been in the evolution and refinement of open source software and related platforms.

20 years ago, there were only proprietary software offerings from SAS, SPSS, Statistica, Minitab, and others. An entire generation, or possibly two generations, of psychologists, social scientists, mathematicians, and analysts grew up using these software systems in undergraduate- and graduate-level academic programs. When entering the business, research, and governmental workforces, those people brought their favorite tools with them.

More recently, open source systems like Knime, RapidMiner, and others offer community versions for free. In addition to the many open source tools and community versions available, the rise and evolution of the R and Python languages have provided a rich toolset for people to build advanced analytics applications without purchasing expensive proprietary software.

Most people stop at the point in the discussion where the community version of the open source tools does not have a license fee. That is missing the point. As the coauthor of my first book, *Analytics: How to Win with Intelligence*, Shawn Rogers, is fond of saying, *"Open source is free like a puppy."* Yes, it is great to get the puppy and it is free at that moment, but there are many expenses that come along with the free bundle of joy. In almost all cases, if you are going to use open source software for production purposes, you will need to buy support, the enterprise version, management software, and interactive development environment or other software and/or services to make the environment effective, efficient, productive, secure, and collaborative.

The truly important element of this market characteristic for the purpose of our discussion is that the proprietary software, open source delineation in the market splits the age of the people you will be looking to hire by age.

From my informal research and observation over the past 5 to 7 years, most data scientists that are over 40 years old will predominately want to use proprietary software. The vast majority of data scientists under 30 years old will use open source coupled with R or Python.

This simple observation and the fact that data scientists are typically allowed to use the tools that they feel most comfortable with means that to have a collaborative team, you want the majority of the team to use tools that foster the sharing of code, approaches, and methodologies.

In practical and simplistic terms, this means that you will either end up with an older team using proprietary tools or a younger team using open source tools supplemented with R and or Python. Again, like the evolution of the team, you can let this organically develop, but acting in this manner will cause you and your team lost productivity, team conflict, and other management headaches.

Pick one approach or the other. Do not mix and match.

Summary

Building an advanced analytics and AI team is the same as building any other high-performance team in several respects, but in other crucially important respects, it is the converse of what you would expect. There are also nuances and subtleties that, even today, elude executives and senior managers.

Analytics teams, and those individuals that comprise those teams – the highly talented and skilled people involved in scoping, designing, building, testing, implementing, deploying, and in some cases, maintaining advanced analytics applications, systems, and environments – are unique.

In this chapter, we have examined the organizational context and considerations that may not be obvious when building an analytics team. We have provided a framework to use when thinking about the type of analytics talent that you may want to hire and how that talent can come into the new organization and have a positive impact in a matter of weeks or days. We have outlined how you can consider hiring people outside the typical population when building your team.

With the organizational and market context set and the foundations defined, let's move on to *Chapter 3, Managing and Growing an Analytics Team*, where we will continue our discussion of how to build an analytics function that transforms an organization at numerous levels.

Chapter 2 footnotes

1. *Dell Autism Hiring Program*, Dell website, January 3, 2020, `https://jobs.dell.com/neurodiversity`

2. *Why Dell Is Making Neurodiverse Hiring A Priority*, October 16, 2019, Danielle Hughes, `https://www.catalyst.org/2019/10/16/why-dell-is-making-neurodiverse-hiring-a-priority/`

3. Ibid.

4. *In a Tight Labor Market, a Disability May Not Be a Barrier*, September 5, 2019, Ben Casselman, `https://www.nytimes.com/2019/09/05/business/economy/recruiting-labor-force.html`

5. Ibid.

6. Ibid.

7. *Novartis CEO Steers Drug Maker Back to R&D*, February 2018, Wall Street Journal, `https://www.wsj.com/articles/novartis-ceo-steers-drug-maker-back-to-r-d-1518962400`

8. *8 AI trends we're watching in 2020*, January 7, 2020, Roger Magoulas, O'Reilly Artificial Intelligence Newsletter, `https://www.oreilly.com/radar/8-ai-trends-were-watching-in-2020/`

9. *Smarter with Gartner, Gartner Keynote: Do you Speak Data?*, March 5, 2018, Christy Pettey, https://www.gartner.com/smarterwithgartner/gartner-keynote-do-you-speak-data/?utm_medium=email&utm_source=topic+optin&utm_campaign=awareness&utm_content=20191230+ai+nl&mkt_tok=eyJpIjoiTVdNd01qZzzFOVE kzWkRrNCIsInQiOiJ4UDFVb2xEOXRCOG-NiWENsZjZpWU1WTkc1b3dtdVdEbnRFNXBH eW9LcHVqQTRFbmdYN09scHJibnlWMnI0blwv b2d6VWZTR1pDaHZjWVA4Q2xSM2R5T1NPaXFR NWhvM1wvZ0ZcL3d0SHduU2VKSEJZZ0ZRQk5 VZnJrZE90VEZpWW5YiJ9

CHAPTER 3

MANAGING AND GROWING AN ANALYTICS TEAM

"Nothing is as powerful as an idea whose time has come."

—Victor Hugo

After completing the previous chapter, you now have a good idea of what it takes to build a high-performing advanced analytics and AI team. It is obvious that after building the team, you also need to begin to manage the team to build team cohesion, connect the analytics team with stakeholders in the organization, and to begin the journey of delivering operational improvements through data and analytics.

In this chapter, we will examine the hiring process, the varying types of talent that you should consider adding to your team, the organizational dynamics of building a team, stakeholder management, and a number of other aspects that are critically important to a solid start to managing and growing your new team.

Managerial focus and balance

Managing and growing an advanced analytics and AI team is rewarding, challenging, and one of the most gratifying and frustrating endeavors I have ever been involved in. I would not trade my experiences and history in hiring and managing these brilliant minds for any other professional experience.

I have had the experience of being directed to manage groups of people who have been involved in executing highly routine work. I am not sure how people maintain interest in managing these groups and the work those team members execute. Also, I am unsure how people who do this work find it engaging and interesting past the first or second cycle of the repetitive process that is required of them, but we, as a society, are fortunate enough to have people among us who will do this work, but these are not the people you want on your analytics team nor would they want to be involved in, or qualified for, the highly variable, intensely challenging work of an advanced analytics and artificial intelligence (AI) team.

Managing an analytics team, like any organizational unit, requires the analytics leader to have a simultaneous focus on the internal management of the collective and an external focus on managing the analytics group within the overall organization or company. As the analytics leader, you need to be adept at the management of multiple parties and partners, including junior and senior analytics staff, your peers, stakeholders, senior managers, and executives. Managing upward in the organization, inside and outside of your group in the broader organization is a critical responsibility and you must make time to ensure that senior managers and executives support your plans and mission. If you have never had to manage this wide range of stakeholders and sponsors, you may be saying to yourself, yes, of course, that is required; all management roles require this level of engagement and direct connection, but that is not the case. At least it is not the case at the level of active and sustained involvement that will be required for success in this role.

Sponsor and stakeholder management

Your personal success and that of the analytics team lies partly in your ability to connect and effectively partner with a wide range of people in the organization. The skills you possess, employ, and deploy in the area of emotional intelligence are paramount in this aspect of your work.

In a global organization, if you have a global role, you will need to meet with a substantial number of people, and depending on the culture of the organization, you may need to meet with those people either in one-on-one settings, small departmental groups, or in large auditorium/stadium settings, or perhaps in all of those settings. In a previous leadership role, I ran the global advanced analytics and AI effort and the associated teams. In the first year, I held over 630 meetings around the world. Those meetings included C-level executives, division managers, team leaders, individual contributors, external vendors, supply chain partners, and customers/patients in each region and country that the company operated in and included multiple company representatives from every operational function across the organization.

All meetings are important to the subsequent success of the analytics team and the engagement you will need from each constituent that you meet. Meetings with C-level executives and senior managers are especially important. These are the individuals who will direct their downline organizations to work with you and your team or to thwart your team and efforts. This group of people needs to know that you and your team are working on their behalf to improve the outcomes, operational metrics, and an organizational future that aligns with and delivers on their objectives, goals, and compensation plans.

Without agreement and alignment, functional managers and executives will meet with you and they will be polite, but they will not direct their teams to engage with you and your team.

It won't be obvious to the organization, or maybe even to you, but it will become apparent after a year or more passes where you have been successful in engaging the executive level and where you have more work to do to bring them on board with the analytics, innovation, and transformation journey.

The good news is that you will be successful in engaging a subset of executives and teams. With those teams, you will execute projects, modify processes, develop applications, and deploy models. These will be your quick wins or success stories that you will use to demonstrate the experience and expertise of your team.

Creating internal demand

Word-of-mouth networking by those that have collaborated with you and your team is crucial for sustained success. The people that your team has helped reach and exceed their goals will talk about your team, the projects, and the value that has been delivered. The stories being conveyed at sales meetings, functional gatherings, in the cafeteria, and in formal presentations will make or break the ability of your team to expand its connections and influence internally.

Word-of-mouth – internal and external – marketing, can be thought of as a flywheel effect. Once momentum is achieved, it becomes self-sustaining. Executives and senior managers will tell their staff to seek you and your group out to solve a wide range of problems. Many of those challenges will not be appropriate for your group to address, but if you can direct those team members to other internal groups or external consultants or provide solutions that they can build themselves, you and your group will gain a positive reputation for being the go-to team to solve simple and complex problems.

One piece of advice I will offer for you to employ in the process of starting and accelerating the word-of-mouth effect in an organization that has worked exceptionally well in the past is that you should tell the functional managers to not overthink the problem or challenge that they are attempting to solve. You should not underestimate the concern of the people who want to approach you but feel that they cannot convey the problem well enough or that they have not packaged the discussion in the "right" way. Communicate to people of all levels that they simply need to contact you or your team to start the dialog. It does not matter to you, and it should not matter to you, how articulate they are in describing the challenge or how refined the idea is; you simply want to start the dialog and with as many people as possible, at as many levels as there are in the organization. Always encourage people to bring ideas forward.

This is your demand creation function. You need to encourage people to speak up the moment they have an idea and you want the entire organization to think of you and your team as the architects of solutions when a challenge arises. The issue with people overthinking the problem is that they start to refine the discussion, which is not the optimal approach; you want them to ramble and discuss tangential ideas and talk about the perceived ramifications of the problem and all the unusual and unorthodox approaches that might come to their minds. These holistic descriptions provide a complete picture of the challenge.

You may find that the organization needs multiple advanced analytics applications to solve the complete problem. In general, functional teams and their managers are focused on the problem that causes them the most discomfort or is the most pressing. Once the analytical team engages with the functional team and the dialog begins to flow, you may find that the problem presented is the tip of the iceberg. To solve the immediate challenge presented, the analytics team may need to develop a number of applications based on descriptive statistics to adequately describe the operations and operating conditions.

Once the operating conditions are well documented and described, then the analytics team can build predictive applications to provide a forward view of operational metrics, and then if it is of value, the analytics team may design and build a simulation and/or optimization tool for end users.

You are better served when the entire global organization sees the advanced analytics and AI team as an innovative group of practical and pragmatic thinkers who are pro-active, easy to engage with, and interested in their individual success and that of their team and group.

In the past, I was approached by the corporate communication team because they felt that advanced analytics and AI was a hot topic that was trending internally and externally. The initial conversation was simply informational and exploratory; neither of us had an idea of where the dialog would lead. The result of that discussion was an agreement that one of the analytical applications that had been built and was driving a new level of effectiveness and efficiency was of internal and external interest and we wrote and edited a story for the company newsletter. That story was then edited and posted to the new corporate mobile app on multiple news channels. The story was then pitched to an external expert who wrote a new story that ran in a top business publication in the US and finally the story was excerpted and included in the annual report. All this activity and positive exposure came from an initial conversation because a team member in corporate communications *thought* that the topic might be interesting.

Typically, we, in analytics, do not think about where our work comes from. When you consider the idea of where work is sourced from, wouldn't you want the work to come from strategically aligned areas of the business that result in measurable, significant positive improvements in the way the firm operates, patients are treated, customers are engaged with, and the level of profit generated? There is a larger topic here that we will examine later, but let's keep the focus on demand generation.

The way you, as the analytics leader, show up in the company and in each meeting determines who will engage with you and your team. The impressions you make determines how successful the team and you will be because it determines the people who will engage with you and your team and the level of funding, effort, and resources they will dedicate to the projects that you and they jointly undertake. That engagement results in success that is discussed around the organization, and it begins a wave of new cycles that carry the process forward and can carry you and your team forward for years.

So, when you think that you want to phone it in on a meeting or postpone a meeting, or just outright cancel a meeting because you can't immediately see what will come of it, think again.

Let me outline a couple of examples of activities that analytics teams I was part of, or led, undertook to create interest and incent participation across a broader cross-section of the organization. These activities and events can be particularly valuable if you can create buy-in from your leadership peers.

While at Dell, we created an **Analytics Innovation Day and Contests**. Teams from across the organization showcased their use of data and analytics. One of the primary and most visible results was the cross-pollination of collaboration from areas that, previous to the event, were not aware of each other.

At CSL Behring, I organized a **Data Science Summit** (**DSS**) and asked team members from around the world to present their vision, views, and projects in data and analytics. Nearly 150 people attended a 3-day event that showcased over 35 different areas of focus related to data and analytics. The DSS not only spurred collaboration, it created new groups focused on data and analytics and created new projects to drive change across the company.

Projects and initiatives like these elevate team members in the analytics team and across functional groups as well as creating tales of winning with analytics that can really go far in getting more buy-in and engagement momentum.

Every meeting is a chance for you to show up and put your best self forward. Don't squander that opportunity. Not everyone gets the chance to make a difference.

To command or to collaborate

Recently, I had the opportunity to speak with a person who has had a highly successful 30-year career in the US public sector, at the federal level, who had successfully transitioned to a new role as a C-level executive in one of the most iconic American brands. The company has been in business for over 150 years and has been an innovator throughout that time. When he provided the opportunity to ask a question or two, I asked, "What is the most common reason people do not succeed in their endeavors in advanced analytics?". He responded, "Hubris. Thinking that they know more than their stakeholders and/or customers do about the businesses that the stakeholders are running on a daily basis."

Let's contrast that with another executive, in a global organization with over 25,000 employees operating around the world in a firm that has over 100 years of successful operating history. This C-level executive who is capping off a 20+ year history in large organizations recently joined a new company and is making his way around the globe communicating his vision for the firm. He recently said something like, "We need to stop listening to the business. They do not know what they need. We need to tell them how to run their business and operations."

Both of these comments were made in the same week.

There couldn't be more distance between these diametrically opposed positions in how to approach engagement with sponsors, stakeholders, and subject matter experts. I find it interesting and slightly ironic that the person who has spent multiple decades at the senior levels of one the most advanced military organizations in the world is the individual espousing humility and collaboration and the corporate executive is raising his voice and promoting a dictatorial style of management and a unidirectional approach to communications and operations.

I have been subject to both approaches and I am here to explain and communicate that the world, for at least highly evolved and intelligent people, is well past the top-down command and control approach. In extraordinarily successful organizations that aspire to succeed over a period measured in decades and centuries, demeaning people and offending them by telling them what to do is an outmoded approach.

This is especially true for knowledge workers. It is worth noting that this overbearing approach is an absolute non-starter for the best Millennial and Gen-Z talent. I suspect that Gen-X would still put up with it if the pay was exceptional, so it's doable but pointlessly expensive when managing Gen-X talent, but it is not even a possibility for the next generation.

An open or fixed mindset?

As we now have four generations in the workforce, a more collaborative approach to all phases of projects and work overall is required. We do see some leaders in organizations being more disconnected from the reality of the workplace than we do in other areas, but this dynamic is not a function of age. Of course, it can be, and we do see a correlation between age and an unrealistic view of how the workplace operates, but it is more a product of being closed and narrow-minded rather than having attained a certain age.

How do you know which end of the spectrum people are operating from? How do you know if they hold the detestable view that they know better than almost all others? It is an important element of their world view to understand. People who feel that they are smarter than others have a wide range of views and beliefs that are less than optimal in the workplace.

One way to discover how people think is to ask questions. Sounds simple, but, in general, people do not ask enough questions. You will often hear people exclaim, "How could I have known?"

You could have asked. That would have helped uncover some of the mysteries that seem to evade our view and comprehension.

One of the reliable indicators of whether someone leans toward the open-minded, collaborative end of the spectrum is whether they hold a view that lifelong learning is a key to being and remaining relevant. Not only do they *say* that they believe in lifelong learning, but do they engage in it? Do they support their teams in learning on the job? Do they send their employees to other business units to immerse themselves in operations to learn how things work on a day-to-day basis? Do they ask questions of others and genuinely seem interested in learning from other people on a consistent and continual basis?

An open mindset has little to nothing to do with enrolling in classes or obtaining a degree or degrees. Actually, some people who are most strident about getting additional degrees have the least amount of interest in learning. They are concerned with showing how smart they are, not about learning. This segment of the population is characterized by a fixed mindset. They were told, or have come to believe, certain fixed principles such as they are always the smartest people in the room or that they do not need to listen to the opinions and ideas of others. This is the type of person that you do not want on your analytics team. Their obnoxious, individualistic, and corrosive views only diminish the value created by the advanced analytics and AI team.

An additional characteristic to be wary of in people with a fixed mindset is that, in their view, all trouble, failure, and delay emanates from others. It is hard for this group of people to see that they can be the source of poor ideas, and the way that they approach a task can increase the probability of failure, and how they act and show up in a group can be a primary or a substantial contributing factor in the group not achieving its goals. It is difficult to impossible for these people to take responsibility for their role in failure or anything less than complete success.

This mindset manifests itself in paranoid reactions, blaming others, and an inability to accurately view their roles in projects and outcomes.

Lifelong learning is a mindset, a world view that is about being curious, engaged, and inquisitive about life, business, people, and their realities. These are the best people to have on your team.

Productivity premium

There has been a great deal written about the productivity gap between the most talented and those possessing less talent. For the most part, it is true that highly skilled, talented individuals can produce 10 to 20 times more, and better, work than those at the bottom of the scale [1]. This discussion started in the late 1960s and was focused on programming when the dialog began, but research over the past five decades has illustrated that this phenomenon is prevalent in a wide range of human endeavors. "A study by Norm Augustine found that in a variety of professions – writing, football, invention, police work, and other occupations – the top 20 percent of people produced about 50 percent of the output, whether the output is touchdowns, patents, solved cases, or software." [2]

This dynamic is the same and may even be more pronounced in advanced analytics and AI teams. Talented and skilled people are better at all aspects of the job and there are a significant number of nuanced aspects to the role of senior or principal data scientist: stakeholder management, technical skills, project management, project estimating; written, verbal, and presentation skills; emotional intelligence, empathy, persistence, diligence, patience, and more. Not everyone is at the top of the scale on all measures, but those that are at the top of the scale in relation to multiple factors will be more adept at learning how to improve in the areas where they need to improve. Not only are the most talented the most productive, they are the least problematic.

In one of my analytic leadership roles, I had a data scientist who was just barely above a junior data scientist in all technical skills, below a junior data scientist in stakeholder management, and poor in verbal and written communications and presentations, but in their mind, they were the best on the team in all the aforementioned skill areas. Also, they produced the least amount of work of the lowest quality, required the most management attention, and generated the most stakeholder complaints and dissatisfaction. I had inherited this employee from the previous management team. This employee was nothing but headaches. I wish I could report that I was able to help this employee see the self-sabotaging behavior, the fixed mindset, and the lack of perspective, but I could not. I could only help this person move on to a new role in a new company and wish them the best on their journey. They have a long way to go, but, in the end, we all have a long way to go. We all have different starting and ending points on those journeys.

The rhythm of work

As discussed in *Chapter 1, An Overview of Successful and High-Performing Analytics Teams*, high-performing analytics professionals are different, in a good way, but it is also true that high-performing analytics teams are the same as all teams; no one wants to work hard and see a team member who does not. However, that is not to say that everyone needs to be and should always be working at 100% utilization; no one can sustain that level of work or that pace of delivery. Such an expectation is unrealistic and can be cruel if pushed too far.

After working for approximately 5 years, about the time that I completed my MBA, I began to view my career as a marathon that requires a moderate and steady pace. Before that realization, I worked full out, all the time; each day was a sprint. Let's be clear: I am not a marathon runner and I am only using the marathon as a metaphor; I am not commenting on people who run marathons competitively or even as an area of casual interest.

Over the course of a career, a project, or a period, the pace will need to quicken from time to time. You cannot expect to run at the most comfortable pace all the time; you and the team need to keep up and match the needs of the project and or company. The ebb and flow of the pace of work is to be expected and proactively managed to increase the productivity and well-being of all team members and the team as a whole.

After I had run multiple analytics teams, I realized that no advanced analytics and AI project runs smoothly on a forward basis. They all encounter some type of friction and delays. This is nothing unique to analytics projects, but the types of delays can include delays unique to advanced analytics and AI projects and delays that are common to every project.

The solution that I have developed and have successfully employed in multiple roles is that every member of the analytics team undertakes and manages their personal project portfolio of work. Sounds obvious when you say it, but I have never seen or read about anyone else managing an advanced analytics team in this manner. It works exceptionally well.

Personal project portfolio

Junior data scientists will likely come from the intern and co-op participant pool. Hiring people for full-time roles who have spent time with the analytics team and have been exposed to the broader organization is a much better way to hire full-time staff as compared to the traditional hiring process, especially in such a heated and frothy market as the data science market is today and looks to be in the foreseeable future.

If junior staff members do come from the intern and co-op participant ranks, then you understand their hard and soft skills and you know what they can and cannot do well. You, and they, understand the team dynamics and type of work and the cadence that is expected from them and the team. The ramp-up time to productivity is shorter and less time-consuming.

Junior members of the advanced analytics and AI team should be expected to undertake one main project and one or two service requests, to engage with the Community of Practice on an assigned basis, to own and manage a Special Interest Group, to develop and maintain an area(s) of technical knowledge and expertise, to engage with the other team members in project reviews and technical consultations, to engage with interns and co-op participants, to be part of the hiring process, to attend staff and team meetings, and do all of this with a positive attitude and enthusiasm.

In the beginning, you or senior data scientists should plan on attending meetings with the junior team members where sponsors and stakeholders will be in attendance. You can use these meetings as opportunities to show the junior data scientist how to interact and engage with personnel from functional areas of the business. Over time, junior data scientists will develop their own rapport and style, and become comfortable attending meetings on their own.

Senior members of the advanced analytics and AI team should be expected to undertake two main projects and multiple service requests, to engage with the Community of Practice on a regular basis, to own and manage a Special Interest Group, to develop and maintain an area(s) of technical knowledge and expertise, to engage with the other senior team members in project reviews and technical consultations, to mentor junior staff members, to manage interns and co-op participants, to engage in the hiring process, to attend staff and team meetings, and to do all of this with a smile.

Let's break down the list of activities a bit further to ensure that we have a common understanding of the management of the prioritized personal project portfolio for our analytics team members:

1. **Two main projects**: The projects are significant to the company and have implications for the functional area. They are high-profile projects where line-of-business staff members are assigned their time and the expectations are that the results of the project will be used to improve the operations of the company. The projects can vary in duration from a few months to a year or more.

2. **Multiple service requests**: Service requests are formulated by the functional areas. The functional area staff may believe that these requests are projects, but in reality, the request can be satisfied in a few hours to a day or two. Senior data scientists can field and stratify most service requests without consultation or discussion with anyone other than the requestor.

3. **Engage with the Community of Practice on a regular basis**: The Community of Practice has a number of elements that are similar to social media and need to be attended on a regular basis to ensure that the community remains interesting to the members and is worth engaging in. Senior team members should be writing and posting on technical topics, project developments, publishing results, and generally keeping the organization aware of all the developments that are transpiring in the company and in the analytics market in general.

4. **Own and manage a Special Interest Group**: A Community of Practice will comprise a few hundred members/employees. A **Special Interest Group (SIG)** will comprise 10 to 100 people. A senior manager will own and manage a SIG. They will set the cadence of meetings and the focus of discussions, and ensure that the SIG remains interesting and a forum and group that encourages the relevant interests of the members and provides an engaging forum for dialog, discussion, and innovation.

5. **Develop and maintain an area(s) of technical knowledge and expertise**: Advanced analytics and AI is a complex collection of technical and mathematical fields. Each senior member of the team should have an area or multiple areas of technical expertise where they are the go-to person for the team. Areas like neural networks, natural language processing, Bayesian statistics, and more.

6. **Engage with the other senior team members in project reviews and technical consultations**: No one can be an expert in all areas. The team needs to consult with each other to ensure that projects, solutions, and applications are being built in an optimal manner.

7. **Mentor junior staff members**: We are discussing the use and management of the Artisanal model for a data science team. There are many aspects of the team to manage and grow. It can be difficult for junior team members to focus on the most immediate and important elements of their projects and their development. Senior staff members need to help the junior staff members stay on track and ensure that they are making progress across all fronts.

8. **Manage interns and co-op participants**: Interns and co-op participants are a great way to grow the team and, as we discussed in *Chapter 1, An Overview of Successful and High-Performing Analytics Teams*, internships and co-ops are great ways to get to know younger candidates. These extended engagements enable interns and co-op participants to gain experience in a real work setting and to see how the company functions. It also enables the team to see and experience these possible new hires in action and to see how they think, act, and react to the day-to-day cadence of an office.

9. **Engage in the hiring process**: Hiring new team members is critical and all senior staff members need to engage fully in the process and weigh in on who is the best fit to join and grow the team.

10. **Attend staff and team meetings**: Collaboration and cooperation are key and much of the foundations of both are established and fostered in staff and team meetings.

The first time I implemented this workload and mix, it was received with skepticism and a more than a little criticism from the analytics team. It was perceived as being too much. And, I suppose if anyone was fully engaged and moving all these work elements forward each day, it *would be* too much, but no one is involved in every activity each day. As noted in the previous section, projects slow down, sponsors move on to other jobs, companies undertake reorganizations, management team members are replaced, datasets are not available, and the reasons for project slowdowns and/or cancellations go on and on.

One of the primary reasons for developing this personal project portfolio approach for the analytics team is that if a project is slowed down or canceled, it is truly a management headache to find work for someone who suddenly finds themselves made idle by external circumstances. If you have a backlog of work, it is made easier, but even a backlog of work does not ensure that the work in the queue will match the experience, expertise, and abilities of the staff member that is now not fully engaged.

Another contributing factor or reason for assigning a portfolio of projects to junior and senior staff members is that you need an overt methodology for evaluating who can and will move up the ranks of the staff. Over time you will need to grow and promote a specific soft and hard skills mix to meet the needs of the organization and as you manage the mix of the team from a pure Artisanal team model to a Factory model and ultimately to a Hybrid model.

As a quick reminder, the Artisanal model for an analytics team is where you start out with a small number of highly skilled staff members who handle all aspects of the project from start to finish and the Factory model is where you hire a larger number of specialists who focus on singular tasks in a series of tasks that are assembled as part of a larger process to complete each project.

In the interest of continually upskilling and exposing analytics team members to new areas, an option for job enrichment is to find and assign challenges where the challenge sits outside of the norm of what might be a typical project. Examples are taking on projects for charitable causes, engaging with a high-level externality that the board or C-suite might bring up, tackling an analytics contest, and so on. These are options for projects or initiatives that could be incorporated into the ongoing diet of projects.

And finally, the last reason for the creation, assignment, and management of a portfolio is that people get bored with the monotony of singular tasks, which leads to a lack of job fulfillment, which leads to dissatisfaction, and ultimately, to employee turnover.

Given the wide mix of personalities, powerful intellects, the possibility of neurodiversity, and the speed at which people assimilate new knowledge and their hunger for more, the implementation of a personal portfolio approach to work assignment and management makes the entire team work more smoothly and engages the emotional and intellectual intelligence faculties of the analytics and functional team members in a way that is difficult or impossible to do without this approach.

Managing team dynamics

Hiring and managing a high-performance analytics team presents interesting and subtle challenges. There are areas where you have options to choose between multiple courses of action and there are areas where it may seem like you have options, but in reality, you do not.

One of my primary objectives in the upcoming sections is to save you time, effort, and in some cases anguish. Read on for guidance on how to make progress in hiring and managing in the most effective manner possible.

The front end of the talent pipeline

Interns and co-op participants are a viable and valuable way to grow your advanced analytics and AI team. One aspect of internship and co-op programs that I feel strongly about is that you need to pay participants. Pay them the fair or market rate for top talent relative to their tenure and experience, which admittedly is almost non-existent at this point in their careers, but it is hoped and expected that the people being brought into internship and co-op programs hold great promise as the next generation of new staff members on your analytics team, correct? The trend over the past few years for unpaid internships is a ridiculous approach to what should be a relatively serious element of the talent acquisition process. If you are going to request or expect that someone undertakes productive and valuable work, why would you not pay them? And if the "work" you are asking them to do is meaningless, why would you bother?

If you can afford it and your team can manage it, you should assign an intern or co-op participant on a one-on-one basis to a senior data scientist. Assigning more than one intern or co-op participant to a data scientist depends on the ability of the senior data scientist to assign meaningful work to the multiple interns and manage the relationships in a competent and productive manner.

One of the challenges of internships and co-op programs is the time interval. Internships and co-op programs are relatively short in duration. For some senior data scientists, it is difficult to decompose work streams into discrete tasks that can be understood, undertaken, and completed in the window of the intern or co-op engagement.

Also, it can be challenging for the intern or the co-op participant to grasp the work, get started; engage with the senior data scientist, and the broader analytics team, and possibly a subject matter expert from the functional team; and complete the work. It is a great deal to ask of an undergraduate student and even a significant hurdle for some graduate-level students.

Another challenge is that you want the work to be comprehensible and achievable given the personal and technical skills, mindset, and maturity of the intern or co-op participant. The data science teams need to rely on the work, but not put so much responsibility and expectation on the young person that they crumble or freeze in their execution of the work.

And the final challenge is that while the work needs to be meaningful, it cannot be mission-critical. An example of this nuance in definition might help. Data engineering is usually required for every analytics project. Interns and co-op students have typically had to execute this type of work in numerous Kaggle competitions, academic projects, class exercises, and more. This is work that is necessary for the success of the project and the intern and/or co-op participant has the ability and experience to undertake and complete the work.

Interns and co-op participants should be very comfortable with this type of assignment and be willing and able to complete the work in a time-bounded and even time-pressured environment. An example of work that should not be assigned to an intern or co-op participant is the selection of the analytical approach to use in the project. The selection and execution of the analytical approach is a mission-critical task and can make or break the success of the project. The intern or co-op student, in most cases, has never had to look at a refined dataset and select an analytical approach with such important consequences attached to their decision. The work assigned to the intern and co-op participant should be meaningful, useful, and contribute to the success of the project, but not be able to derail the project if it is not executed perfectly.

It takes a team

Talented and skilled individuals are better at collaboration. In general, they have a more evolved world view or mature understanding of human nature. They are less possessive of the ideas that they may have generated or those that they may have borrowed in the process of understanding and solving multi-step, interconnected, and interrelated challenges. This is important for several reasons.

First, most challenges that are appropriate for the advanced analytics and AI team to solve are mission-critical, difficult, and wide-ranging, thereby requiring more than one person to develop solutions to them. By nature, the challenges faced by you and your team are best solved by a team, or at least a sub-team, and hence collaboration and communication within the analytics team and between the analytics team and the functional team that has "hired" your team to solve their challenge are required and crucial to the success of the majority of projects.

There is a subset of the overall population of people that you could hire who are very good at the technical aspects of the role and may have been incredible individual contributors but who are ill-equipped to collaborate. These possible staff members might be good junior data scientists, but they will not be successful as senior staff members unless they can grow their ability to be part of a larger effort. You may even choose to hire them, but they need to understand the team model, structure, their current and expected role, and the skills that they need to develop and master before they can become senior members of the analytics team.

Second, the best solutions are designed and developed in an iterative manner where the sub-team presents their initial and interim findings and work products to the larger analytics team for evaluation, discussion, and iteration. If the team member cannot present their work products in a cogent manner, the broader team cannot help in improving the project.

If the team member's ego will not allow them to hear and receive feedback, the impact will be felt beyond the project and will impact the team dynamic and the work environment. In some cases, you and other analytical team members will attribute this inability to the presentation and communication skills of the employee, and in some cases that may be the reason for their lack of sharing, but you need to delve more deeply into the root cause of the lack of sharing. In a few cases, you will find that the lack of sharing is due to feelings of paranoia or superiority. Both root causes need to be discerned in the interview process and if people possess these views, you are best served by not bringing these individuals on to your team. The root causes of these behaviors are beyond the ability of most managers to lessen or eliminate.

Third, beyond the analytics team, the sub-team needs to present their iterative work to the sponsors and subject matter experts for review and revision. They need to engender confidence and engagement from the functional team that has entrusted the analytics team to build a solution to the challenge that the functional team is facing. The sub-team leadership needs to be open to the input of the business team, but also needs to be cognizant of keeping the project on track and remain true to the charter that has been agreed to. If the project sub-team is not open to the ideas of the business, the collaboration and the quality of the project will suffer and, even worse, future collaborations and projects may never come to fruition because the business team will experience the lack of openness and receptivity of the sub-team leader or the entire sub-team.

And finally, no one person can know the entirety of the knowledge base in the wide-ranging and interconnected fields of study that are required to build the optimal and complete solution to any of the challenges presented by the functional areas of any business.

Just as it is difficult for any medical, legal, or professional practitioner to keep up with the volume of research and innovation in any field, it is impossible for an analytics professional to be knowledgeable about all of the changes and innovations in the technical and functional areas of the multiple fields that they may work in on the many projects that they will undertake.

A key takeaway is that no one can be everything in a project, team, or sub-team. Collaboration and communication skills are key to the initial, immediate, and long-term success of the analytics team.

Over the past 30 or so years that I have been involved and engaged in this market, I have seen the evolution of analytics and technical professionals getting a pass on communication skills, emotional intelligence, and other soft skills. To some extent, many of the less functional team members and those with designated disabilities or special conditions will still be granted dispensations to compensate for those syndromes and conditions, and appropriately so; but those that want to succeed and grow in this market need to be operating at the highest level of their abilities on both sides of the equation – technical and soft skills. The bar has been raised, and to be a top performer, you need to meet or exceed those expectations.

Simply the best

One of the most valuable, unique, and rare qualities individuals that make up a phenomenally successful advanced analytics team possess is the ability to understand the constituent elements that encompass, comprise, and come together to cause or perpetuate an outcome.

On the face of it, most people think that they know why processes happen, what the process actually is, and what the outcomes are, but do they really know? Are they truly aware of the nature and driving forces of why processes work and why a company operates in a certain way? Typically, "common knowledge" is not accurate or a true representation of how the world works.

Many people operate on intuition and gut feelings. A number of these people have been world leaders and have written best-selling books on the topic of managing in this manner. The problem is that these leaders are the exception, not the rule. The majority of people are operating under misguided perceptions of how processes really work. Being inquisitive and delving into how things really work is a skill that can be developed and it should be developed in a broader cross-section of the population, but that is a topic for *Chapter 7, Selecting Winning Projects,* and *Chapter 10, The Future of Analytics – What Will We See Next?.*

The best analytics professionals ask questions like, what are the context and driving factors that combine to create an outcome? Why does this process run in this manner? Why does the team use this source of data? Why is the forecast formulated in this manner?

The most talented analytics professionals are keen, unique, and in some cases, unusual observers of life, processes, people, and the world in general. They look beyond the surface of a process, result, or model. They look at the precursors. They look at the economic and organizational context of the phenomena to be dissected. They look for elemental causes and effects.

This manner of looking at the world is a skill, and like any other skill, it can be fostered and improved, but the most talented people that I have met do not need to work at this skill. They seem effortless in seeing processes, problems, and challenges in a way that presents the best options for how to analyze, understand, and improve how these operations function. They are amazing in this manner because this is their natural way of seeing the world. This quality is one of the primary capabilities needed to be a highly successful advanced analytics professional.

Advanced analytics systems are about providing solutions to improve the yield in manufacturing plants across numerous industries; enabling predictive maintenance in cars, planes, windmills, bridges, dams, and pipelines; providing for the widely discussed anticipation of autonomous vehicles, and much, much more.

This is the essence of why there is so much hype about advanced analytics systems – because they provide the opportunity to change *everything*. Not just a few things, but everything.

And, if we are endeavoring to change everything, the teams that design and build these systems are critical to the success of the systems and our overall efforts. Therefore, it behooves us to understand the people we are entrusting to construct these systems in the broadest and most detailed way possible.

Managing egos

Talented people can be humble and possess humility and they can also be insufferable jerks. There have been books written on the no jerks policy in hiring and team-building and if that is a problem for you, or the people that you are attempting to manage or work with, then I recommend you pick up one of those books – they are entertaining reading.

Fortunately for you, I have managed and tried to help a substantial number of jerks. I have tried being transparent and honest with them when they are failing. I have worked with human resources to design plans to help them build skills and see themselves in the broader context of a sub-team, the analytics team, and the overall company, and I have managed them out of the company.

Through it all I have learned one thing; they are not worth the effort.

The best approach to the self-absorbed and self-important is to not hire them; to screen them out and never bring them into your organization.

How do you screen them out? First and foremost, make it clear to everyone in the interviewing process that company and team cultural fit is one of the most important aspects of the hiring process. Of course, you want to hire the best talent available, but cultural fit is key and overrides any measure of technical skill.

Interviewing is time-consuming and you want to grow the team and move on to other interesting tasks, but do not rush the process. A poor hire will cost you more time, effort, and anguish than a well-executed hiring process ever will.

In the hiring process, have a wide range of people interview the candidates; not only you and your advanced analytics and AI team, but staff from Human Resources, and members of one of the operational areas that you have collaborated with and have been successful in developing and deploying an analytical application. The more people that you can have interact with the candidate the better. The advanced analytics team can vet the candidate from a data science and technology view, but your stakeholders and Human Resources will give you a better read on the fit of the candidate for your team and the company overall. Listen to external opinions on the questions of cultural, team, and company fit; they hire more people on a regular and on-going basis than you and your team.

What to do when you inherit someone of this type of profile? Most people act out when the work environment puts them on edge or creates stress in their inner world. Perhaps their preferred manner of being managed and your management style do not mesh. That makes the collaboration difficult and means that there is not a great fit between the two of you, but it doesn't reflect badly on the employee. Perhaps you can meet each other in modifying your respective styles and behaviors, but that usually doesn't work well for the long term. And as we all know, if you and your manager do not get along, change is usually happening to you, not for them.

When inheriting someone who is just not going to work in the new environment, it is best to determine where they would be a good fit. You will need to assess their strengths and weaknesses. If those can be determined, you can encourage and openly support their move to a new area of the business. If they are just a problem, then it is unethical to try to move them to another area of the business.

You, and they, are better served for them to move on from the organization to find a role, manager, and company that is a better fit for them.

Organizational maxims

I have learned valuable lessons over the decades of being an analytics professional and manager/leader.

These lessons are better understood and acted upon rather than pondered. In the next three sub-sections, I will lay out a few of these lessons that apply in a global context.

Take these as truths.

People do not change in the time required

I know that this is a controversial statement and one that raises the ire of some people but hear me out. You and your team are tasked with selecting, undertaking, and succeeding with projects that will drive positive change in the organization. This is your responsibility and you are accountable for the achievement of the goals and objectives. You have about a year to execute on the first cycle that results in positive and measurable change.

People can change, but usually the window for change at a deep personal level, which is what is needed to affect the personality traits that are problematic, is measured in decades. People do change, but over the arc of a lifetime; not in the time needed to be successful in their current role.

Ask yourself, why do we have fables and parables? Why has the story of the scorpion and the frog [3], or the scorpion and the tortoise, been told for hundreds, if not thousands of years? People will modify their actions and behavior in the interest of self-preservation or self-interest, but they will always revert to their core nature.

I have tried to help people change multiple times; it always ends the same. They blame you for the situation and the poor environment that they find themselves in. They rarely, if ever, look to themselves as being a factor in how the situation plays out. Never give someone a second chance to blame you for their failure; cut early and cut fast.

What happens if you do not remove them from the team and or the organization? First, you will lose the high-performance nature of the analytics team. Hard-working team members will start to avoid the problematic team member. Second, the positive team dynamics will degrade and you will find yourself managing the loss of talented staff, your ability to hire will be impaired and, eventually, your team will lose its reputation as being a great place to work in the local market.

Giving them another chance does not work. Manage them out as fast as the company and local, state, and federal law will allow. Do not hesitate to pay a severance package. The money that you pay will be saved many times over by removing the friction in the daily operations of your team and the broader organization.

Cultural change

Certainly, there are times when you want to hire people who will be agents of change, but keep in mind this fact: organizations are comprised of people. Therefore, organizational change is gated by the amount of change individuals can understand and assimilate. People will listen and determine how much change is good for them and that they judge to be good for the organization and they will reject and work against change that exceeds this perceived threshold.

Culture is slow to change. Culture can and will change, but those that are brought into drive or affect change will be rejected and fail if they press too hard, too soon. Be aware of the organizational rate of change that can be accepted and work toward being at the forward edge of that threshold, but not beyond it.

In the metaphor of change, you want to be the river, not the rock.

Don't hang on, move on

Remember our discussion from *Chapter 2, Building an Analytics Team*, everyone should be in a job and role that they love.

If you don't like your job, move on. Don't hang on, move on.

If you are unhappy with the job that you have, find a new one in the organization or move to a new organization. If there are people on your staff who are continually unhappy, help them move on.

There are numerous people who would love to have the job you or your staff members are grumbling about.

By hanging on, you and they are depriving someone of having a job that they would enjoy.

Be brave. Find a job that you would enjoy – those jobs are out there. Go find them, and make two people happy – you, and the person who fills the job that makes you unhappy.

Summary

In this chapter, we covered a wide range of topics that set the context and provide a constructive corporate environment to begin to build a high-performing advanced analytics and AI team. As the leader of this new team, it is important that you connect with sponsors (executives), stakeholders (management), and subject matter experts (functional staff) and have a positive, collaborative, and cooperative relationship with all those groups.

It is crucial to your success and that of your new team that the executives and their downline organizations embrace analytics and engage in the process of building analytical applications that will be the leading edge of change and transformation in processes, people, products, and more.

Hiring the right people and ensuring that the leadership is oriented to an open mindset, ready for experimentation and change, are necessary environmental elements to evoke and realize the benefits of advanced analytics.

You are now aware of the foundation that you need to build for your team. You understand how to create a diversified personal project portfolio for your team that will enable them to operate with a level of independence and allow them to have an element of self-determination in their work that is the basis of fulfillment and true enjoyment in the execution of the craft of analytics.

The value of youth can be a renewing force in the team, and I hope you have an organization that sees this value and supports bringing in a new generation of creative thinkers and architects of analytical applications and change.

You may have found my counsel on managing difficult people a bit harsh and you may have a different approach. I urge you to try what you think is best, but I can tell you that my advice comes from decades of experience with analytics professionals and analytics teams. I offer my hard-won years of experience and mistakes so that you don't have to relive the errors yourself.

The world has changed and will continue to change in every aspect you can consider. Even today, it can be valuable and rewarding to spend decades in one company or organization, but if you are like me and don't find yourself settling into one firm for the long haul, don't worry. Make yourself valuable and useful. Be interested and interesting. Work hard, work smart, and there will always be work for you to do.

Now that we have your team sorted, let's talk about what analytics leadership can be and should be like. We will also delve into what it should not look like too, but we will spend most of our time in the subsequent chapter outlining and describing what the best leadership can be.

Chapter 3 footnotes

1. *A good programmer can be as 10X times more productive than a mediocre one,* December 2013, multiple authors and contributors, `https://softwareengineering.stackexchange.com/questions/179616/a-good-programmer-can-be-as-10x-times-more-productive-than-a-mediocre-one`

2. Ibid

3. *The Scorpion and the Frog,* `https://en.wikipedia.org/wiki/The_Scorpion_and_the_Frog`

CHAPTER 4

LEADERSHIP FOR ANALYTICS TEAMS

"Show up early, it pays off."

—Edward Tufte

What are we talking about when we use the term leadership? What makes leading an advanced analytics and artificial intelligence (AI) team different than any other high-performing team? In what ways are the team dynamics different in an analytics team compared to software development teams and other project teams in general?

Leadership is a well-worn term used in a highly varied and diverse set of contexts. In this chapter, we will use the term to describe and discuss the people who attract, evaluate, hire, manage, fire, lead, and otherwise direct and encourage all the aspects of the daily operation of an advanced analytics and AI team.

The people in the leadership positions who will be the subjects of our discussion and examination undertake activities related to defining the vision, direction, application, implementation, maintenance, revision, and continuation of analytics programs and projects.

They also ensure the ongoing relevance of advanced analytics to examine, develop, predict, prescribe, and affect change in their immediate organization or department, functional group or division, and the entire organization and the organizations that are related to and interact with their companies.

The leaders we will describe and dissect are involved in developing and exerting a positive influence on their advanced analytics teams, other operational and functional teams, the management of those teams, the peers of the leaders we are discussing, and the senior and executive management teams who are responsible for the strategic vision and daily operation of the firm.

We are defining leadership as a role that encompasses daily managerial duties, extends through the annual business cycle, and touches and influences the strategic direction of the business.

Exemplary leadership of an analytics team is a uniquely multifaceted role. To be a good – and possibly great – leader of analytics teams and of peers and superiors, an analytics leader needs to have a mastery of analytical techniques. Without this foundational knowledge, the leader will not gain or maintain the respect of the more technical analytics team members. Also, an analytics leader needs to possess business expertise, knowledge, and acumen. Without this, the leader will not be able to illustrate and demonstrate a vision of why analytics can and will be valuable to their functional peers and superiors. Finally, the analytics leader needs to understand and be able to communicate the best path forward, melding the requirements of data, analytical techniques, and technology with business operations and market needs to deliver practical, pragmatic operational improvements in daily operations.

Leadership in analytics requires the person assuming the role to have the ability to understand, synthesize, and communicate the value of all these respective streams of work to a wide range of people in the analytics team, across the organization, and outside the organization with vendors, partners, and possible collaborators. The role is demanding and rewarding.

There are readers and listeners who will be comfortable with this expansive view of leadership. However, there will be others too who, due to their stage of career development, age, personality type/traits, scale of ambition, or any other individual or varied combination of traits and characteristics, will not want to consider or embody this level of leadership or engage with this broad spectrum of organizational operational units and/or personnel; that is perfectly fine and acceptable. Our discussion of leadership in the field of advanced analytics will be modular. You can pick and choose what works for you today and leave the rest for future use and reference, or leave it out of your personal and professional repertoire altogether.

If you do choose to embrace this expansive view of leadership, this book can be utilized as a reference guide over time to help you be the best leader you can be or to understand and work with the analytics leadership you encounter in the most advantageous method possible. If you choose to embody a different combination of traits as the focus of your efforts, perhaps at the departmental level, this book can help you maximize your efforts in being the best you can be for your chosen focus and purpose.

Artificial intelligence and leadership

Given that we are engaged in a discussion about advanced analytics and AI teams, and we are in the midst of examining the topic of leadership, we need to ask the question, "Will AI take over the leadership of corporations and the leadership of AI teams?"

The management consulting firm McKinsey has remarked that:

> *"...the role of the senior leader will evolve. We'd suggest that, ironically enough, executives in the era of brilliant machines will be able to make the biggest difference through the human touch.*

> *By this, we mean the questions they frame, their vigor in attacking exceptional circumstances highlighted by increasingly intelligent algorithms, and their ability to do things machines can't. That includes tolerating ambiguity and focusing on the "softer" side of management to engage the organization and build its capacity for self-renewal."[1]*

There is no question that computers and software have evolved and have embodied powerful mechanisms for simple reasoning across broad and deep sets of data, but even though we use terms like machine learning, deep learning, reasoning, and decision making, computers and software still do not make decisions the way people do. Computers and software do not really "learn" and "reason" in the same way and they do not possess the same capacities as people. Software can predict what will happen next, but it cannot, at this time, explain why predictions are true. We need to keep in mind the "artificial" portion of the term "artificial intelligence."

In the 1967 *McKinsey Quarterly* article *The manager and the moron*, Peter Drucker noted that:

> *"the computer makes no decisions; it only carries out orders. It's a total moron, and therein lies its strength. It forces us to think, to set the criteria. The stupider the tool, the brighter the master has to be—and this is the dumbest tool we have ever had."[2]*

We have developed and evolved beyond computers and software being at the "total moron" stage, but computers and AI are not ready to take over leadership roles just yet. In late 2019, and going into 2020, we have seen several AI augmentations in the workplace, including board of directors-level advisors; diagnostics in healthcare; document search, retrieval, and triage in law; and more.

The common theme in each of these instances is that the AI is supporting human decisions. For more on the theme of AI augmenting human capabilities, I suggest that you read *Augmented Intelligence: The Business Power of Human–Machine Collaboration.* [3]

Today, AI is augmenting and improving processes, not leading them. AI-based autonomous leadership is many decades away. AI may be able to help today, but it is best if you keep improving and leading teams using your intuition, intelligence, creativity, and drive.

Traits of successful analytics leaders

Being a leader of an analytics team and function is in some ways like leading any other function in an organization, but it is also unique in several ways. Let's outline the traits that make an analytics leader stand out in the minds of subordinates, peers, and superiors.

Consistency

Consistency is an element of work or an approach to interacting with a wide range of people that has been valued and respected in all the roles that I have held and all those that I have worked with around the world. In Chicago, London, Stockholm, Tokyo, Sao Paulo, Melbourne, and all the other cities that I have worked in, being consistent is reassuring to people, whether those people work for you, or you work for them, or whether you are collaborating across functions, across organizations, or across continents.

Consistency is not only globally applicable, but it is also a relevant personal trait in organizations of all sizes. From start-ups to multinational corporations, consistency is prized and valued in all sizes of commercial, academic, and governmental organizations.

Being a consistent force and applying your core principles in a consistent manner enables people to trust you. Consistency can be the foundation that enables people to build multi-dimensional relationships that can last for years, and possibly a lifetime.

Sounds simple – be consistent. But think back to the people you have worked with that you really did not enjoy working with, and possibly did not trust. I would expect that in that mix of personality traits and actions that you recall, there is an aspect of being arbitrary and inconsistent. At first glance, and on the surface, what can look like arbitrary and capricious behavior is really a deeply held belief that ethics, honesty, and truth do not matter; that lying to achieve objectives and goals is acceptable.

Consistency is an outward manifestation of being honest, ethical, and having core principles that guide your actions. As was outlined in the final words of *Chapter 1, An Overview of Successful and High-Performing Analytics Teams*, being transparent and honest changes the way you act and shows up in your personal and professional relationships.

Consistency is a trait that you should strive to cultivate and one that you should seek in people you work and collaborate with.

I think it is obvious that not everyone who is consistent is good. There are consistently evil people that want to take advantage of others, at every opportunity, but those people are easy to spot and avoid, therefore I do not plan to spend any time on that unfortunate topic. Many books have been written about sociopaths. If you need help in working with someone who embodies this condition, there are other books and resources that can help you on your journey.

Passion

Be passionate, yet even-tempered. I have always been passionate about the elements of life that I am interested in and care about. My interest in and passion for data, analysis, and advanced analytics has never wavered. My passion for my family has been the bedrock of my entire life. But the even-keeled or even-tempered part has been a developmental goal and objective for me since being an adolescent.

In a professional setting or context, situations and challenges are typically complex, with numerous groups and individuals being involved. Each group and subset of individuals will be working to advance their agenda and interests; this is natural and to be expected. A helpful assumption to begin with is that a complete understanding of each party, their agenda, and motivations is useful and needed to develop a full picture of the project, program, or situation. Try to go into each discussion with an open mind and ask as many questions as possible to gain a clearer view of the relative positions of each participant in the dialog. Remain detached and centered as you gather the required information. Once you have developed an entire, or nearly complete, understanding then you can engage fully to help mold the solution by employing your knowledge, experience, and passion.

I believe that I have heard most of the coaching advice and the well-timed slurs against being "emotional" or "over-enthusiastic." I can remember the day that I decided that I would stop listening to all the people who told me that my way of reacting and engaging was wrong. It was a flash of insight that made my personal history in this make sense in a moment. I hope that you have at least one of these moments in your life. They are literally life-changing. Let me explain a bit about my experience and epiphany.

I had conceived, and had been working on, an idea that would produce a product/service similar to what LinkedIn enables people to do today. I was bootstrapping the company and I felt deeply passionate about the firm and the potential for the product/service to be a significant success.

I had been working on the idea for over a year, and I decided that I could make more progress if I brought in one or two partners. I spoke with a person that I had known for over 20 years. We had worked together on a variety of consulting assignments. He agreed that the core concept was good, and we decided to work together.

In that same meeting, the new partner suggested that we bring a third person into the collaboration. Within a week, there were three of us engaged in moving the idea forward and we had begun the process of forming a company.

A few months later, we were having a meeting and I thought that these were two people that I could trust and express myself without filtering what I was thinking. I had known them for decades. In the middle of a heated discussion, one of them turned to me and said, "Oh, you are always so emotional, can't you just calm down?" In that moment, I had a flash of realization that my anger and passion were a driving force but expressing them in such an animated manner gave people a tool to use against me. In that moment, I resolved to liquidate the company, leave the venture, and to moderate my external expressions, but not dampen my internal feelings from that day forward.

I must thank that person someday; this change has been very helpful and useful to my continued and accelerated success in the working world.

I have concluded that anger is a good thing. Anger is motivating and is a driving force. What is to be avoided is expressing anger in a forceful manner. Anger scares people and anger is off-putting to many. The expression of anger is to be avoided. The feeling of anger and the experience of anger is to be embraced and controlled, channeled, and used to achieve greater goals for you and your team.

You must be careful about how you discuss anger and passion. First, the terms related to anger have dramatically different meanings and connotations to people of varying cultures. Misunderstandings and changes in relationships can result from discussing these personality traits that are undesirable to some. Second, certain cultures teach people that these traits only exist in people of inferior character and lesser levels of development.

None of this is true, but by describing your inner state, you can be subject to judgment and behavior from others that puts you in a disadvantageous position or eliminates you from future opportunities. The adage "better to keep one's thoughts to oneself and maintain the mystery, rather than open one's mouth and remove all doubt" is apt in this instance. Keep your thoughts and feelings about anger to yourself.

If you are like me, this will be a lifelong pursuit of personal development and improvement that is best kept to yourself. Use the energy to propel you forward, use the internal drive to achieve your goals, but keep the descriptions of your inner state to yourself.

I am aware that many in the analytics community will find this previous section baffling due to the fact that they see the world and everyday situations in a very different way. That is good – we are all unique. But believe me, people do feel this way; they have just learned to not show it.

Curiosity

I am consistently amazed that people do not ask questions about things in the world that they do not understand at a deep and intrinsic level. I am surprised when people illustrate little to no curiosity whatsoever. Hummingbirds fly by, AI systems produce intelligence recommendations, babies are born healthy, planes fly overhead, electricity flows each time you flip a light switch, and people keep walking down the hall to the next meeting.

I flew over 200,000 miles last year. I am aware that my carbon footprint in this area is not optimal. I am working on reducing my impact on the climate in this area. As I was sitting on one of those flights, I was looking out the window and I realized that I did not really understand how an airplane wing worked.

I spent the remainder of that flight reading articles on lift, drag, wing shapes, and how airplane wings work and how wings are being made more efficient. Why? Because I am endlessly fascinated by life, people, genetics, physics, math, emotions, personal development, human relationships, and almost every other topic that you can conceive of.

Good leaders are curious. Curious about their staff, the organization they work in, the improvements they and the advanced analytics team are endeavoring to bring into reality, the people they meet, the people they are collaborating with, and all aspects of their work situations that have an impact on the project they and their team are engaged in. A certain level of curiosity is warranted and, dare I say, required.

The saying "curiosity killed the cat" is curious in and of itself. The saying is meant to imply that inquisitiveness can lead one into dangerous situations. I did not realize that curiosity had such a long lineage of negative connotations associated with it. Curiosity hasn't received good press over the centuries. Saint Augustine wrote in Confessions, AD 397, that, in the aeons before creating heaven and earth, God "fashioned hell for the inquisitive."[4] Perhaps this history is a contributing factor as to why we routinely try to shut down the stream of questions from children as they run down the path of trying to understand the world around them.

Take time to be curious about all aspects of life. If you can't muster the interest or energy to be curious about all of life, then cultivate a curiosity for the people you work and live with. They will thank you, and you will be a happier, more engaged, and connected person.

There is no more intoxicating drug for people than asking them questions about themselves. I am not speaking metaphorically. It is scientifically proven that the brain releases more dopamine when people talk about topics that they care about, and no one cares more for any other topic than the topic of themselves. People literally get a rush when they are given a chance to talk about themselves.

"On average, people spend 60 percent of conversations talking about themselves—and this figure jumps to 80 percent when communicating via social media platforms such as Twitter or Facebook."[5] If you can flip the script and ask more questions, people will think you are more interesting, and you will learn about yourself in ways you cannot imagine.

Stop talking about yourself and ask questions. Try it. Observe what happens. You will be astounded. I was and continue to be.

Leaders need to be curious. Leaders cannot know everything that there is to know. Knowledge is like a map. The vast majority of people believe that maps are static and unchanging. That is not true. Maps are updated constantly. Some more than others, but all maps vary over time and so does knowledge. Knowledge is based on facts and reality and those underlying elements evolve to fit the current circumstances.

One of my analytics teams was working with a leader of a business unit. The analytics team was performing the first data-driven segmentation of the customer base for that business unit. The leader had over 30 years of experience in the business. The historical view was that there was a segment of the population in the US that was younger, more affluent, and highly educated. The operational view was that the team needed a unique and separate marketing strategy, plan, and budget to attract and manage this population. The data illustrated a completely different view. Yes, this segment did exist, but in numbers that were so small that it made no appreciable difference to the operational numbers.

The analytics team learned that 20 years ago there was a significant segment in the customer base, but it no longer existed. We met with the business leader in a small setting and explained the evolution of the customer base in this area. The reaction was not positive and our findings were not accepted. It took the leader another month before he and I had a subsequent discussion where he agreed that he needed to change his view to match the new reality.

How many years and how much money have been spent in a non-optimal manner due to a lack of curiosity?

Ownership

You are reading or listening to a book about how to build, manage, and grow high-performance advanced analytics and AI teams. This fact alone says a great deal about who you are.

We all have our leading edge of development, aspects of our personality, and way of being when we are acting in alignment with our best self, bringing our best views, characteristics, and thoughts to the current situation. And, of course, there are times when we are not our most developed and evolved self. We fall back to earlier coping mechanisms and learned patterns or habitual patterns of behavior.

We are all human and this is simply a fact of life. In some cases, it is unfortunate and has consequences, and in other cases, our ability to rise to the occasion and be the best person we can be simply slips by and we have only to deal with the minor irritation and feeling of regret of our inability to live up to our potential.

The one lesson that you need to take away from this section of the book and our discussion is that how you take up and handle things matters. People who have not attained a level of personal development cannot see that how they act, engage, and behave impacts situations in important, and sometimes, dramatic ways.

You need to know that your every act and action has an impact and redirects the situation in a positive or negative way. If and when you find yourself talking about how the main factors contributing to a current, typically negative, outcome are outside your control, stop and think about how you contributed to the current environment. Taking stock of your impact is crucial to being a good leader and being able to improve and redirect nearly all outcomes.

Taking the position of a passive participant, or even worse, a victim of circumstances, is not how you want to act or be perceived as acting. Show up and be proactive, engaged, and an empathetic part of the solution.

Variety

One of the great joys of a career in analytics is the variety of subject areas that you are invited to discuss, examine, reinvent, and possibly improve.

Most people go to work and they address a certain functional area. People work in accounting or finance, or they are experts in supply chain operations or manufacturing. For the most part, people take pride in the fact that they have specialized in their field of endeavor and they feel good when they are consulted as being knowledgeable about their area of specialization.

Due to my nature and the fact that I am curious, love to learn, get bored quickly, and have lots of energy, I was a challenge for all of my managers early in my career. I apologize to all of them for the heartburn I caused them. These traits also combined to have me labeled as a job hopper in the early stages of my professional life. People that I interviewed with were scornful of my inability to hunker down and stay in a role for 10 years or more.

It was not planned, and I certainly did not see it at the time, but what I was gaining by moving around was a deep education in multiple functional areas and vertical industries. I was involved in solving or solved problems in supply chain operations, discrete and process manufacturing, cross - and up-selling optimization, retail store operations, marketing strategy, infection minimization, protocol compliance, and more. I have worked in industries such as Consumer Packaged Goods, Utilities, Semiconductor Manufacturing, Automotive, Finance, Software, Professional Services, and Management Consulting.

I have had the joy of working in the USA, Canada, Mexico, Brazil, the UK, Sweden, Norway, the Czech Republic, France, the Netherlands, Poland, Germany, Japan, and Australia.

Unwittingly, I became a management consultant. It would never have happened if I hadn't fallen into a deep infatuation with analytics. There are very few paths that can lead you to have as broad and deep understanding of business, people, and the world as analytics. It has been and continues to be a pleasure and an honor.

OK, we have covered all the relevant traits that make for a solid and positive leader of an analytics team. Let's turn our attention to an organizational concept and a current debate and discussion of how organizations assign leadership duties, responsibility, and accountability to get things done in relation to data and analytics.

Optimism

I have found that an optimistic viewpoint on life, its possibilities, and people to be a valuable mental construct. However, it can also be a limiting view that causes problems too. I used to think that I was a realist, seeing the positive and negative sides of the situation equally, but over time, I realized that I was, and remain, an optimist. However, there are two clear downsides to this.

First, being an optimist can lead you to ascribe skills, talents, and levels of competence to people who do not possess them. Someone's age, current position, background, professional experiences, educational pedigree, or other personal and professional traits can lead you to believe that they possess and have mastered valuable technical, professional, or soft skills. To put it another way, you give people the benefit of the doubt that they are at a certain level of professional achievement and personal development; many are not. You would be better served to start from a position where you hold out the benefit of the doubt until the people you meet exhibit and prove their level of competence and abilities. This is learned behavior for optimists.

One mistake people who work in analytics make is that they want or need to prove that they are smarter than those they meet and, often, they try to do this in their first encounter. To put it indelicately, they engage in a pissing contest. This is childish and immediately puts you at a disadvantage.

Think of it this way. If you are not going to work with or encounter this person again, why do you care what their level of competence is? You will rarely or never see them again. It is a waste of your time to even think about their abilities in relation to yours. If you will work with them again or see them on a regular or semi-regular basis, you will have ample opportunity to probe their skills and areas of opportunity for improvement. Life, and your career, is a marathon, not a sprint. You have plenty of time to assess the people who you will collaborate with, and in some cases, compete with. Take your time and assess carefully and from multiple perspectives; each person could be a collaborator and ally, or a competitor and adversary, or maybe both at different times.

The second mistake, is assuming that because you do something easily, naturally, or almost effortlessly in some cases, most others can do it as easily and as well as you do. I used to think that only I did this, but that is not true. A significant number of people hold this view. They devalue hard-won and learned skills, or even more commonly, they devalue easily won skills and traits simply because those traits and skills came so very easily to them.

I commonly hear, "Well, anyone can do that, right?", "I picked that up after reading about it in an academic journal that is simple and easy to understand", "Everyone knows that," or, "That is obvious and is common knowledge." The fact is that people who are in analytics do this with surprising regularity in relation to very technical topics that are incredibly hard to understand and embody an immense amount of complexity.

I had a conversation with someone who had worked for me for just over a year. We were having a casual conversation over lunch and I mentioned that the night before I had read an article on Bayesian-based analytics and that I thought that Bayesian probability theory was fascinating. This person responded that he had completed his master's studies in Bayesian theory. I had no idea. He then downplayed the skill and his deep understanding of the topic by saying that everyone in analytics knew about Bayes' theory and that it was no special skill or ability. I took the opportunity to gently remind my lunch companion that Bayes' theory is very powerful, complex, and nuanced, and that Bayes' theory is not widely understood. Finally, one of the primary reasons that Bayesian theory has not been widely used in the business world and in practical application is that there are a limited number of people who understand the subtleties of the theory and the underlying math. We went on to discuss how we could improve one of our existing predictive applications based on an upgrade using Bayesian theory.

It's better to assume that the people you meet are competent and possess a modicum of skills, but best not to attribute to them more than a person of average ability would possess, and not an average person in analytics, but an average person on the street. It's even better to carefully observe how many people possess and utilize the skills that you embody and use on a regular basis. By leveling a skeptical eye at the world and the people you encounter in one-off situations and those that you will work with regularly, you will gain perspective on your skills and abilities and those of the people around you. I am betting that you will be in for a pleasant surprise. Try it – it will be fun.

A clear-eyed assessment is more than a simple understanding of the landscape of skills and talents. By having a realistic understanding of your relative skills and abilities, you can serve the teams you work on and the stakeholders of your projects in a much more effective manner.

By realistically assessing the skills and abilities of the people you will be working with in the short and long term, including managers and subject matter experts, analytics teams, vendors, consultants, and others, you will have a greater understanding of the culture and environment in which you will be constructing, growing, and managing your high-performance analytics team.

Building a supportive and engaged team

What do analytics professionals want their working days to look like? What do professionals who are engaged in advanced analytics want from their projects, teams, and leaders? Multi-faceted and meaningful questions, those are. A bit of Yoda there for you, Star Wars fans...

Let's start with where we just arrived in the previous section. Let's begin with assessing and understanding how to lead the team that you have. You must be aware that not all analytics teams are the same. The mix of skills and abilities of team members will, to some extent, dictate the projects you can undertake, how quickly you can move, and the level of impact you and your team can have on the firm. You need to understand the current technical, professional, and soft skills of the team and the teams that are ancillary to the core analytics team.

Traditionally, analytics teams were comprised of a significant number of highly autonomous individual contributors, and to some extent, for many teams, there remains a bias in this area. This is a problem. Especially now that we are welcoming in new employees and retaining valuable employees, and this staff mix can span four generations.

This mix of employees needs to collaborate effectively and share knowledge that spans the domains of technology, projects, communication protocols, organizational and historical awareness, operations and data, and other tangible and intangible topics.

Without the ability to fluidly and easily transfer knowledge and information, analytics teams will be constricted in their ability to deliver value.

As leaders, we need to foster a respectful, open environment where all personnel feel comfortable in expressing their ideas and approaches to difficult technical, process, and organizational challenges. This is becoming more challenging. We have smaller and smaller universes of shared experiences, worldviews, levels of personal development, and cultural lenses that we are looking through as a group. When trying to move quickly in a diverse group to solve challenging problems in a time-constrained operating window, people can have misunderstandings and be misunderstood.

This is where, as a leader, you need to ensure that you have taken the time, and made time for the group, to spend time together before the harried pace of projects becomes too intense; to have each of the team members share their personal experiences, professional accomplishments, areas of expertise, experience, current areas of study, and more. You need to give the team time to get to know each other as people and as professionals.

As new people join the group, they need a chance and an open and welcoming forum to acclimate and join the team; not to just physically join the team, but also socially and psychologically. The first few months of any new person's tenure are critical to them feeling like they belong. As a leader, you need to spend time ensuring that this process is being actively attended to for each new employee.

This type of activity has been a challenge for me for several reasons, but mostly because I have a strong bias toward action.

I have assumed at various times that people:

- Are much more talented and accomplished than they are

- Have the same level of energy and drive as I do

- Want to do the best work they can
- Are all in and not distracted by other developments in their lives
- Are honest and transparent in their motivations, insecurities, and personal and economic needs

Most, if not all, are bad assumptions.

To build a great team, you will need to understand all of the factors above for each person on your team. This takes time and, for some readers, it may seem like an impossible task. The good news is that it is fairly easy to do; it just takes time. It has taken me decades to come to this view.

My personal pattern started out as hire quickly and blast into action. This has evolved into hire slowly and carefully, understand the individuals, discover team dynamics, move the misfits out, assess the strategic goals of the company, find projects that fit both the strategic goals and the skills of the team, design a portfolio of projects, engage with stakeholders, and manage the execution carefully for the success of all involved.

Let's take a minute to address a couple of points that have probably invaded your mind as you have been reading.

First, these steps are not prescriptive; they are merely a descriptive and representative list and they are not as linear as they have been described here. Of course, you and your team will iterate, refine, revise, and move back and forth in the process. That is normal and natural. Think of the entire process as being circular and recursive rather than linear and unidirectional.

Second, some of you will be thinking, "It will be weeks to months before we do anything if you must do all these activities upfront before starting to execute any "real" work." To clarify, this *is* real work. This is the work that will enable you and your high-quality team to execute projects in a high-performance manner in the near and long-term future.

You have heard derivations of the "culture constrains strategy" or "culture eats strategy" quote that is widely attributed to Peter Drucker. [6] What you are doing here is building a team that will embody the culture of the advanced analytics and AI team. This is critical to your success and the success of the team. Do not shortcut or shortchange this process or you will pay with time, energy, and possibly anguish, later.

Managing team cohesion

In *Chapter 3, Managing and Growing an Analytics Team*, we discussed managing talented jerks and the need to hire the best possible people. The previous points were made, and the discussion remains valid. It is worth reiterating that a bad hire will dampen and diminish the cohesion of the team and the team's ability to collaborate. Once you realize that a person is a poor fit with the group, move to collaborate with the human resources department quickly to manage them out of the company or, to put it more plainly, to fire them.

It is important that you do not equivocate or waiver. You may think that it will take time away from other tasks, and it will, but acting quickly and decisively will be better for you, the team, and, in the end, the employee who is not working out.

The most dangerous element of this situation is that if you attempt to help this person in fitting in, you will waste your time, the team will see that you have made a poor decision, the team will have to work around the person, and at some point in the very near future, the misfit employee will go to human resources and accuse you or someone on the team of being the source of their failure to fit into the team.

As with all people, if it is a choice between them being the source of the failure or them being able to blame someone else for that failure, and that someone who will have the blame pinned on them could easily and probably *will* be you, then that is an easy choice for the misfit employee – it is your fault and problem. This then initiates a process that is very time-consuming for all involved.

Take my advice and guidance, fire them at the first sign of a poor fit. They will not be able to keep their true nature hidden for more than a few days to a week and you and the team will know it. Do not dismiss the first signs of their inability to work as part of the team; realize that those signs are there as a gift to you and the team. Act quickly and act courageously. Everyone will benefit from it.

As we have discussed before, analytics teams are the same as other teams in numerous respects, but very different in others. Let's discuss how they are different than other teams and outline and describe the challenges and opportunities that these differences present for a leader of an advanced analytics and AI team.

Being the smartest person in the room

Let's be clear about one thing. If you *need* to be the smartest person in the room, then you will need to find a very special company, start a company of your own, or get over the feeling that you need to be smartest person in the room. The last approach is the one I would recommend.

I hope for your probability of success in leading an advanced analytic and AI team that you are not the smartest person in the room. If you are, then you are either an incredible person, or you have hired poorly, or maybe a bit of both.

I am certain that at one point in my career, I needed to be the smartest person in the room and I am certain that I embodied all the less-than-desirable personal traits of such a worldview. With these beliefs and views, you will not be seen as a leader and you will not be able to lead a team to sustained success.

Competing with your team to be crowned the best and brightest is one of the fastest paths to team discord and employee turnover.

Good (and bad) ideas can come from anywhere

If you are lucky, you will have a team of highly skilled, highly trained professionals who have technical acumen in varied areas that include math, technology, data management, process design, user interaction design, and more. For your success and your team's well-being, you need to celebrate their expertise. Also, you need to bring value in several ways.

One way that you can bring value is by bringing the perspective of a novice to the discussion.

About 15 years ago, I was on the executive team of a start-up. My role was marketing and corporate development. The development team was trying to solve a problem related to fraud in credit card use. The technical team had camped out in the conference room and they were furiously debating how best to draw a curve through the data space that described all the possible uses of a credit card. The line illustrated the risk frontier for the credit card issuer. The team had the data space built and described.

They had also determined how to mathematically deduce and draw the line through the data space, but they were having a challenging time determining how to move the line based on refinements in the data and changes in user behavior. As I sat in the room and listened to the impassioned arguments for a variety of approaches and techniques, I also heard how each of those proposals was debunked for technical and process reasons.

It struck me that the team should not try to move the entire line, but they should break the problem down to local minimums and maximums and determine the optimal local movements and then draw the complete line from the newly moved segments. I occasionally attended the technical meetings and I rarely spoke in them, but after I went to the whiteboard and explained my idea, the room fell silent. Each team member considered the idea and then they started nodding and quickly agreed that this was a workable solution. They made a few snarky remarks about me, my lack of education, and the surprise they all felt that I had a good idea. I took a quick metaphorical victory lap, and I immediately left the meeting. I know when to take the win and go.

The point being that I had no detailed understanding of the technical underpinnings or of the math of the problem being discussed, but I could bring the view of an informed novice to the discussion. That perspective broke the log jam and enabled the group to move to action and implement a solution to the problem. And we all had a good laugh about how we arrived at the solution.

I had new credibility in the eyes of the analytical leaders of the company. I was welcomed into future meetings and when I spoke, everyone paid attention. That one moment of insight changed the team dynamics and I could have only done that by realizing that I was not the smartest person in the room, but I was clearly considered to be a valuable employee in the room by the analytics team – until I wasn't.

Emerging leadership roles – Chief Data Officer and Chief Analytics Officer

Leading organizations are beginning to create C-level positions to direct, grow, and manage the emerging and evolving functions related to data and analytics. Some organizations are focused on the data side of the function and hence they start their efforts by creating the Chief Data Officer role, while others begin with the Chief Analytics Officer role. Either starting point is valid and useful.

The creation of these roles and opportunities for the people assuming these roles illustrates the importance of these functions and the corporate recognition that these roles are strategic and are crucial to drive the company in a defined direction. These roles will grow in number and sophistication. The creation of these roles signals a tipping point in corporate history and illustrates that the data and analytics function is a core strategic capability for leading corporations.

On or around November 11, 2019, I posted the following multi-part question on LinkedIn:

> *"I am curious about Chief Analytics Officer roles. I believe that we will see more of these positions in the near future. Is your organization beginning to design such a role? Who seems best suited to fill the role? Is there an overlap with the Chief Data Officer role or are the roles combined into a Chief Analytics & Data Officer role? Looking forward to the dialog."[7]*

This question elicited 41 comments and over 12,000 views.

The following is an edited version of the discussion that resulted from posing the question:

Bill Hoggarth

I'm interested in what happens when, as I guess all CAOs might hope, analytics becomes so entrenched that every CXO is in effect a Chief Analytics Officer for that X? Finance and People are already thus entrenched, and we still have CFOs and Chief People Officers, but will we still have CAOs, or by the same logic CDOs?

John K Thompson

I am often asked when we will be done with analytics. My response is never. There will always be people who see math and data as a competitive advantage and a way to move ahead of the market. Kind of like asking, have all the songs been written? Quite clear the answer is no.

Alek Liskov, Director, AI + Data Office at Verizon

While I agree with the nuance, there will always be a need for a dedicated function. Just because CTOs are getting MBAs and are becoming proficient in Finance and other business functions doesn't mean we won't need CFOs. Everyone has major and minor strengths.

Fantastic question. Plenty of great responses. The key theme for me is fit for purpose with regards to the aspirations and strategy of the company.

Winston Sucher – Aspiring CDO, Data Envoy, Enterprise Solution Architect

For me, the Chief Data & Analytics Officer (CDAO) is the Holy Grail outcome.

Using a sports analogy, there's the offensive (CAO) and defensive (CDO) side to the equation, two sides of the same coin. There's the opportunity for more CAO roles as the view on advanced analytics capabilities continues to evolve.

To start their journey, many companies will hire a CDO who has experience and a taste for analytics to address the most common data hygiene issues while delivering analytics outcomes. Over time, the role will change to more of a CAO focus whilst maintaining data hygiene.

There's no right answer. It's a business-focused discussion about what the business needs at the current point in time. Politics, I feel, is more likely to dictate if more opportunities of CAO will be forthcoming.

Doug Gray – Accomplished Analytics | Data | Digital Executive

The CDO role is about data management, data governance, and data security, which is a full-time job, certainly for larger organizations.

The CAO role is about extracting and delivering business value and economic impact from data using analytics, data science and AI and is also a full-time job.

I believe the roles CDO and CAO, and if you combine them into a CDAO, depend as much on the individual person as the organization.

Data and analytics are complementary and go well together, but the skills of the CDO and CAO roles are very, very different.

You would need to be equally skilled and equally passionate about data and analytics to be effective as a CDAO. The CAO and CDO roles might be combined for organizational efficiency, but if you are a CDAO, then your direct reports should complement your skills.

If you lean more towards data or analytics in your skills, experience and passion, then your team needs to fill in your gaps.

The CDO role needs analytics to deliver the most business value from data, and the CAO role is wholly dependent on the availability of clean, quality, integrated data to function.

Tim Negris – Advanced B2B Technology Marketing Strategy Leader

Good questions. There is a necessary collaborative overlap between CDO and CAO roles, but combining them is a bad idea, as they represent two different skill sets.

The CDO has a part to play in assuring that analytical processes have the data they need, but the strategic CDO role is in managing data provenance, privacy, and protection, plus, increasingly, leveraging "outside" data resources for both analytics and process management.

Similarly, the CAO must work closely with the CDO to find, qualify, and utilize data assets, but the strategic CAO role is involved in developing effective analytical models for solving functional and business problems, plus, increasingly, working with DevOps to implement model-driven business processes.

CDO is an asset management role and CAO is an action management role.

John Thompson

Well put Tim. I agree completely. I see the CAO as the driving role. Almost like an internal consulting organization to the company with a focus on realizing operational and functional insights leading to change and improvement.

Gautham Nagabhushana – Practice Area Business Partner – AI & Analytics at Cognizant (Pharmaceutical/Lifesciences Practice)

In my mind, the demarcation between the Chief Data Officer (CDO) and Chief Analytics Officer (CAO) roles is that the CDO is more of an enablement function while the CAO role focuses on developing the right analytical methodologies to address key business issues.

The CDO role's internal client is the CAO role. The CDO role needs to understand what key objectives and approaches/methodologies the CAO is focusing upon to drive the business.

Based on this, the CDO role can organize the data and provide the appropriate tools for the CAO to provide insights and recommendations to the business stakeholders.

With respect to having them as separate roles or combining them into one role, it depends on the maturity of the organization in making data-driven decisions, what type of organization of data has been accomplished thus far, and whether the function is a part of IT or the business.

I hope that this perspective makes sense and look forward to further dialog.

John Thompson

Agreed. You and Tim Negris have a very similar take on the functional duties of the CDO and CAO, which I agree with wholeheartedly. Thanks for commenting on the thread. Very valuable perspective.

Steve Friedberg – Experienced Corp Communications Strategist, Analyst Relations Expert

John, the question will be over how many companies want to combine the two roles; one being tactical, as noted elsewhere in this thread, and the other being far more strategic. In other words, can a CDAO delegate the administration of the data, across multiple formats and locations, to a director/ manager level, while retaining the more strategy-focused role of him/herself?

I'm betting you're going to see a bunch of companies at least try this approach.

Brian Gillet – Senior Director, Platform as a Service at MedeAnalytics

I've been seeing on a weekly basis, news posts in the health system and health insurance space that announce a new CAO and how this position is newly created due to the need to help contribute to the digital transformation these organizations are going through. Looking forward to hearing others' insights on this question.

> **John Thompson** – Brian, I am seeing the same thing. At an initial glance, it looks like healthcare/pharma industries are moving quickly on this front. Perhaps a bit of a herd mentality. Thank you for your insights.

Matthew Prozaki – Sr. Specialist Sales, DB & Analytics at Amazon Web Services (AWS)

More common to see Chief Data Officer as the title but playing the same role.

Cindi Howson – Chief Data Strategy Officer at ThoughtSpot

I agree with Matthew Prozaki. Although, this does not seem to be the prevailing opinion on this thread. Interestingly, when I first joined Gartner 4 years ago, we were debating which role and title would ultimately prevail in the marketplace. The CDO title has become more popular.

However, simply collecting data serves little purpose unless you are going to analyze it – more to Alek Liskov's point. It's one reason why I preferred the CAO title.

With that said, I do see two types of CDOs. The less mature ones are primarily focused on getting the data house in order, the more mature ones are focused on leveraging that data for business value. Whether this is an evolution or skillset from the outset is debatable. But I'd say that suggesting that a CDO is only responsible for storing data is pigeonholing that role.

John Thompson

Cindi Howson – a great reply and remarks. I like your addition of the nuance of the evolution of the CDO role. Thanks for jumping in.

Dr Simon Carlino – Analytics Director / Chief Data Officer (CDO) / Data Lead

There is a lot of overlap between CDO and CAO. I recently had experience of an extremely non-technical CAO (which was an experience!). Fortunately, I was able to do the tech bits and Power BI, or the client would have been considerably worse off.

In terms of CDO/CAO, I was taken on purely as I had extensive board experience and good technical knowledge (which is apparently quite rare, I'm told). It's interesting to look into the criteria for these roles. CDO criteria differ by generation and organization maturity.

Monther Alhamdoosh - Sr. Mgr. Bioinformatics & AI at CSL Global Research Data Science

CAO would be critical to achieving end-to-end analytics. The greatest thing an organization can achieve is when data and analytics are fully connected and drive the business forward... not many organizations manage to achieve this.

It requires a good vision for data and analytics at the top levels, as well as a cultural change at the lower levels of the business. I think the separation between data and analytics roles is inevitable for organizations that are newly transforming in the digital world, but at some point in time (when the data culture has changed), the two roles need to converge into one role to add more value to the business.

Armin Kakas - Analytics Executive

I echo much of Winston's response.

CDO's ensure that you have the right analytics ingredients (over-simplified). CAOs drive the analytics agenda for the company.

From what I have seen, CDOs are largely IT roles, while CAOs have a seat at the table with the senior executive ranks (as they should). Particularly if an organization is in its infancy from an analytical maturity standpoint, the CAO role has to be part analytical innovator, part salesman extraordinaire (for example, funding for growth, support for the right use cases and so on).

Most analytics folks miss this last part: they tend to get enamored with ML/AI-driven solutions while minimizing the importance of selling and convincing internal and external stakeholders.

Hiring the Chief Data Officer or Chief Analytics Officer – where to start?

Building an analytics team can start at any number of points: bottom-up, top-down – either approach can work. Let's assume that the organization is just beginning to build the data and analytics capability; they can start by hiring the Chief Analytics Officer or the Chief Data Officer. As supported by the dialog above, and my decades of experience, and if we are using probabilities to make a choice of where most organizations will start, the majority will start by hiring the Chief Data Officer.

The Chief Data Officer

Hiring a Chief Data Officer is seen by most as a choice that is safer, easier to understand, and easier to gain consensus around. This is a valid starting point, but as called out above, it is a decision and starting point that will begin the organizational journey by looking inward – inward at the data, technology, and processes that the company currently has and maintains, rather than outward at opportunities.

The primary implication to be aware of is the progress toward implementing analytical models that change the way the company builds products, changes processes, and improves the efficiency and effectiveness of people will be delayed by a year or more. Let's examine why this is the case.

Chief Data Officers are tasked with examining the existing and potential universe of data owned, managed, and processed by the organization and its partners. The Chief Data Officer will need to hire a team, assess the organizational readiness, assess the state of the existing data universe, assess the need for technology purchases and upgrades, and build consensus around the need for change and improvement. After all these projects and considerations have been resolved in the organization, the team can then begin to consider how the organization will start to plan to build analytic applications upon the new and improved data environment that the Chief Data Officer joined the company to revise and build.

The Chief Data Officer, in most cases, will be focused on issues related to processes and technologies such as metadata management, change management, data governance, and other related matters. All important issues and items to be addressed, but they are all infrastructure related not change and action oriented. Also, Chief Data Officers, for the most part, are concerned with internal data. I have only met a couple of Chief Data Officers who consider external data or third-party data on par in importance with internal data, if they think of external data at all.

The Chief Data Officer position, by definition, is an infrastructure and process-oriented position. The Chief Data Officer needs to have this view and these attributes to be successful, but the overall process that a Chief Data Officer will design and drive will have a longer inherent delay in realizing organizational change that manifests itself in additional strategic insight and profit improvement than starting with a Chief Analytics Officer.

The Chief Analytics Officer

Hiring a Chief Analytics Officer starts the process at a point where the development of an overall organizational transformation initiative is the strategic starting point and objective.

The Chief Analytics Officer will immediately begin to build consensus around the need to develop analytical applications that drive improvement and change in all business functions. The impetus for the Chief Analytics Officer and their team is to partner with the executive and senior management teams to identify where the organization can change and improve at a strategic level, to help develop a proprietary advantage for the company that can be built and defended over time and find more routine opportunities to ensure that the company achieves competitive parity or superiority in processes and operations in relation to its market competitors.

The Chief Analytics Officer will use data and resources that are owned by the company and external data, consulting, and technological resources that can be licensed or purchased by the company.

The starting point for a Chief Analytics Officer is change and competitive advantage. This mindset and starting point is required for a Chief Analytics Officer to be successful. Even with this mindset, change and success are not guaranteed and are not instantaneous. The most ambitious and assertive Chief Analytics Officer can be expected to take at least a year before any level of success can be achieved.

Why will it take a year to see success? The Chief Analytics Officer needs to meet with the executive and senior management teams, and not just in an introductory meeting; the Chief Analytics Officer needs to meet with executives and senior managers to build rapport and to learn where the organization has latent opportunities to build a defensible competitive advantage. At the same time, the Chief Analytics Officer needs to hire a team, set the priorities, build the global community, find the people who will be the day-to-day drivers of change, and gain their confidence that they will have a chance to make a difference and receive credit for their efforts.

In approximately 1 year, the organization will have the first case studies to show that advanced analytics and AI are not just topics of discussion, but real drivers of change and corporate advantage.

Summary

Leadership is the topic of many books, thousands of lectures, and much discussion and conjecture. Leadership is an industry unto itself. It is funny how many leadership gurus have never been leaders in the fields that they profess to hold the pinnacle of knowledge in. Nonetheless, they have followers and people who believe in their teachings. That is good for all involved.

Analytics leadership is a subject that has not been discussed much and has been written about even less. This is not surprising given the state of evolution of analytics leadership. Analytics leadership is emerging as an area of study and practice.

In this chapter, we have examined why analytics leadership is different from leadership in information technology, software development, or general leadership. We have enumerated the traits that make a good analytics leader and we have examined the point of evolution in the current market for new analytics leadership roles in corporations.

In this chapter, we have examined the fundamental nature of the characteristics of successful leaders of analytics teams and analytics functions. We have delved into the nature of analytics leaders and looked at what they need to do with executives, senior managers, peers, and subordinates to deliver on the promise of a high-performance advanced analytics and AI team and capability.

In this chapter, we sketched the outlines of the new leadership roles of the Chief Data Officer and the Chief Analytics Officer and a possible hybrid role of the Chief Data & Analytics Officer. Personally, I prefer the more strategic and proactive role of the Chief Analytics Officer, but there are as many, or more, professionals who prefer the data-oriented approach of the Chief Data Officer. No matter – there are, and there will be, numerous roles in a wide range of companies that align with the personal preferences and skills of practitioners in the data and analytics fields.

Analytics leadership is new and is being recognized as a growing need in leading corporations around the world. It is a great time to be an experienced leader in the field of data and analytics.

As noted in this chapter, this is an expansive view of leadership that spans an entire corporation and reaches out to partners and providers. To many, this is a bridge too far, and that is fine. Use this book as a reference guide as you develop as a leader. Read a little, work a lot, make mistakes, and learn along the way. That is how most of us do it.

Now we'll move on in our journey from understanding our roles as analytics leaders to examining how analytics leaders can effectively engage and work with executives across the organization.

Chapter 4 footnotes

1. *Manager and machine: The new leadership equation,* McKinsey Quarterly, September 2014, By Martin Dewhurst and Paul Willmott `https://www.mckinsey.com/featured-insights/leadership/manager-and-machine?cid=other-eml-cls-mip-mck&hlkid=0b00d5ae4c264dd0821632a30c90eb75&hctky=2020931&hdpid=5de210fe-6adc-4201-9d10-1e5f9c04e8ef`

2. Peter Drucker, *The manager and the moron*, McKinsey Quarterly, 1967

3. *Augmented Intelligence: The Business Power of Human–Machine Collaboration First Edition*, by Judith Hurwitz, Henry Morris, Candace Sidner, and Daniel Kirsch, `https://www.amazon.com/Augmented-Intelligence-Business-Human-Machine-Collaboration/dp/0367184893`

4. *Curiosity killed the cat*, `https://www.phrases.org.uk/meanings/curiosity-killed-the-cat.html`

5. *The Neuroscience of Everybody's Favorite Topic, Why do people spend so much time talking about themselves?*, Adrian F. Ward, July 16, 2013, Scientific American, https://www.scientificamerican.com/article/the-neuroscience-of-everybody-favorite-topic-themselves/

6. *Culture Eats Strategy for Breakfast*, https://quoteinvestigator.com/2017/05/23/culture-eats/

7. On or about November 11, 2019, I posted the following question on LinkedIn, *"I am curious about Chief Analytics Officer roles..."* https://www.linkedin.com/posts/johnkthompson_i-am-curious-about-chief-analytics-officer-activity-6605458399830298624-1Ac1

CHAPTER 5

MANAGING EXECUTIVE EXPECTATIONS

"Plans are worthless, but planning is indispensable."

—*Dwight D. Eisenhower*

Working across the organization is a critical element of the success of you and your team. Engaging with and gaining the support of executives is a requirement for success. In this chapter, we will delve into the details of capturing the imagination, attention, and support of executives across the organization. We will examine the relevant factors that will guide and shape your communication and engagement with your direct reporting line executives and those executives that own and manage related corporate functions.

Executives and senior managers are important to the ongoing success of any company and they have a significant role to play in the early and ongoing success of advanced analytics and AI teams and your personal success as well.

Working with executives to support their needs in order for them to support your needs is a fact of life. Embrace their needs, support and feed what they need, and you and your team will have a much easier time navigating the organization and obtaining the support and funding that is required to do the work you love.

Executives may not understand what you do or what motivates you, but that doesn't really matter. They do not need to understand you, your team, and the work you do. You need to illustrate to them in terms that they can understand that you and your team are a good investment that will deliver valuable results and impact at a faster and higher rate than other investments. It is that simple. Do this and your life and work will be much easier.

While I do not advocate spending too much of your time selling up, you will be required to engage in selective and strategic selling and sales activities to convince the upper echelons of the firm to secure and maintain funding for your personal efforts and to support the efforts of your advanced analytics and AI teams.

In this chapter, we will examine how to develop and deliver a clear and compelling message to the executive team that will engage their imagination and pull them into the analytics journey. We will also discuss how to position the various types of work you and your team can and will do and how to handle the discussion about which part of the analytics workload can be outsourced to external parties. We will conclude with information on how the daily operations of your team can be presented to the executive level of the organization. The core of this chapter is about how to engage with executives.

Personally, I have reacted negatively to the thought that I needed to sell up to have my organization and projects funded, but it is a reality of life in a large organization. Rather than resisting this activity and notion, which I did for years to the detriment of my overall efforts and success, you need to embrace and engage in the process if you want and need funding and support, and if you do, then you will need to "sell" up.

Keep in mind that an organization is a collection of competing strategies, projects, and functional areas. You need corporate sponsorship from executives just like Leonardo da Vinci did from the powerful Medici family. [1] The reality of the matter is that you need sponsorship and money and you need to ensure that the executive team or at least your sponsor on the executive team continues to support and fund the efforts of your team.

You are not the only game in town

Executives have many teams reporting up through organizational structures and those teams have numerous initiatives underway and those initiatives contain a diverse set of projects. Just because *you* are living and breathing the portfolio of analytics projects, doesn't mean that your senior management team and sponsoring executive have more than a cursory understanding of the projects and initiatives that you and your team are engaged in.

This organizational separation is part of the reason why we have been discussing the need for the analytics team to be connected to a larger overall process of organizational improvement and transformation. Executives can only keep a certain amount of complexity and breadth of activity in mind at any one time. When they see that your efforts, and the efforts of your team, are supporting strategic initiatives, then you are aligned with their thinking and you will have their support.

It took me years to get my head wrapped around the fact that not only did they not know what I was doing, but they didn't really understand how it was being done and, in some cases, were dubious about the probability of success and the scale of the impact.

Let me help you not make the same error in judgment. It is not their job to understand what you and your team are doing. It is their job to lead the company and make strategic decisions and to be accountable for those decisions.

It is your job to ensure that they understand how the efforts of you and your team align with where they are attempting to take the company. You must work hard at keeping them informed, and to you, it may seem like a waste of time and you may also think that it is not "work" since it is not building something of value. Well, let me tell you, it is an important – no – it is a *critical* portion of your primary work duties. You need to support your team in securing the support of the executive team or at least your executive sponsor. Without their support, you will not have a team or the resources to do the work you love.

In this respect, executives are like everyone else; they need to have messages put into a context and language that they understand and connect with. You need to put those messages in a language that they can hear and comprehend quickly.

I know that it is exciting to tell people how hard you worked and how smart you and your team are, but that is not going to help you in this task; it actually detracts from your effectiveness.

Be assured that the organization and the executives hired you and your team because you are intelligent, can solve complex multifaceted problems, build incredible models, and improve the organization in a multitude of ways. You do not need to prove that again and again. Your intelligence and ingenuity are the price of entry, and you have paid that price. The executives and senior managers who have met you and know you respect your abilities and talents. This is without question and you can rest assured that you are viewed as a valued member of the organization.

Your focus and efforts, at least in this area, need to be on refining and honing your ability to connect with senior managers and executives on their level in a voice that they can hear. Speak their language and your success will come much more easily.

Know what to say

Executive communications are easy to understand but can be challenging to successfully navigate. For the most part, executives want simple, fast, easy-to-understand answers that convey that the work you are undertaking has a significant positive impact that will be realized in the corporate or financial reporting period that they have on their mind at the time of your discussion, but what does that mean?

Your answers should be short and convey the strategic area in which you and your team are working in and that the quantified positive impact will be above the financial or operational threshold they care about in the next reporting period, which is typically a calendar quarter or possibly in time for the next board meeting, or both.

I was in a meeting recently where an executive told a team leader that he was not interested in the project if it did not deliver a positive $20 million impact in the next quarter. In the following month, the project was sidelined and eventually shut down.

This turn of events was devastating for the team leader and as we could tell from their facial expressions, completely unanticipated. This person had joined the firm within the previous year with a very publicly stated purpose and mandate to undertake the initiative and process of establishing this new corporate function. Not only was this a seemingly great opportunity, it was a passion project for the team leader. The team leader had moved across the United States and had been working diligently on the project.

You can argue failure on the team leader's part to gather the required data from the executive to understand the level of significance required to gain executive sponsorship, but you can also argue that the fault lies primarily with the organization that hired the team leader.

The organizational structure in this area had not changed significantly in over 5 years. Hence all the senior managers knew what projects were raised to the level of interest of this C-level executive. However, no one told the team leader, or the team leader was not astute enough to discern this fact. In the end, this person had taken a new job, moved across the country, threw significant energy into the project, and used much time and energy to develop a plan for this new function, only to have it eliminated in the span of a few minutes. Within 4 months of this meeting, the team leader had resigned and left the company – truly a waste of time, resources, employee engagement, and motivation.

The message was delivered bluntly. That is typical of some corporate executives, but it was callous as well. The tone and tenor of the message were unnecessary and hurtful. Corporate executives are not known for being compassionate messengers. I doubt that we will see a dramatic change in this communication dynamic in the short term. Of course, it will change over time and it has changed a great deal in the past 3 decades but be ready for harsh criticism of your efforts and projects.

You need to know what the expectations are from the executives and senior managers that you will be engaging with. If the expectations are in line with the scenario above, you need to be certain that you, and your team, can deliver at the required scale and speed. If you cannot, for whatever reason, find a different functional area to engage with or a project to undertake.

Know how to say it

People ask me, with fair regularity, why analytics teams, analytics projects, and all things related to analytics are unique. As we have described along the way in our discussion, analytics initiatives rely on a mind-boggling array of moving and interrelated parts: technologies, corporate strategy, functional tactics, data, external suppliers, executives, senior managers, and the analytics team.

This constantly moving collection of elements is complex to understand, manage, and drive in a coherent direction.

It is even more complex for people who have little to no understanding of any of the component parts, let alone the whole of the ecosystem. You need to assume that the executives you are engaging with have little to no knowledge of any part of this environment, and at the same time, they have very little interest in the topic. They may have a strong interest in the possible outcome(s) and changes that can be driven through analytics, but it may be dangerous to assume anything more than a passing fancy for the topic.

Complexity combined with little to no knowledge, and a small amount of interest mixed with a healthy dose of executive ego makes for a volatile mix. Never underestimate the cycle of lack of understanding/interest, followed by confusion, quickly leading to embarrassment, concluding with lashing out and condemnation. As we all know, and have experienced, it is a near-universal reaction – if I am confused and you are presenting or representing something that I cannot understand and the choice is between me being unable to understand the topic or you being wrong or incapable, then the second option is an easy choice. Executives are exquisite at making this snap judgment in a matter of seconds. Being embarrassed or confused is Kryptonite for the vast majority of executives.

To be clear, you are, in all likelihood, much smarter than the vast majority of executives you will encounter. If you engage them in a battle of wits, you will win, but you will never receive the funding and support you need to be successful.

Be clear, concise and on message. If you can say it in 45 seconds, that is great, but 30 seconds is even better. You can do it.

Think of the famous quote from Blaise Pascal, "If I had more time, I would have written a shorter letter."[5] Being concise can be thought of as being a gift that some have and others do not. That is not true.

Being concise is the product of focus, effort, and the refinement of what you want to communicate. Work on refining this skill – it will pay off.

Shaping and directing the narrative

Early in my career, I was attending an annual sales meeting for Metaphor Computer Systems, at the Silverado resort in Northern California. There was a senior manager, Jay McGrath, leading the discussion. He was addressing a group of system engineers, and I was one of them. I was approximately 2 years into my consulting career. I had just completed my MBA and I thought that I knew it all, forward and backward. Jay ended a section of the discussion with the statement, "Telling is not selling." I was perplexed by this statement. I assumed that most of the people that we were talking with were smart, informed, reasonable people and all we had to do was tell them of the benefits and value of our proposition and they could make the best decision possible.

All of that is true, but it certainly leaves much unsaid or undone in the process of arriving at the destination you desire.

When you are presenting to executives, you need to show them what is good and explain why it is good. I was recently in a meeting reviewing a presentation illustrating the initial results of a predictive application. The first pass of the model produced an error margin that was less than 4% when compared to the actual operational results; we were ecstatic. We knew that the model would improve and produce even lower error rates in the future, but when I spoke with one of the operational executives in an impromptu hallway conversation, he looked at me with curiosity. I asked what he thought. His response was "Is less than 4% good?" I smiled and said, "Yes, very good, and it will get better." He smiled in response and said, "That sounds great."

Do not assume executives and senior managers understand what you are talking about. If it is good news, tell them, and show them why, ensuring to frame the story in the way you want to define it.

Know before you go

Cultivating, assessing, and obtaining executive support starts even before you join the organization. When interviewing for a new role and when new executives subsequently join the organization who have a direct or indirect impact on your team size, funding, and future plans, you need to evaluate the executives and senior managers to understand their history, perspective, and experience with analytics teams.

I have heard executives express the following views:

- We need to see significant changes resulting from the analytics teams in the primary operating functions in a matter of weeks.

- The analytics team should be staffed and running efficiently by next quarter.

- Our company has never been good at continual improvement; the analytics team will fix it.

- Our company has never been good at innovation; the analytics team will change that.

- We will have the advanced analytics and AI team build dashboards and reports in their "spare time."

- We will have the advanced analytics and AI team build robotic process automation workflows in their "spare time."

- We have all the data we will ever need; the analytics team needs to find it and make it work.

- We need some machine learning/AI/predictive applications.
- We can outsource all the data and analytics work.
- This is so simple, we could have two interns and a dog do it.
- Listening to the functional teams is a waste of time; the analytics teams need to tell them what to do. The executive that said this thinks he is Steve Jobs...you, sir, are no Steve Jobs...
- Building an analytics community across the organization to increase awareness, understanding, and engagement with data and analytics is a waste of time.
- If the functional teams are not adopting the new analytics, just force them to do it.
- Why do analytical models need to be updated? If they are right when they are implemented, why aren't they right all the time in the future?
- We have lots of smart people in the organization, including scientists, doctors, and PhDs: have them do the data science work.
- The advanced analytics team looks like a technology team. Have them report into the technology function.
- Budget? The advanced analytics team needs a budget. Why?
- The analytics team can change the technology systems and process models to implement the analytical models into production processes, right?

These viewpoints indicate that your role, and that of your team, is not well understood, and it is more than likely that neither you nor the team will be valued and funded.

If you are considering joining an organization where the executives say the things I have listed above, you are probably talking with them because someone at the executive level is advocating for advanced analytics, and that is good, but if other executives hold the views expressed above, it will only be a matter of time before the sponsor and the other executives will be infected with and succumb to the same views.

Of course, it could go the other way too, but I am a firm believer in planning for the downside.

The downside is easy to describe. The executive sponsor who is advocating for the funding and hiring of an analytics team will fight for the funding and hiring of a leader and a team. The executive sponsor wins the ability to fund a small team. The analytics team leader and the analytics team work diligently to engage and illustrate success. The skeptical and unconvinced executives work consistently to undermine the efforts of the analytics team. The executive sponsor loses the will to continue to fight with the other executives. The funding is reduced for the advanced analytics and AI team, the best team members leave, the leader leaves, and the entire effort becomes part of the company history, a footnote of a failed effort. This failure could have been easily avoided if the analytics leader had conveyed the project scope and efforts clearly to the executive team and convinced them.

How many of us are out there?

One of the realities of advanced analytics and AI is that, at the current time, conversations in the business press, popular press, in governments at the cabinet and ministerial levels, in universities, in think tanks, in venture capital firms, in private equity firms, and in the minds of nearly everyone that is interested are focused on the changes that advanced analytics will bring to our businesses and societies.

The interest in advanced analytics and AI has never been higher and has never been discussed on such a wide platform with so many diverse sets of people.

The number of people who truly understand the multiple factors that need to come together in a specific way to deliver positive operational improvements from analytics is a very small number.

I have been part of several large and small companies. In one of the larger firms, with over 26,000 employees, there was approximately a third of 1% of the entire staff around the world that understood the value and actual definition of advanced analytics and AI. That minuscule percentage might have included one executive. The number of firms that possess a significant concentration of executives with a strategic vision, managers who understand how to leverage data and analytics, capable and experienced technical professionals, diverse and well-managed data, and valued/supported analytics professionals who all pull together in a synchronized way to deliver operational improvements where it matters is strikingly and exceptionally low. The small number of staff members who understand analytics and are actively engaged in the process of furthering the analytics effort and agenda does not indicate that success cannot be achieved. Certainly, leading firms are hiring people, aligning resources, charting the long-term process and transformation, undertaking projects, and changing their operations on a daily basis. The task is difficult, but not impossible.

Let's change gear and discuss the proactive actions to be taken to increase the probability that our efforts will be successful.

There is a proven path to success

There is evidence that when firms can and do align these varying groups, employees, and functions, the results are amazing. This is one of the reasons why we see the leading firms that have invested seriously in analytics pulling away so dramatically from the majority of the firms across multiple geographies and industries.

A global study by McKinsey in 2019 illustrated:

"that a small share of companies—from a variety of sectors—are attaining outsize business results from AI, potentially widening the gap between AI power users and adoption laggards. Respondents from these high-performing companies (or AI high performers) report that they achieve a greater scale and see both higher revenue increases and greater cost decreases than other companies that use AI. McKinsey defines an AI high performer as a company that, according to respondents, has adopted AI in five or more business activities (is in the top quartile for the number of activities using AI), has seen an average revenue increase of 5 percent or more from AI adoption in the business units where AI is used, and has seen an average cost decrease of 5 percent or more from AI adoption in the business units where AI is used." [2]

Also, from McKinsey:

> *"research suggests that a technology race has started along the S-curve for AI, a set of new technologies now in the early stages of deployment. It appears that AI adopters can't flourish without a solid base of core and advanced digital technologies. Companies that can assemble this bundle of capabilities are starting to pull away from the pack and will probably be AI's ultimate winners. Executives are becoming aware of what is at stake: our survey research shows that 45 percent of executives who have yet to invest in AI fear falling behind competitively. Our statistical analysis suggests that faced with AI-fueled competitive threats, companies are twice as likely to embrace AI as they are to adopt new technologies in past technology cycles."* [3]

When a company is managed in a way to bring all these disparate factors together to work in concert, the results are impressive, and the flywheel begins to turn, and success begets success. We talked about the word of mouth effect in *Chapter 3, Managing and Growing an Analytics Team.*

The advanced analytics team is responsible and accountable for delivering analytics that drive operational improvement, but they cannot do it alone. Once they deliver projects that make an impact, the broader organization needs to talk about those successes; subject matter experts from all functional areas need to engage with the advanced analytics and AI team, fund the analytics team and hold those results up and demand more of the same from the analytics team and the broader organization.

In October 2019, the CEO of Novartis, Vas Narasimhan, announced that Novartis and Microsoft would team up to establish a lab to develop AI technologies and approaches for the pharmaceutical industry.

In establishing the lab, he said, "We know that data science and digital technology will play a pivotal role in the future of medicine. The AI innovation lab will be our go-to place to innovate, experiment, and scale AI-based solutions in our efforts to transform the way we discover and develop medicines for the world." [4]

What are you hoping to accomplish?

I have spoken with executives who believe that all data and analytics projects and efforts can be outsourced. That is possible, I suppose. I have never seen this type of effort deliver strategic impact and value, but that does not mean that it cannot happen.

One of the problems of outsourcing anything – not only analytics but any project – is that you need to know what you want to have in the end before you start. How can you expect an external vendor to deliver exactly what you want, when you want it, at the expected cost when you don't know what you want or how to achieve it? Sounds straightforward, right? You would be surprised how many executives, firms, and teams have little to no idea of what they want to do.

This is a particularly acute problem in analytics currently. With the land grab mentality that some firms have, it is challenging to define what they want. Remember the statement, "We need some machine learning." That is an actual quote from an operating executive in a Consumer Packaged Goods company; shockingly ill-informed.

One of the challenges in defining exactly what you want is the multidimensional nature of the problems that we seek to solve or challenges we seek to overcome with analytics. A related challenge is the Gordian knot [6] of whole problems or related factors that are bound together. Often the challenges that analytics teams attempt to undertake were previously considered impossible to solve.

Decomposing these interrelated elements into their source elements or first principles enables the analytics teams to formulate solutions that are not obvious at first glance through what can be a very creative process.

In one project, we started with the stated goal of having a better market-based and competitive forecast. That was too broad of a project mandate. We re-scoped to address the demand side of the market. We then found that there was no reliable, easily accessible core data on the activities of many of the smaller competitors. We then decided that we would focus on a demand forecast for the firm and the top three competitors. We built a solid and accurate forecasting model for the described entities and, over time, built on that platform to move toward the original objective.

The definition of objectives and goals has always been challenging when collaborating with subject matter experts from the functional areas of any business. The process described above works quite well, but it can be fraught in the effort to bring together the analytics, functional, and technology teams to arrive at a consensus regarding the problem to be solved. And, once you have reached a consensus on the scope of the objectives, then the discussion turns to the ability to actually formulate a workable and practical solution based on the technology, data, and analytical skills available to the organization. Just because you can describe the problem doesn't mean that you can solve it.

This raises an issue that you need to be aware of and have the ability to address in a concise and cogent manner. Executives and senior managers that embody the various characteristics, mental constructs, personal idiosyncrasies, and more also have an issue in that since they do not understand the data, analytical approaches, and/or technologies, they do not have a good understanding of what is possible. For some executives and senior managers, analytics is akin to alchemy or magic.

Many executives have no basis for discerning the possible from the impossible. You need to be aware of and know the practical and possible and be able to discern between the possible and the impossible. You need to possess the wherewithal and composure to be able to explain what can and cannot be done. Of course, you want to respond in a tactful and respectful manner to what you know to be an impossible request and you need to avoid embarrassing the source of the request or questions, but you must also not set you and your team up for failure by agreeing to work on an intractable or impossible problem or challenge.

Outsourcing

In general, we are moving away from the "not invented here" model where organizations believe that they need to build everything themselves, but there are still pockets of this view. It is the opposite view of the situation described above where some executives think that everything can be outsourced. As with most things in life, the ends of the continuum are the extreme cases and, as such, are typically found in a smaller number of organizations.

In most cases, you can outsource portions of the analytical process. Let's break it down for clarity:

- **Easy to outsource**: You can outsource the following activities with the lowest risk: data acquisition, data integration, data profiling, data loading, and data visualization steps are the easiest to outsource and can lower the overall cost of operations.

- **More difficult to outsource and success is difficult to achieve**: Feature engineering can be executed by an outside vendor if the company you are outsourcing to has not only technical skills, but also skills in the business or functional domain related to the analytical models to be produced, but this combination of skills is hard to find in a service provider.

- **Hard to outsource and hard to achieve repeatable success**: This is the modeling phase. I have had very little success and have seen even less success when other companies attempt to outsource the model building function. Numerous firms present and represent that they can build models and I am sure that they can build models, but the question is, are they effective models, are the models easy to update, and do they contain a solid foundation that can be extended to include a broader operational domain as you learn more and more about the data, operations, and strategic direction planned by the executive team? This can work if the domain you are focused on is one that is generic, well known, and widely applicable. The need to build an analytical or predictive system in this instance is probably driven by the need that all other relevant competitors have this type of system and the company needs to implement the system to simply remain competitive. In those cases, outsourcing may work.

- **Nearly impossible to outsource**: The integration of predictive models into production processes is so unique and individualistic that outsourcing nearly always fails or is more expensive and time-consuming than staffing and undertaking the effort internally. I suppose that if a vendor is running the production process in a cloud environment that is outsourced to the external vendor and the vendor is an expert in managing and extending the process, this is possible, but that is a very specialized case. I have not seen success in outsourcing the modification of proprietary processes that are managing a factory or a supply chain or an operating room.

Typically, the modification and changing of these processes are quite unique and require the expertise of multiple groups within an organization. Also falling into this category is model management. It takes significant skill and expertise to know when to change models and it takes even more skill and knowledge to know which model is the best to move into production next. Outsourcing these tasks are done at your peril.

These are the steps to consider outsourcing data acquisition, data loading, data profiling, data integration, and data visualization. The steps that carry more risk if outsourced are model selection, modeling, model tuning, hypothesis definition/testing, pilot/prototype/production, and model management.

Another way to make this point is to think of it in terms of the core versus context framework. Areas that deliver competitive differentiation for a specific company would not work well for an outsourcer as these are core business factors. Core business processes are typically unique and are not able to be generalized across many organizations. Rather, areas aligned with a common commodity function or context are opportunities for working with an outsourced partner. Corporate functions (for example, HR and Legal) and analytics related to those functions are good places to look for this type of partnership. Unless you're doing something really special with those functions, pushing them out to a group who can do it cheaper would free up resources for focusing on core functionality.

To sum this up concisely, when you are asked to outsource a portion of the analytics process, you need to know what you can easily outsource without compromising quality.

Elephants and squirrels

Executives are just like other people in many respects; in other respects, not so much, but we must remember that executives are people too.

One characteristic of people that inhabit the executive ranks that I find interesting is that they are typically split into two groups on the ability to retain and remember facts over time. Perhaps it is my selective memory at play here but it seems to me, from my decades of experience, that executives either are like elephants, in that they remember everything (they remember where the conversation was had, what was said, who was there, the weather outside, the stains on the carpet – all in great detail), or they are like squirrels in that they can't remember much at all. They say the same things repeatedly and repetitively. They ask people to do the same or similar projects within days or weeks of each request. They seem to be surprised when most of the people in the room understand immediately or seem to have the same idea. Well, it's not hard for people to come to an agreement when you heard the same thing a week ago. It is intriguing to me.

I am like an elephant. I remember conversations for years and can play them back almost verbatim to what was originally said. Funnily enough, I have trouble remembering names. It is an odd memory that I have, but it works well in recounting what was said and what was agreed to.

Elephants are easy to work with. You come to an agreement and you work toward that agreement. Squirrels are harder. You never know what they remember, how they remember it, or how much they will change the memory over time. Be alert, be humble, and ask lots of questions of the squirrels. Typically, they remember with enough accuracy when they have been prompted and probed enough. Ask lots of questions, and they will remember bits and pieces of the previous conversations the more you talk and move them in the right direction.

Squirrels do not like to be reminded that they cannot remember past conversations. As suggested, ask the executives questions and bring them along slowly. Do not say, "We agreed to x, y, and z last week, don't you remember?" Not a winning formula with squirrels.

Daily operations

Managing the daily operations of the analytics team can be done in a manner that increases your probability of success. In the next four subsections, we will examine how to set up the focus and cadence of the analytical team's daily work to ensure that they are engaged in the right type of work and are delivering in a manner that optimizes their productivity and the visibility of the work to the relevant executives, senior managers, and subject matter experts across the organization.

Quick wins

Everyone agrees that quick wins are good. Everyone wants to get off to a fast start and to deliver value and positive results as soon as possible, right? Not a trick question, the answer is yes. Yes, in all cases.

But you need to ensure that you and the executives you are conferring with are on the same page and have the same expectations. I was fortunate enough to be assigned to live in the UK early in my career. I lived in London and worked in the London office. It was great. I was young, had no commitments – not even a house plant. Moving was easy and simple.

The London team was great and included me in all sorts of challenging and interesting projects. I remember sitting with an English executive. We were talking about the value of building analytical applications and how much he supported the idea. He said, "I can see the value in data and analytics. I am excited to see the company moving in this direction.

I am certain that in the short term, we will engage in these types of projects." I was so excited; I was certain that we would be engaged in a project in a matter of weeks to maybe a month or two. I asked, "When you mentioned the short term, what time frame were you thinking?" He replied, "Within the next 5 to 7 years for certain." I was crestfallen. Make sure that you have an agreement as to what terms like quickly, short-term, very soon, and other related terms mean to the executives you are engaging with.

A more typical situation in the United States is the following. You have discussed the project. You have agreed with the subject matter experts the scope, definition, timeline, and related parameters that will govern the project, and now you are providing an update to the sponsoring executive. She expects that this project will be a quick win and so do you, but what is her definition of the timing aspect of a quick win? She might be thinking a week and you are thinking that it is 6 to 9 months. The sooner you reconcile this implicit misunderstanding the better. In many cases, the misunderstanding stems from the fact that analytics projects are new to many executives. They have no experience of understanding what is reasonable in an analytics project. It is up to you to be noncommittal until you have a reliable and accurate assessment of the duration and phasing of the current project. But, once you know, it behooves you to get those dates, durations, and resource allocations out into the open as fast as possible.

What is a typical and expected duration of a quick win? From the time of project inception to delivering results, for a service request, it could be a couple days to 2 weeks. For a small project, it could be a couple of months to 6 months.

Clarity and open communication on these facts are paramount to creating and maintaining trust with your executive sponsors.

Service requests

We defined service requests in *Chapter 3, Managing and Growing an Analytics Team*. Hence, there is no need to define the term again. Why bring service requests up in the context of managing executive expectations?

We have discussed at length the lack of interest, knowledge, and experience in analytics that besets most executives; that is not a good or a bad thing, it is just a fact. There are executives who are not detail oriented. They like to stay at the highest levels of discussions. Not a problem. You can make this dynamic work in your favor.

Service requests can be thought of as small projects – projects that you can use to create goodwill and trust with executives that you are just meeting and getting to know. Often, executives will have a list of problems or challenges or curiosities that they have not been able to obtain answers for. In many cases, the advanced analytics and AI team can quickly and easily answer these questions for them.

I encountered a situation where a company was exploring new markets to enter. The strategic work had been done with external consultants to determine where the best markets and targets were for the long-term viability of the company. For the most part, the company enthusiastically supported the chosen markets.

The new functional business units were named and staffed, and the teams went about learning about the new markets. We received a call asking if we could help in narrowing down the research domain of one of the new functional areas. The new leaders of the functional area were stuck. They were experienced professionals, but none of them had worked in this new area. They came to us expecting a project that would take a few months.

They explained that they needed to know out of the universe of over 1 million research papers, monographs, presentations, and grant applications scattered around the internet which documents were the most relevant to their task in that the relevant documents contained or mentioned one or more of their top terms. They wanted to know which documents would provide the most insights to the team in their quest to understand the market and the state of the art.

They had what they considered a desperate need and a seemingly insurmountable problem. Searching via Google and trying to find the relevant corpus by brute force did not work. They were frustrated when they came to the advanced analytic and AI team.

When we understood what they wanted and needed, we discussed it to ensure that we understood the challenge and need well enough and then we explained that we would provide the answer that they were seeking by the end of the week. We had an intern complete the project in 3 days.

They were amazed and pleased, and they talked about this service request and how it solved their problem across the organization in an extensive manner. The word of mouth was incredibly valuable in raising the profile of the advanced analytics and AI team.

The strategic use of service requests has engendered a reputation for the advanced analytics team as being customer-focused and responsive to the needs of the organization. Service requests are your friend. Use them often, judiciously, and expeditiously with executives.

A sense of urgency

Velocity in delivery is important for you and your team and in the eyes of the executive team. On a daily basis, it may seem puzzling as to why you keep gently pressing the advanced analytics and AI team to be creative, solve small problems, and to show progress on all projects and service requests and to communicate that progress to you, stakeholders, and sponsors.

One of the primary assumptions of this book is that you and your team are reasonably new to the organization. You and your team need to build a reputation and an expectation across the organization, and especially with the executive team and your executive sponsor, that you and your team deliver success and results in small and large-projects on a repeatable and consistent basis.

You need the executives to have it as a background belief, an almost unconscious view, that you and your team succeed in everything – well nearly everything – that you undertake. That view should lead the executives to almost reflexively ask when intractable problems arise, "Have you had the advanced analytics team take a look at this?"

Before you know it, a year will have passed and you want to be able to sit down in front of or with an audience of individuals and discuss with comfort and confidence the projects that have been undertaken and delivered for the business. You want to be able to discuss in practical terms the difference that has been made in operations and you want your subject matter experts and business sponsors to agree with what you are representing.

For example, in one of my roles, in the first year, the advanced analytics team delivered successful results on 10 major projects and 12 service requests. When anyone asked, I outlined the number of successful projects and the teams we collaborated with and offered for the audience to pick and choose any project that they were curious about or interested in, and I would explain and describe the project in any level of detail that they found useful.

Velocity and delivery are necessary for success. Also, a side benefit is that you develop a high-performing team. In this case, we started out with a level of assigned work for each team member that seemed a bit excessive. Even I thought that we were pushing the limit and risked burning the team out, but when asked if the advanced analytics team wanted to reduce the level of work, the team was unanimous in their view that they did not, that they enjoyed the pace of work and being engaged with subject matter experts and business sponsors, and in a few cases, executives.

The business will demand results, after all. They did commit funding, and like all funded projects, they demanded a return. It is much more fun and enjoyable to talk about the positive use of those funds and the results delivered than the alternate viewpoint.

Innovation

Executives signed off on the investment for you, your team, and the supporting infrastructure, technology and related expenses. Given all that we have talked about in the current business and general climate around advanced analytics and AI, there will, in all likelihood, be an expectation that innovation will result. Operations will change and the executives will be able to represent in interviews to the press, and in meetings with stakeholders, and in investors calls, that they have invested in the hot new space of data and analytics.

Fortunately for you, innovation is almost an effortless byproduct of the work you and your team execute on a daily basis. Be ready to talk about and produce stories that the communications team can revise and package for the executive team.

Innovation that is interesting to the executive for external audiences will typically be focused on innovation in products, people and/or processes.

Remember our discussion about the level of impact that is interesting to executives and be able to craft stories from your work and the work of your team that support the narrative that the executives want and need to express to the outside world.

Celebrating learning (some call it failure)

You have undoubtedly heard, and have been part of, discussions about failing fast or the corollary expression, succeeding quickly.

You and your team will undertake projects that fail. This is a fact and one that you need to understand and manage. You need to manage the process of failure for the sake of your team and the reputation of the group and your personal reputation.

How failure is handled, tolerated, or celebrated depends on the organizational culture, and culture does vary widely.

In one of my previous roles, failure was expected and embraced. There was a widely known process for failing. Failing in a project, failing to meet the sales numbers, failure to complete any process or project within the expected timeframe, or not achieving the stated objectives, or failing to reach any of the relevant project or process goals was expected.

The steps in this process are:

1. Acknowledgment of the failure
2. A description of the failure

3. A description of the chance of recovery or remediation

4. A discussion of the best path forward

5. A decision on whether to regroup and work toward obtaining the original objective or to move onto the next challenge

6. Back to action

This process was well known. People coming in from the outside of the organization either could understand and execute the process, or they could not. In many organizations, failure is followed by condemnation or rejection.

At first, when I encountered the structured and overt process for managing failure as outlined above, it was uncomfortable and unfamiliar. Typically, in organizations, failure was understood, but rarely acknowledged and even more rarely discussed openly and constructively. Once I understood the process and how the organization managed it, I enjoyed having a failure mode or process. The process was overt and known. Everyone fails – if they are trying to push the envelope, they encounter failure more than others. The real question is how you deal with failure, how you recover, and how the organization around you and your team support you in that process.

If your organization does not have a process for failure, I suggest you set one up in your team and use it with your management. It is refreshing. No one who sees and experiences the process will be disappointed to see you and your team acting in that manner and working through the process. Try it – you will like the results and so will your team and your management.

Summary

This chapter has been about engaging with the broader organization in a constructive and productive manner with a focus on gaining attention, understanding, and support from the executive team.

The executive team is critical to the success of you and your team. The executive level in every organization is accountable and responsible for the overall strategic direction, operational health, and long-term viability of the organization. Working with the executive-level team is unique and requires that you adopt and exhibit a certain attitude, style, stance, tone, and tenor in your actions and in your written and verbal communications and presentations.

In outlining how you and your team can and should engage with the executive team, this chapter has provided a guide to productive engagement with executives as a group and as individuals. As with any skill, you will improve with time and practice. You will be more comfortable in this mode of operating the more you engage with the executive level.

One last piece of advice in entering the executive suite: go in with confidence and go big. Executives, for the most part, like big ideas and they want to hear about ideas that will change the course of the company. Go big – plan for and present initiatives and programs that will require risk, investment, and time. By going big and presenting a vision, you will have their attention, and, in many cases, they will fund and support your plans.

Now that you know how to engage with the executive team to gain their attention and support, let's look at how to engage with the broader organization, including managers, peers, subject matter experts, and the rest of the organization, to undertake projects, and drive change and improvement across the organization.

Chapter 5 footnotes

1. *The House of Medici* [English: /mɛdɪtʃi/ MED-i-chee or British English (UK): /məˈdiːtʃi/ *mə-DEE-chee* (https://en.wikipedia.org/wiki/Help:IPA/English), Italian: [ˈmɛːditʃi] (https://en.wikipedia.org/wiki/Help:IPA/Italian)] was an Italian banking family (https://en.wikipedia.org/wiki/List_of_banking_families) and political dynasty (https://en.wikipedia.org/wiki/Dynasty#Political_families_in_Republics) that first began to gather prominence under Cosimo de' Medici (https://en.wikipedia.org/wiki/Cosimo_de%27_Medici) in the Republic of Florence (https://en.wikipedia.org/wiki/Republic_of_Florence) during the first half of the 15th century. https://en.wikipedia.org/wiki/House_of_Medici

2. *Global AI Survey: AI proves its worth, but few scale impact*, November 2019, McKinsey, The survey content and analysis were developed by Arif Cam, a consultant in McKinsey's Silicon Valley office; Michael Chui, a partner of the McKinsey Global Institute and a partner in the San Francisco office; and Bryce Hall, an associate partner in the Washington, DC, office. https://www.mckinsey.com/featured-insights/artificial-intelligence/global-ai-survey-ai-proves-its-worth-but-few-scale-impact

3. *Artificial intelligence: Why a digital base is critical*, July 2018, McKinsey Quarterly, Jacques Bughin is a director of the McKinsey Global Institute and a senior partner in McKinsey's Brussels office; Nicolas van Zeebroeck is a professor at the Solvay Brussels School of Economics and Management, Université libre de Bruxelles. https://www.mckinsey.com/business-functions/mckinsey-analytics/our-insights/artificial-intelligence-why-a-digital-base-is-critical

4. Novartis/Microsoft establish an AI lab for join collaboration, October 1, 2019, Vas Narasimhan, chief executive officer of Novartis AG, `https://www.instagram.com/tv/B3FFzCNg808/?utm_source=ig_embed`

5. *If I Had More Time, I Would Have Written a Shorter Letter*, Blaise Pascal, "Lettres Provinciales", 1657, `https://quoteinvestigator.com/2012/04/28/shorter-letter/`

6. Gordian Knot, `https://en.wikipedia.org/wiki/Gordian_Knot`

CHAPTER 6

ENSURING ENGAGEMENT WITH BUSINESS PROFESSIONALS

"Everyone has a plan until they get punched in the face."

—*Mike Tyson*

We have discussed engaging with and convincing executives that there is value in data and analytics. Now, let's turn our attention to the managerial levels of the organization below the C-Suite and above the front-line workers.

We are now interested in exploring and understanding all levels of management from senior management to front-line managers. In most organizations, these are the levels where work can be immediately stopped, delayed indefinitely, or approved and moved forward.

In this chapter, we will examine the most common causes of analytics not being developed or adopted. We will look at the variety of areas in which you will need to be armed with knowledge and expertise, to convince your functional stakeholders that these roadblocks need to be overcome. This will help them realize the potential and value of analytics for the organization. Most of your stakeholders want to leverage and utilize data and analytics, but they do not know how to achieve this goal. Part of your job is to help them understand how to navigate this journey successfully.

As we describe and examine each of the roadblocks and organizational areas, keep in mind that we are describing these areas so that you will have them in mind and be able to formulate your own views on how you, your analytics team, and the broader organization can surmount each of these obstacles.

Let's lay out the case and path for how we can engage even the most intractable and least fluid parts of organizations to move them in a direction where we can build and implement systems that will drive operational change through data and analytics.

Overcoming roadblocks to analytics adoption

Tom Davenport and his co-authors have offered the following observation: "More than a decade after the concept of big data became part of the lexicon, only a minority of companies have become insight-driven organizations..." [1]

In using Davenport's quote about the passing of a decade, I want to ensure that we understand that analytics and analytical approaches have been around for a significant period of time— certainly longer than the decade we have been talking about "big data" for. To be clear, we are not talking about big data and we have not been talking about big data anywhere in this book.

Davenport's quote is employed here to illustrate that data and analytics have been in our orbit for far longer than a decade. Data and analytics have been with us for centuries, and only in the past decade has there been widespread recognition and interest in serious and active utilization of data and analytics to improve business operations, government, society, and our world as a whole. We need to ask: why is this so?

We have, within our reach, large amounts of relatively easy-to-access data and algorithms that are invoked through user interfaces that guide even the most novice users to a safe and reasonably accurate path. This is coupled with more than ample network connectivity/bandwidth, and compute cycles are, for all intents and purposes, infinite.

So, why is it that we are not doing more with data and analytics? What are the limiting factors? What can we do to lessen the impact of, or completely eliminate, those impinging factors on our efforts to drive change through data and analytics?

Davenport and his co-authors go on to assert that:

> *"The amount of data available to organizations every*
> *day continues to proliferate at a staggering volume. But*
> *technologies such as analytics and artificial intelligence*
> *(AI) have the potential to help businesses make better*
> *use of these massive volumes of data. In an age of*
> *collaboration between humans and machines—what is, as*
> *Tom and his coauthors call, "the Age of With"?" [2]*

In *Chapter 1, An Overview of Successful and High-Performing Analytics Teams*, we discussed the future of advanced analytics and AI as being one where AI will be used in conjunction with human judgment and skills. We cited Judith Hurwitz and Henry Morris' new book, *Augmented Intelligence*, which outlines how integrated hybrid human and AI systems will permeate our business operations, social media, and other services that we utilize daily. [3]

The team that I lead at Dell Software created an impressive system to predict which patients had a higher probability of developing sepsis after surgery. Post-surgical complications are a serious and relatively common occurrence. In fact, they are the most common reason for unplanned readmissions to the hospital in the United States.

The advanced analytics team at Dell Software worked with the University of Iowa Hospitals and Clinics to develop an analytics system that predicted which patients were at greater risk of suffering an infection from a surgical wound. The system used a variety of data, including details of the surgery itself, such as the patient's vital signs (blood pressure and heart rate, for instance), and information from the person's medical records—whether, for example, he or she has diabetes or hypertension.

By analyzing an ensemble of data in real time, the system could predict the likelihood of infection while the patient was still on the operating table. For patients who were at higher risk, doctors could then use a different technique of closing or treating the wound, or prescribe a more effective regimen of post-surgery medication.

The results of this sophisticated analytic environment have been impressive, with the rate of infections for patients following colon surgery plummeting by more than 75 percent over a three-year period. [4]

This is an example of an augmented intelligence-based approach to surgery. We did not and do not talk about this as a human surgical team augmented by a robot, but some people have described the system in those terms. We see it more as the augmentation of the intelligence of the surgical team with an AI based system that provides guidance and counsel in a non-intrusive, supportive manner in a timeframe that can improve surgical outcomes for the surgical team, the hospital, and most importantly, the patients.

On a positive note, all the necessary elements or building blocks are in place and generally available to all corporations and a significant portion of the general population to build and leverage advanced analytics: hardware, software, high-speed networks, a proliferation of detailed and real-time data, powerful data management, far-reaching data integration, an increasing level of data literacy and analytical skills, and a growing awareness of the need for and value of advanced analytics and AI.

Organizational culture

Currently, we are experiencing an intense wave of interest in the possible positive and negative impacts of advanced analytics and AI. We have seen waves similar to this in the past, but previous episodes have not been as widespread, nor have achievable and practical results been as possible to so many organizations. We certainly did not have as many success stories to convince people that analytics can make a difference in their lives, work, school, government, or communities.

Interest is required, but interest is not enough to drive action. We need to enter discussions with stakeholders and sponsors under the assumption that the advanced analytics systems being developed will be implemented and will change the way that operations are executed.

It seems odd for me to write this and probably strange for you to read it. You would never enter into a major technology project or process re-engineering effort thinking that the end users may or may not use the results of the project; the organization is committing to whatever project it is, and therefore it is assumed that the end users will adopt the results without question.

That is not always the case with analytics projects. Often, the advanced analytics and AI team approaches a problem, diagnoses an issue, and shows the end users the results and a path forward to eliminate a problem, improve an operation, or find some other possible improvement in the operation and management of the functional department. The end users may find the results interesting, but they will not always engage in the process of change.

I would expect that if managers were shown an obvious and better way, they would, of their own volition, adopt the improvement and change the systems to incorporate the insights and new information. Typically, that is not the case. This was surprising and disappointing to me.

One way to improve this situation is to extend the projects being executed by the advanced analytics team to be included in organizational change management processes. The advanced analytics team does not need to run them—the processes can be run by project management teams—but the advanced analytics team needs to consult on the changes to ensure that processes do change and that the organization gains the benefit of the investment and engagement in advanced analytics projects.

In addition to the issue of complexity that we just discussed, there can be political or communication issues at play. Political issues come generally from turf battles or not-born-here aspects of the organization that the analytics leader must address directly. Communications issues can come from the analytics team not clearly explaining the relative value delivered by the change, or from perhaps not promoting it to the right audience. For example, projects that result in potential improvements by reducing the labor required to complete a process or task can turn to confusion when the functional leader doesn't implement the change. The functional leader may not make the change due to a perception or belief on their part that doing so would adversely impact their personal career progression.

Analytics leaders may need to walk the functional manager through the change and expand their thinking into what new possibilities for value creation emerge as you free up their team and their future for more creative pursuits.

Organizational culture is a powerful force, and that force, in the majority of organizations around the world, tends toward stasis or even active resistance to deep structural change. While many of us think that if a good idea is developed and presented, the organization will adopt it, that is not true in most cases.

Again, we in analytics are different: we like complexity, we like change, and we do not only like change, we *seek* to change things in a proactive and engaged manner. Most people do not have that mental orientation or personal constitution; most middle managers seek to actively avoid change.

While it may seem, on the surface, that organizations are in a constant state of change, corporate cultures and the majority of managers and executives work proactively against change. It is true that superficial change is nearly constant. An example is moving from a vertical industry focus to a horizontal process. Nothing changes except the superficial organizational structure. The culture doesn't change, the majority of processes do not change, and the pricing structure remains essentially unchanged.

Analytics leaders and analytics teams look beyond the superficial. They look at the data, the operations, the efficiency, and the effectiveness. Analytics teams analyze and produce fact-based illustrations of why organizations, team structures, processes, prices, and more need to change for an organization to improve. While superficial change is abundant, deep structural meaningful change is rare.

So, we must recognize that we have a mismatch in modalities. That is fine—we just need to realize that where the analytics team seeks and sees change, middle managers see danger.

The analytics team needs to design a change process as part of every project and the analytics team and the project management or change management team needs to help the functional teams to move through the prescribed change.

Although we argue that engaging the data science team to manage and drive this change is a waste of time and money, the organization needs to have another group, like a project management or change management group, that is chartered with driving the process and operational changes required to realize the value of the insights and intelligence generated by the advanced analytics team. The project management team is, in all likelihood, not part of the advanced analytics and AI team, but they are the team or group that the analytics team can hand off change management processes to.

Most people find change hard. The processes that the advanced analytics team changes with data and analytics might represent especially hard changes for an organization. The analytics team needs to consider the reticence of the organization and plan for how to overcome the tendency to the status quo.

Data or algorithms – the knee of the curve or the inflection point

We have reached, and passed, an inflection point in our engagement with data and analytics.

We have heard the arguments that algorithms and math are the seat or source of competitive advantage. We have been told that if you are smart, innovative, and own your own algorithm(s) or approach, then you have mastery over all your competitors and the road to success is nearly assured.

Also, we have heard, sometimes from the same experts who asserted the previous point, that the pathway to all success in analytics is through the ownership, control, management, and proactive use of data—large amounts of typically fast-moving data.

Why are we discussing data and algorithms now, as part of a chapter on organizational engagement? The topic is salient and relevant at this juncture in our discussion. I have had to refute the argument from functional managers numerous times, and I expect that you will as well. Functional managers will advocate for investments in data or algorithms, but rarely both. The analytics leader needs to be cognizant and aware that investing in and focusing on data at the expense of algorithms or vice versa will lead to less-than-optimal outcomes. The analytics team and the organization need to focus on both simultaneously.

People are continually invoking velocity as a way to create urgency in why investors need to hand over their money, or why an enthusiastic advocate needs to build a team and start today: because the competitors are already moving and each moment that you do not move, you are losing to the fictitious "them." As with most arguments or discussions, there are kernels of truth in each of these positions; they are true, in part.

The inflection point has illustrated to us that we need algorithms and data preparation techniques and methods, but that owning them is nearly impossible. Math is infinite and the ways to reach solutions to problems are manifold. If you go to all the time and trouble to protect a methodology or an approach or a math function, someone else will reach the same point of efficiency and effectiveness, or probably exceed it, through a different approach that you have not secured through legal means. Your best path to success in this area is to combine innovation and secrecy. Given the ephemeral and limited nature of the ability to protect sources and methods, constant innovation coupled with obfuscation is the best option when thinking about the math side of the ecosystem.

Of course, as with all situations or positions, there are unique or special cases. In our discussion, I am assuming that you do not work for or control a global technology company like IBM, Microsoft, Alibaba, or Hitachi.

Those companies, and companies like them, have made multibillion-dollar commitments to develop, maintain, and extend patent creation engines, which are a source of competitive advantage. If you work for a company in this class, then you can protect your intellectual property through legal means, but for our discussion, we are not assuming that you work in one of these firms.

We also learned after passing the inflection point that we need data, and we all know that data is essential to our efforts. But for data to be truly valuable to us in our efforts, data must be free of the common problems that we have faced in the past. Let's talk, very briefly, about some of the problems with data that have held us back in the field of analytics.

Four of the most foundational problems are:

- **Synthetic data; example or trial data**: Creating test data in the volumes needed to enable the valid testing of our analytical applications is challenging to the point of being nearly impossible. Generating the data needed from a small sample or seed set of data is typically not representative of the real world. If you have ever tried to create example or trial data, you know the pitfalls and problems that exist in this exercise. It seems so very simple on the face of it, but it is not. It is a fraught exercise. It is becoming easier to obtain large volumes of test data from external sources, but if you and your organization are seeking to test a unique application with data specific to use cases that are limited to your organization only, the cost and effort involved in creating or obtaining truly representative test data is not to be underestimated.

- **Bias**: Bias is baked into both the synthetic data that we create and the real-world data that we might want to use. Taking a small amount of limited data from limited datasets of patients, customers, partners, citizens, consumers, protestors, and/or other groups institutionalizes bias. Patterns that would occur in natural systems are difficult to create in, and generally do not exist in, synthetic or limited sets of data. How do we solve this in a way that is fair but realistic? We will turn our attention to a more complete treatment of bias in *Chapter 9, Managing the New Analytical Ecosystem.*

- **Limited breadth**: Most people have been inculcated with the belief that a large amount of uniform data is the best way forward in analytics; that is not true. Diversity of data produces the best results. You need internal and external data integrated together to understand the multiplicity of phenomena that occur in the real world. In the real world, almost nothing occurs in an isolated vacuum. Relationships and relative change in one area impact the results in another area. While it is impractical to think, at least in the short term, of modeling the entire world, we can model smaller, related systems and analyze those ecosystems to understand how interactions occur and how they impact the results and operations we seek to improve and optimize.

- **Volume and velocity of data**: In the past, we had data, but not enough of it and certainly not enough variety of data sources we needed. We did not have the tools, technologies or the skills to integrate data at scale, and we certainly did not have access to real time data or the ability to get data fast enough to act upon within a timeframe to make a valuable response to the relevant people and processes.

An entire book could be written about these problems and limitations, and other people have done so successfully. We will wrap up this topic by summing up this aspect of our discussion with the following observation: these problems can and still do inflict limitations on analytics projects, but they do not need to. We are well aware of these problems and we can avoid them or solve them where necessary.

To sum up these key points and insights:

- Algorithms have been with us in a recognizable form for centuries

- Data has been generated since the beginning of human existence

- Compute power is now ubiquitous and cheap

Never before in history have we had the combination of math, volumes of diverse and readily accessible data and the power to compute it that we now have at our finger-tips.

When we have all three of these fundamental elements working together in real time and on a continuous basis, we can produce valid scalable results in real time that can be used to monitor and manage almost any process in an automated fashion.

The main point is that it is not data or algorithms, it is data *and* algorithms. They each reinforce the value of the other and amplify their impacts in an evolving and dynamic manner. Don't let people simplify the equation or need for investment and focus to one or the other—both are required for success and successful change.

A managerial mindset

I completed my undergraduate degree in Computer Science (it was called Data Processing back then) in 1983. When people asked me what I was studying, I replied, "programming and computers." The most common reply to that was, "There is a future in that?" My son received his degree in Computer Science in 2018 and my daughter will receive her undergraduate degree in Information Management in 2022. A common joke that we share is, "Those computers; there's a future in working with them?"

It seems a silly observation, but think of it: there are still a significant number of executives and managers who graduated from their undergraduate programs in the 1980s and 1990s. Many of those people have a cursory understanding of computers and programming, and even less of an understanding of data and analytics.

Generally, people do not enthusiastically embrace what they do not understand. You won't find many, if any, of that generation of executives and managers who will freely admit that they do not fully understand basic computing technology. Ask them how a computer transfers data from disk to memory to a processing unit and I am quite confident that a blank stare will be the result in the majority of instances. If this is a mystery to them, I am certain that there is an infinitesimally small percentage of that managerial population who understand basic descriptive statistics, let alone advanced analytics and AI.

> *"...a recent Deloitte survey, Analytics and AI-driven enterprises thrive in the Age of With, The culture catalyst, of U.S. executives that found that only 10% of companies are competing on their analytical insights, and that the most popular tool for analyzing data — used by 62% of companies responding to the survey — is the spreadsheet?" [5]*

Given that this is a reality for the next 7 to 10 years, what do we do about it? Patience and clear communication are recommended for a start. Normally, I would have said concise communication, but in this case, a serious and significant amount of talking, writing, coercing, and convincing will be needed on your part.

Recently, the advanced analytics team that I am responsible for built and implemented an analytical system for a functional group. During the development of the system, the advanced analytics and AI team met with the functional team each week. After the prototype, pilot, and production implementation cycles, the analytics and functional teams continued to meet and talk on a weekly or bi-weekly basis. After a year of engagement, the third version of the production system was in place.

Representatives from executive management asked to see a demonstration of the system. The analytics team was excited to see the request. The functional team was less excited. The analytics team was curious about the functional team's reticence. When the analytics team asked the functional team and their management how the analytics team could help prepare for the meeting with the executives, the functional team asked for a detailed walkthrough of the system and a very detailed explanation of almost every metric in the system. It was as if the functional team had never seen the system or metrics before. The analytics team was flabbergasted at the lack of knowledge, engagement, and ownership of the data, analytics, and metrics.

The meeting with the executives was a success. The functional team explained the analytical application and demonstrated how the predictive and descriptive capabilities helped the functional team save time and money and be more efficient in the newly redesigned business process. The executives were happy to see that data and analytics were being used to change how the business operated.

The analytics team met internally after the demonstration sessions by the functional team for the executives. The discussion among the analytics team centered on how the analytics team could be more effective in organizational change management (encouraging greater adoption of new applications) and in knowledge transfer (training).

It was surprising to the analytics team how little ownership that the functional team had developed for the new application. It was clear that the functional team understood the value of the new application, but they had not fully embraced the application. Part of the issue that was uncovered was that the management of the functional team had been managing the business process in the same manner for over 25 years. When asked about changing the process to more fully incorporate the use of data and analytics, the manager of the area replied, "I had not thought of changing the process." A stunning remark given that the manager had been in most of the meetings over the previous year.

Do not underestimate the lack of awareness in existing middle managers of the need for changes in processes, training, job content, and performance management to fully leverage and utilize data and analytics.

The skills gap

Another real and present reason for the lack of progress in developing and leveraging data and analytics is the talent gap. The talent gap has been discussed widely in academic circles, within data science teams, and in the press that is oriented toward the science and engineering communities. In the popular press, the conversation is typically discussed in terms of the lack of students in **STEM (Science, Technology, Engineering, and Math)**. There is definitely an issue with the lack of qualified students in this broader area, but when you narrow the focus, the problem for advanced analytics teams becomes even more acute.

Hiring managers cannot find and hire enough talented people to build, manage, and maintain a rich, growing, and evolving analytical ecosystem across all of the industries, geographies, and companies that want to build out their analytics capabilities.

Tom Davenport and his co-authors also explored organizational gating factors in the adoption of analytics:

> *"Our survey results clearly show that analytical competitors represent a minority of businesses today, despite the number of years technologies like big data and analytics have been readily available. Becoming an organization that's driven by data and analytics is not the result of any single factor; it is multidimensional. For organizations to fully leverage the insights they derive and embed them into decisions and actions, a combination of three drivers is required: data and tools, talent, and culture."* [6]

When encountering multidimensional challenges, timing is important. Each portion of the ecosystem—talent, tools, culture, and more—can be mutually reinforcing or destructive. If you hire talent and do not have tools, the teams will be restless and question whether management is committed to analytics. If you have tools and talent, but no widespread support for using data and analytics, your results will suffer. It is important to build support with management, invest in tools, engage with a broad community to build grassroots support, use data and analytics, and then finally hire more than a handful of talented analytics professionals to begin working on projects with stakeholders and subject matter experts.

Davenport and his co-authors exhort us to work hard to enlist executive sponsors, which, as we know, is important:

"**Aim high for analytics champions**. *Executive sponsorship is vital to this level of organizational change, and the best champion sits in the corner office. According to the survey, the CEO is the lead champion of analytics in 29% of companies surveyed, and these companies are 77% more likely to have significantly exceeded their business goals. They are also 59% more likely to derive actionable insights from the analytics they are tracking. Companies should hire or promote leaders with a strong orientation toward analytics-based strategy and competition." [7]*

Beyond executive sponsorship, we need middle managers to show overt leadership and support for data and analytics projects. We need to:

"Encourage leaders to model examples. In meetings, for example, leaders should demonstrate the importance of analytics by asking for data points to back up business decisions. There is a major opportunity for companies to provide more education and improve the user experience if they want every employee to use insights as part of their work." [8]

"To really succeed with analytics, a company will need to acquaint a wide variety of employees with at least some aspects of analytics. Managers and business analysts are increasingly being called on to conduct data-driven experiments, interpret data, and create innovative data-based products and services. Many companies have concluded that their employees require additional skills to thrive in a more analytical environment.

> *One survey found that more than 63 percent of*
> *respondents said their employees need to develop new*
> *skills to translate big data analytics into insights and*
> *business value. Bob McDonald, at one point CEO of*
> *Procter & Gamble and then head of the U.S. Veterans*
> *Administration, said about the topic of analytics (and*
> *business intelligence more broadly) within P&G: We see*
> *business intelligence as a key way to drive innovation,*
> *fueled by productivity, in everything we do. To do this,*
> *we must move business intelligence from the periphery*
> *of operations to the center of how business gets done.*
> *With regard to the people who would do the analysis,*
> *McDonald stated: I gather there are still some MBAs who*
> *believe that all the data work will be done for them by*
> *subordinates. That won't fly at P&G. It's every manager's*
> *job here to understand the nature of statistical forecasting*
> *and Monte Carlo simulation. You have to train them in*
> *the technology and techniques, but you also have to train*
> *them in the transformation of their behavior. Of course,*
> *all senior executives are not as aggressive as McDonald*
> *in their goals for well-trained analytical amateurs. But in*
> *even moderately sophisticated companies with analytics,*
> *there will be some expectations for analytical skills among*
> *amateurs of various types." [9]*

Analytics is a skill set and core competency that our workforce needs to possess and master. As stated above, we need all employees and managers to be adept and competent in analytics. One of our long-term goals should be that there are no advanced analytics teams, that *everyone* is an analytics expert and practitioner.

And if this really is one of our long-term goals, then we should be working with our local elementary schools, middle schools, high schools, colleges, and universities to ensure that they are all teaching data literacy and analytical competence.

Your local schools will welcome your involvement. Make an appointment to go visit with the principal, the head of the math program, or the head of the applied arts program. You can make a difference. Start today. This effort is longer than your life. We need generations of people to support and further this effort. Start by enlisting your children as well.

Linear and non-linear thinking

Developing analytical applications is a creative endeavor.

The process is characterized by fits and starts, dead ends, sparks of brilliance, and moments of eureka. Who would not want that in their daily jobs? It turns out, lots of people would rather never have to do any of that in their daily role. They are linear thinkers. Linear thinkers are everywhere. You may be one of them. I am not. No matter—we can all work together.

Linear thinkers tend to see things in black and white terms. They want concrete and defined dates. They see the rules as being immutable. No gray areas, or very few gray areas for them. Again, no worries, we can all get along, if we are willing to listen to each other and collaborate.

Working with linear thinkers—and you will have to, because they are the majority of people who are successful in business today—is not as hard as it sounds. You simply need to spend much more time setting expectations for and with them. Think about every date that you can possibly define in a timeline of a project and multiply that by a factor, and you will understand the level of detail that the linear thinkers will want to have.

They have a seemingly endless need for minute detail. Much of the requested detail is never needed, but you will need to calm them down, and a plethora of details seems to do the trick.

This is one of the reasons why if you are taking a new role in a new company and they announce that the advanced analytics and AI team will report into the Information Technology team or the Finance team or the Operations team, you have an uphill battle on your hands. Unless the manager of those functions and your new manager are remarkable, you will have to contend with the modality mismatch we discussed earlier. Not a fatal flaw, but tiring to deal with on a regular and routine basis.

To be fair, linear thinkers are typically experts in an area—areas such as production planning or large system implementations or building complex factories. Rarely are they experts in data and analytics. The intelligent and well-adjusted linear thinkers know that they are experts and they are inquisitive about data and analytics. The obnoxious and self-assured linear thinkers are smugly convinced that they know everything. The latter are the most difficult people to work with, and, in the end, it may not be possible to work with them; they are exhausting.

You will learn through experience that just because a person is a professional, that does not mean that they have a very wide field of vision or curiosity. I worked closely with a lawyer that I liked, and still like, very much. He was very smart, engaging, and fun to work with, but his area of interest was purely legal matters. He wasn't conversant in business operations and he had no interest in data and analytics. I learned a lot from him about contract law and how to protect me and my business interests, but I am quite sure he learned almost nothing from me; he was a strict linear thinker and stayed in his lane at all times. I had no issues with him or his way of thinking or being, but like I said, I think I learned more and gained more of our relationship than he did.

Don't expect linear thinkers to change or open their viewpoints. If you are a non-linear thinker, you can see ways to solutions and approaches that linear thinkers cannot see and cannot even conceive of as being possible or practical. They are like fish—water, what water? They are so enveloped by their view of reality and certainty, they cannot even see it. Perhaps you can help them by leveraging their single-minded focus and disciplined thinking. Help them find the new groove and they can accelerate that line through their complete focus and ability to not get sidetracked. Set them in flight to come back with new ideas on a periodic basis that they can digest.

Do you really need a budget?

Budgets are many things to many people. For most people, they are a way to keep score. Who has a bigger budget? How can you take money from someone else's budget? However, what if you didn't need a budget?

In an advanced analytics and AI team, you really do not need a discretionary budget. Of course, you need money to pay for salaries, incentive compensation, desks, office space, travel and entertainment, and setting up your team with the appropriate technologies, but after you have the team hired, the infrastructure built, and the software installed, do you need a big or any additional budget to be effective and to deliver results? Trust me, you don't.

I have had multiple roles where budgets were tight. Actually, I am having a hard time recalling where budgets were freewheeling and we were let free to spend whatever we wanted. The point is that budgets are always controlled and restricted.

Since the advanced analytics and AI market is mature, evolved, and wide open from a technology perspective, and there are so many options for powerful multifaceted analytical platforms, most teams really do not need to buy software from IBM, SAS, or Tibco.

You and your team can be very effective by using open source software for a substantial portion of your work. Languages such as R and Python are powerful, valuable, and easy-to-access tools. Open source visualization tools like Plotly are easy access and use. The tools from Plotly are powerful and enable people to build very cool, animated, graphically rich visualizations in just a few hours, and, again, they have a really powerful open source offering.

Of course, you will need databases, interactive development environments, deployment-grade software, and a number of other tools to enable and empower your team, but most of those tools will have already be licensed if you are working in an established enterprise-class business. Someone somewhere in the company needs these tools too, and the other teams were probably in the organization before you and your team arrived. You can leverage the master services agreements that the firm already has and piggyback off the departmental licensing deals to get started. Once you have found where the tools you need are licensed and you have contributed your portion to pay for the licenses, there really isn't much for you to spend money on.

It will seem strange to your colleagues, and if you have never managed an advanced analytics team, this lack of a need to jockey for budget funds may seem strange to you too. In most technology projects, people think that analytics projects are technology projects, but since you are reading this book, you know better. People think that you need to buy hardware, software, professional services, management consulting services, and more, and in some cases, you need to—but in the majority of analytics projects, if you have hired the right team members, you will not need to spend any additional funds.

Budgets can be a roadblock to success. Budgeting can be a divisive process. Budgets can take a great deal of your time, especially when you are politicking to gain more money or to take money from someone else. Budgets can be contentious and they can be a problem, but not for you.

Budgets can be no big deal; that is how I deal with them. Set up your team, hire the right people, the budgeting cycle can be put on autopilot. This approach saves you time, money, and anguish. Who doesn't like that? No one.

Not big data but lots of small data

I am certain that my views in this area are informed and shaped by my early consulting experiences. I was fortunate enough to work with experienced professionals that knew how to acquire, integrate, and analyze a wide range of related but disparate datasets. They never worried about bringing together a couple of databases to create new information and analytics. They saw this activity as quite natural. As a consequence of spending so much time with them and seeing the incredibly powerful and insightful results, I too came to believe that integrating data together was an incredibly valuable activity that provided tools and insights that other people just did not see or even think of.

In the beginning, we would integrate datasets that were obviously related. We would integrate shipments information from the client company systems with the consumption data from grocery stores. Consumption data or scanner data from Nielsen and Information Resources, Inc. (IRI) would be integrated with survey data from Simmons on what consumers purchased and how they used our client's products and products from their competitors. No real stretch there; we were looking for a complete picture from the supply of raw materials, through production, to shipment and storage, to retail stocking and sales, to stocking in a pantry, to the ultimate use.

That was easy and it was clear what we were looking for. Now we have moved well beyond the obvious. To be clear, we still do the obvious for obvious reasons, but we now are looking at integrating far-flung data sources. We are searching for non-intuitive connections.

We are looking for sources of competitive advantage that have not been thought of, discovered, or tapped yet.

To be clear, this point is important for you to understand. There will be functional managers and executives who will argue for using limited data sources, possibly in large volumes, to analyze the phenomena that you are seeking to understand. They will do this for a number of reasons, which may include cost reduction, a simplistic view of the problem statement or area, or other motivations. What matters most, and the reason that we are discussing this point, is that you as the analytics leader need to advocate for the use of a wide range of disparate internal and external data to develop solutions that are differentiated from the competition and that provide a lasting basis for competitive advantage.

One of the talents and traits that you want in your advanced analytics team members is creativity in thinking about data and the wide range of internal and external data sources that you can access, integrate, and use. If your team does not have at least one person who is passionate and curious about how to leverage data, your team will unlikely be able to reach their potential.

Currently, we are routinely integrating data from a significant number of disparate internal sources. We use survey data, sales data, website visits, complaints, compliments, production yields, safety data, quality data, price and volume data, forecasts and actuals, financial data, supply chain data, test results, reject rates, and more. Also, we integrate a vast array of data from external commercial suppliers; local, state, and federal government sources; academic sources from research studies; primary and secondary research; and more.

One aspect that you need to be aware of is that collecting these sources of data may span a wide range of departments in the company you work in or are consulting with. Why should you care about this fact?

The more people who are involved in the process, the more explaining, teaching and approving that is required. The more departments and managers that are involved, the bigger the need them to budget for the acquisition of expensive data sources from commercial suppliers.

Government and academic sources involve much less overhead and can generally be obtained and used without many, if any, restrictions.

An operational consideration, and one that analytics teams continually overlook, is that if you are utilizing a dataset once, it is highly likely that you and your team will use it multiple times. More than once in a single analytical application on a refresh basis and possibly for multiple analytical applications. In nearly every case, it makes sense to build the data acquisition, transfer, loading, and integration logic in a modular reusable manner. Building the software, scripts, and utilities in this manner will take a little longer, but you will have an asset that you and your team can reuse for years. It is worth the incremental time and effort.

Introductory projects

It is unclear in certain circumstances if the sponsoring stakeholders or subject matter experts are fully committed to the project that you are chartered to undertake.

Of course, they will say that they want to engage, and they will assign people to support the efforts of the advanced analytics and AI team, but they may not even know the implications of engaging in an analytics project. It is almost certainly the case that they do not know the full implications of engaging in the project and the results that will be shown.

I strongly suggest that the first project you do with a new functional area, a new manager, or an executive that you do not have an existing relationship with should be a short project.

Not short as in small in ambition or scope—you can definitely take on a significant issue or challenge for the company or cause— but you should break down the initial stage of the project into a piece of work that can be completed and presented with compelling results in 2 to 4 months.

It has been true since the time that I began building performance management and analytic applications that end users cannot see or envision the results that they will receive and be expected to work with, and they are even less capable of understanding the cascade of changes that will need to be enacted to realize the full benefits of a data and analytics-based approach.

The sponsors and stakeholders will in most cases be impressed that you and your team are committing to deliver results so quickly. They will have little to no knowledge that you are doing this for your benefit more than theirs.

What happens in most cases is that you and your team will illustrate an interesting insight or find a result that is not intuitive. You can use this finding to open the discussion regarding planning the phase of the work, where the analytical application or predictive model(s) become part of the newly re-engineered production process. Most managers will not act surprised, but I can guarantee you that they will be surprised and may resist implementing the changes, but you need to push forward. You need to gently persist in the belief that the data, insights, and analyses are leading to an improvement in pricing, operations, marketing, or whatever functional business unit you are analyzing.

The organization did not invest in an analytics team to have results be ignored. You may have numerous conversations and you may have to escalate the process to your management, but if the results are not used to benefit the company, you do not want to be the person who did not push for full value realization. I am not a fan of this kind of maneuvering in corporations or companies, but in this case it is unavoidable.

Value realization

I have seen a wide range of reactions from organizations as their own advanced analytics teams have developed and delivered new findings and insights that illustrate the path to positive change in their operations.

A few years ago, I was talking with the manager of an advanced analytics team at one of the leading manufacturers of athletic clothing. The situation that was described was not surprising to me. The analytics team worked on projects for all functions of the company, but most of the projects that the advanced analytics team undertook were focused on marketing and sales. If the project findings supported what the sales and marketing leader believed and had planned to do, the results were embraced and used in building the case or executing the plan. If the analytical findings indicated that there was a better way to execute the plan, then the results were ignored, and the plan was executed as the sales and marketing leader intended. This happens on a regular basis in numerous organizations.

The question is, what do you do? The projects that the advanced analytics team undertakes need to have visibility to your management team, to the management team of the functional area, and to the executive leadership team. This visibility is best achieved through written, verbal, and personal communication. Visibility to the management of the analytics team and to the functional team is best achieved through routine status reports and personal meetings. Visibility to the company is best achieved through company bulletins, newsletters, company app updates, social media channels, and other communication vehicles. I am assuming that you are not more than 2 to 3 levels away from the executive leadership, and therefore your updates to your management should filter up the executive leadership team.

With visibility comes accountability and responsibility. Given that the analytics team has delivered positive messages and solid analytical insights, when you are asked when functional change is to be implemented and value realized, you can point to the level of collaboration with the functional team and their management.

We have talked about how certain managers have little to no appreciation for or understanding of technology, data and analytics, and we also have talked about how people tend to try to ignore topics and discussion where they are uncomfortable. This is the perfect storm of all of those factors. You cannot and should not be party to this. The projects that you and your team are undertaking should all conclude with a phase where organizational change is undertaken or where analytical applications or models are put into production usage.

Typically, good ideas have a long shelf life, and most businesses run on repeating cycles. You do need to collaborate with the functional team to help them understand how to leverage the insights to realize the full value of the findings. In most organizations, it will be the responsibility of the functional team and a change management team to implement the process and operational changes, but you need to have your team ready to consult on the actual changes.

It may be the case that the functional team is too busy to make the change when the insights are produced. The functional team may need to talk and consider their options and plan for the optimal time to implement the suggested changes. The timing of the change is the responsibility of the functional team and their management.

You and your analytics team can move on to other projects, and when the question comes to you as to why the results have not yet been implemented, you can point to the functional team and their timing and process.

In my experience, there is no shortage of project work for the analytics team to undertake. Part of your role, and that of your team, is to set the functional teams up for success and be ready to collaborate through the value realization process. You cannot make them leverage the insights that have been found, but you can be ready to explain to your management, the managers of the functional areas, and the executive leadership your role in the process.

On the other hand, there are organizations and functional groups that are eager to accept that insights have been found and new ways of executing processes are possible and probable. The analytics team collaborates with the functional team and the organizational change management team to implement the changes needed in operational processes to take advantage of the modes and insights developed.

One consideration that we will briefly touch on here and explain in greater detail in *Chapter 9, Managing the New Analytical Ecosystem*, is that with each successful project comes a growing set of analytical applications and models that need to be maintained, extended, and refreshed. Your team will need to keep in mind that all analytical applications should be built in a way that means the functional teams can accept responsibility for interacting with and using the analytical applications and models in their routine and regular processes and operations. If the advanced analytics team needs to run every application, the bandwidth and productivity of your team will grind to a halt quickly.

Summary

Middle managers get bad-mouthed on a regular basis. I am sure that as you read this chapter, some of you may have felt that I was taking unfair aim at some of our middle management compatriots. I meant no harm or disrespect.

This chapter was all about understanding the roadblocks that you will encounter. I have encountered all of these issues and challenges multiple times in various organizations. I have included them because I am nearly 100% certain that you will encounter them as well.

I have described and discussed the issues as clearly as possible in hopes that you will think through them ahead of time and consider your team, the organization you are working for or consulting with, and the best method possible for explaining the challenge, the solution(s), and the benefits of moving past the current roadblock to your collaborators.

These issues can only be overcome in collaboration with the functional sponsors and stakeholders that you and your team are engaged with in advanced analytics and AI-based projects and processes. You may need only their agreement. You may need their agreement and active sponsorship. You may need all of those previous elements and budgetary support too. No matter what level of support you require, it will only come from your stakeholders and sponsors.

Remember, you are the expert and they are the novices. It is your role and responsibility to teach them and communicate with them and convince them that they should come on this journey with you and your team. At first, this may seem to be a waste of your time, but trust me, it is not. You need them and they need you, even if they do not know it yet. Be patient and describe the challenge, solution, and benefit in as many ways as required for them to buy in and join the journey.

I once sat in front of an industry luminary in the early stages of the **Customer Relationship (CR)** market and movement. Yes, I know, it was a movement before it became a market. It sounds odd to say, but it is true. I was explaining the value of driving the CR process through data and analytics. And, yes, I had to explain it to him because it wasn't obviously true to him or the broader market at the time.

I was so very excited to be meeting with this person and I had brought the CEO of our company and a board member with me. I explained the concept in the most straightforward way that I knew—it didn't land. I tried another approach—that did not land either. I was really starting to panic. I tried a third approach and the guy said, "Oh, I get it!" I was about to pass out, but it worked, and we gained a hugely valuable ally in our quest to have the broader market use data and analytics in the CR process.

When we left the meeting, the CEO said, "I thought that you were never going to get him to understand the value of data and analytics, but you kept pitching and it finally landed." I felt like saying, "Well, you could have spoken up rather than sitting there mute." But given that he was my boss, I simply smiled and took a deep breath.

The point is that the burden is on you as the expert to bring the sponsors and stakeholders along on the journey. It is obvious to you, but not to them. Just keep pitching and breathing. You will win out in the end.

Now that we know how to engage with executives, senior managers, and subject matter experts, let's turn our attention to how we should analyze and determine the best projects for our team to undertake and execute.

Chapter 6 footnotes

1. *Analytics and AI-driven enterprises thrive in the Age of With. The culture catalyst,* July 25, 2019, Thomas H. Davenport, Jim Guszcza, Tim Smith, and Ben Stiller, `https://www2.deloitte.com/us/en/insights/topics/analytics/insight-driven-organization.html`

2. Ibid

3. *Augmented Intelligence: The Business Power of Human–Machine Collaboration 1st Edition*, November 1, 2019, Judith Hurwitz, Henry Morris, Candace Sidner, Daniel Kirsch, https://www.amazon.com/dp/0367184893/

4. *University of Iowa Hospitals and Clinics Transforms the O.R. Accessible, predictive analytics results in 74% reduction in surgical infections.* https://www.tibco.com/customers/university-iowa-hospitals-and-clinics

5. *What Separates Analytical Leaders from Everyone Else.* https://www.thelowdownblog.com/2020/02/what-separates-analytical-leaders-from.html

6. *What Separates Analytical Leaders From Laggards?*, February 3, 2020, Thomas H. Davenport, Nitin Mittal, and Irfan Saif, https://sloanreview.mit.edu/article/what-separates-analytical-leaders-from-laggards/

7. Ibid

8. Ibid

9. *INFORMS Analytics Body of Knowledge (Wiley Series in Operations Research and Management Science) 1st Edition*, James J. Cochran (Editor), Thomas H. Davenport, https://www.amazon.com/dp/1119483212

CHAPTER 7

SELECTING WINNING PROJECTS

"Man does not simply exist but always decides what his existence will be, what he will become the next moment. By the same token, every human being has the freedom to change at any instant."

—Viktor Frankl

Before we go further in our discussion, let's take a moment to define winning projects. Winning projects are those analytics projects that are widely understood by business executives, sponsors, subject matter experts, project review members, portfolio managers, finance professionals, and the analytics team. Winning projects are prioritized in the analytics backlog and chosen as areas of strategic and tactical importance to the success and improved operations of the company. The most important and selected analytics projects are then measured and compared to a wide range of other projects that the company needs to execute, and the final selection process is undertaken. The resulting projects have been carefully scoped, vetted, and funded.

Those projects are the projects that will deliver value to the company. Those projects have been shepherded through the selection process and have broad support across the organization. The analytics team and project team from the business function has the support and air cover they need to execute these chosen, winning projects.

Analytics self determination

In most business situations, people are directed to the projects that they will be undertaking. Of course, there are decisions to be made and leeway in how the project(s) will be accomplished and how progress will be made, but for the most part the projects that are to be undertaken are dictated; this is true for large and small projects. People are told to build a factory, or they are charged with upgrading the hardware and software of an application system, like an **Enterprise Resource Planning** (**ERP**) environment, or perhaps they are tasked with improving the user interface or data visualization for an application.

The point that I want to make is that not everyone has the option of selecting the projects that they or their team will undertake. Having a choice of the work that we and our teams will engage in is a fulfilling and energizing element of running an advanced analytics and artificial intelligence team. We should not take it for granted that we will always have as much say and sway over the work that we as analytics leaders, and our analytics teams, engage in.

As analytics becomes a broader skill set in the workforce and it is more widely understood by managers and executives, the practice and profession of analytics will become a more mainstream activity and hence will be subject to an increasing set of rules, procedures, regulations, and governance.

We, as analytics practitioners, want to drive and direct our elementary, high school, and university education systems, training protocols, and management mindset to move in this direction for the greater good of our organizations and societies. While we are driving for this directional change, we need to be aware that, as a whole, our governments, businesses, academic institutions, and our overall society are not there yet, and therefore we analytics professionals and leaders have immediate work to do to ensure that our organizations and institutions make the best decisions possible to obtain the greatest value from the investments and efforts we undertake in our analytics projects and programs.

There are a variety of causal and contributing factors for why analytics leaders and managers are vested with so much leeway and leverage over the work that we are entrusted to prioritize and ultimately undertake.

Communicating the value of analytics

Let's take a look at the top three reasons why we find ourselves in this environment and discuss the best methods for ensuring that we, as analytics professionals, can make this work to our maximum benefit. Let's discuss the ways in which we can ensure that the executives, managers, and subject matter experts we work with understand the value of analytics.

Relative value of analytics

In my view, the majority of functional executives and managers are not aware of, or conversant in, the salient factors relating to the tradeoffs or relative value to be delivered between the possible or potential analytical projects that are being considered. This is an education issue and an issue related to the current time we live in.

Also, it is related to the level of knowledge and interest management and managers have in analytics in general. Most executives and many managers look at analytics projects as technology projects and, for all the reasons we have previously discussed in this book, they do not delve into the details of making an informed decision of which projects deliver the most immediate, and greater overall, value to the company.

Managers consider and evaluate options, such as hiring a third shift at a factory, and compare it to upgrading the SAP ERP system, or they compare the use of funds with the possibility of building an infrastructure for advanced analytics and artificial intelligence (AI). Yes, these are valid comparisons and the decisions that need to be made at a corporate portfolio level, but they are like comparing pomegranates and apples. At some level, decisions and commitments must be made, and projects of varying types must be compared and chosen between, but these decisions should be made with the most detailed information and the deepest level of understanding of all the possible options.

This is a problem for the company, for the executives and managers, and for you. In many cases, the decision makers are kicking the can down the road. You and your team need to reduce and, if possible, eliminate this dynamic in the project selection process. How do we lessen the ambiguity around helping the decision makers understand the relative value and impact of analytics projects in relation to other projects that those managers and executives may have seen multiple times and have a greater level of familiarity with?

We need to make evaluating an advanced analytics project as easy as possible. We do not need to "dumb it down," but we do need make the scope, scale, time frame, resources required, transformational potential, possible range of returns, and long- and short-term value clear to decision makers.

The value of analytics, made easy

Part of the issue lies with the leadership of the analytics team. Recently, I had a conversation with a group of subject matter experts, a project sponsor, and the analytics team members. The analytics team presented initial results from a test that was underway, they explained that we had seen positive and negative operating results from the test. I asked the team as a whole to highlight and extract the effects of the test into the following elemental components – naturally occurring business results; results from known, yet unrelated, operational changes; and results from external events (i.e. competitive activity, natural disasters, man-made or market changes) and from the tests that we designed and inserted into the operational mix. The people who fought the hardest against the request or directive to take the results down to the next level were the data scientists. The analytics team argued that there were no compelling reasons to tease apart these factors and results.

Given that the analytics team works for me, it was easy to see who was going to prevail in the discussion, but it is worth noting that the subject matter experts and sponsor were mute during this part of the discussion. The sponsor and subject matter experts know and knew that they need the additional level of detail to have a discussion with their management, but they did not speak up or support the request to decompose the results.

As an aside, I diligently try to not manage the analytics team with a heavy hand, but when the work is required and the team is not seeing the larger organizational goal, I will step in and dictate the work to be done. I much prefer to manage through a process where the value and need is illuminated for the data science team by their own thinking and discovery rather than to dictate, and they make, in some cases, the begrudging decision that further work needs to be done to ensure a broad understanding across the organization.

Enabling understanding

We, as analytics professionals, often know what needs to be done, but the analytics team either does not want to do the work, because they have plenty of other work to do, or they think that the results are obvious and the further decomposition is not needed to understand the deeper dynamics and the driving forces underlying the high-level results. In the majority of cases, the data scientists rationalize their reasons for not wanting to undertake the further decomposition work because they can already see and understand the dynamics without the further effort, but the business users – the sponsor, who has to explain the project, value, and the need for change to the executives, and the subject matter experts who have to support the sponsor and also implement the required changes – do not understand the core dynamics at a level where they can change the operations in a meaningful way that maximizes value realization for the business as a whole.

This is a problem for the majority of analytics professionals, including me. We as analytics professionals are busy and have a backlog of work to do, and we have a bias that once we see and understand something, we want to move on to the next interesting project, but we must remember that two of our primary functions are – to enable the organization to realize the value of the analytics process and projects, and to ensure that the management and executives of the company understand, at a visceral level, the underlying elements and dynamics of change.

As analytics professionals, we often think that when we and our analytics compatriots see a correlation, everyone else sees it too. In most cases that is not true. We need to constantly be vigilant so that we carry the work far enough to ensure that executives, sponsors, subject matter experts, and all those involved can see and understand what we see and know.

Ensuring that subject matter experts, managers, and executives understand the relative value of analytics, the complexity involved, the competitive advantage, and the personal benefit that will be gained from supporting you and your team is a worthwhile endeavor and activity and one that you and your team need to continually engage in. Bring along the functional team in each project and your efforts will be supported, funded, and rewarded.

Enterprise-class project selection process

The communication dynamic outlined in the previous section – the need to ensure that the functional team understands and is on board – is true and extends to the project selection process as well. Analytics leaders and professionals need to be decomposing projects down to a level where analytics projects can be compared on a like-for-like basis with competing projects and priorities. This is a track of work that we as analytics professionals need to improve on and hone our skills in.

Often analytics leaders and professionals do not want to create the materials or information for review by a project review board or by a portfolio management function because the projects may be rejected, or more information might be requested or the project scope may be changed, all resulting in more work for the analytics team. The bottom line is that this activity and the materials to support it are required by most organizations and must be completed. This is just a fact, but the other consideration is that, in my experience, and given the level of interest and engagement from executives, sponsors, and subject matter experts, analytics projects are typically approved at a higher rate and faster than other competing projects. Currently, the analytics teams have a winning hand, and as such, analytics teams and leaders should be excited about presenting their projects and programs for evaluation, discussion, and approval.

Understanding and communicating the value of projects

The second factor to call out is that the finance organization or the portfolio management function in the organization does not know how to calculate the relative value of the possible projects in the analytics portfolio very well or with the needed level of accuracy. I am not being harsh or demeaning to the finance or portfolio management teams with this remark. The analytics projects being discussed and undertaken are not well defined, or at least not as well defined as they could be. Analytics projects have a great deal of flex and flow in their definition.

It is paradoxical that the analytics team is not very good at defining the details of the project delivery, cost, timelines, and relative value of analytics projects. Given that the primary purpose of analytics projects is the measurement of performance or the prediction of future results, it would be expected that the analytics team would be better at this aspect of the project selection process, but analytics professionals, in general, do not find the definition and description of possible projects interesting. They would rather be executing the projects than describing and selecting them.

Part of this lack of definition comes from the wide range of people involved in the dialog. Saying something akin to, "We want to improve the operations of our supply chain," to the CEO will have a much different meaning and connotation than saying the same thing to a manager of a warehouse. The audience that we are addressing matters. Being clear with that audience is crucial in the project definition and selection process.

Implicit in this discussion is another nested factor: project scope and scale. Analytics projects can take a day or multiple years. One approach that has worked exceptionally well for me is to describe analytics efforts as a process.

We discussed changing the mindset of the organization from a project mentality to a process mentality early in the book – in the introduction, actually. By describing the overall effort as a process, you can set the stage for a larger transformation of the organizational functions that are being examined, analyzed, and ultimately transformed. At the same time, you reserve the right to undertake projects as short as a day and of varying durations that makes sense relative to the effort required to achieve the objectives and goals.

As an example, the complete process of transforming the supply chain of an organization from the suppliers of raw materials including commodities to the delivery of finished goods to the ultimate consumer and customer may take a decade to complete, and as part of that process, understanding the on-time fill rate for each order coming off a production line may take a day.

The point I am making is that the clarity of the size, scope, and scale of the analytics effort comes from you, the analytics leadership, and the analytics team. You and your team need to ensure that you are presenting the information from an entry-level project in relation to competing projects of the same scope and scale. If the total transformation of the supply chain is being considered, then it needs to be in relation to projects of the same importance and impact. To do so otherwise is to lead the decision makers into a situation of making flawed comparisons and decisions.

Your role in communicating clearly and in a concise manner comes down to being able to describe, discuss, and sell a vision for an analytical process (i.e. a complete transformation of the supply chain), while breaking the time line, resources required, investment needed, and relative probability of success into manageable projects (i.e. improving first-time, on-time, and in-full orders) so that the executives, sponsors, subject matter experts, finance professionals, portfolio management professionals, and all related and involved parties can understand, evaluate, and support the analytics team and projects proposed.

Delegation of decision making

The final factor that I see on a daily basis in the project selection process for analytics projects is the delegation of decisions down to lower levels of the organization; executive management delegates the decision-making authority for analytics projects to the senior managers, who in turn delegate to the functional managers, who, in the majority of cases, default to what the head of analytics wants to do, or recommends, to the functional managers.

In one of my previous roles, I spoke with a senior vice president about how to prioritize the company's investment in analytical applications. I suggested that we organize a cross-functional group of executives and senior managers to review the lists of projects and assist in making fair and equitable decisions regarding where the analytics team would focus their efforts. The person thought about it for a couple weeks and when I came back to revisit the discussion, the suggestion was to delegate the decision-making authority to a project review board.

The project review board was made up of middle managers. The members of the product review board mainly reviewed technology projects. In attending the project review board meetings, it was clear that each member of the project review board had their routine questions that they asked of each project sponsor that came before the review board. Some questions focused on cost, or time of delivery, or vendor licensing, others on resources and external consulting involvement. After a few meetings, it felt you could predict which staff member was going to ask which question. The questions were asked and answered and, mostly, projects were approved or deferred until more information could be gathered to address the questions of the staff members and the review board.

When it came to analytics projects, a few of the standard questions were relevant and those questions were asked and dispatched quickly, and every analytics project was approved.

There was no discussion about which projects to undertake or which project would be better for the company as a whole. No dialog about tradeoffs or relative value, or any dialog about which projects should be undertaken.

This is a dangerous situation – if not dangerous, then disingenuous for sure. The executive delegates to a project committee; the project committee, in effect, delegates or defers to the head of analytics. There is a process in place, but in the end, all decisions are made by the head of analytics. This seems like a waste of time, a false decision-making process, and the vesting of the decision power in one person when it appears that there is a committee review being undertaken. We need to ask, why does this happen and what is the problem with it?

This situation evolves and is perpetuated for the reasons outlined above – people are busy, they want to trust in the group, the group wants to trust in the head of analytics, the executive and the committee do not understand the scope, scale, and resources needed and the relative value of the analytics projects being proposed, and possibly other personal motivations that I have not considered.

While it seems like a winning situation where the organization believes that there is a review process but, in the end, the head of analytics is making all the decisions, it is not a sustainable or defensible situation.

There are a number of remedies to this situation and it is not productive to be prescriptive in a detailed sense here, but let us say that the role of the analytics leader and team is to develop, present, and clarify detailed project plans and proposals that can be easily and fairly compared with competing projects, and it is the duty of the project review board or executives or other managers to provide sufficient review, governance, and guidance to all project managers on why projects are being selected and undertaken and why others are being deferred or rejected.

Let's delve into the factors that need to be included to have a healthy review process, an engaged organization, and a cross-functional team making informed decisions on the behalf of the company for the overall betterment of the company.

Technical or organizational factors

For the remainder of this chapter, we will examine and discuss the factors that play into selecting winning projects. Our discussion will center on two areas of important factors – technical and organizational. We will address the technical factors first and then move on to the organizational factors.

Data – does it exist, and can you use it?

As we have discussed, we are data scientists and analytics professionals, not alchemists.

If there is no data that directly or even indirectly describes the operational aspect of the company or behavior of the entities – people, processes, products, machines, etc. – that we are to examine and analyze at least once, then the advanced analytics team cannot assist in the improvement of that process, operation, or area.

All analytics professionals experience this situation regularly: the discovery of the lack of data is often accompanied by a sense of surprise, and possibly disbelief, from the executives and in some cases from the sponsors and managers. After the analytics team tells the subject matter experts that there is no relevant or useable data, it is recommended that the analytics team lead a discussion of how the functional team can begin collecting and or buying the relevant and required data so that in the future the analytics team can come back and analyze the operations.

The analytics team can provide an overview and a high-level roadmap of how to instrument the relevant processes, collect the data, and work with the information technology team to build an operational data environment that will feed the future analytics process.

If there is data and it is only one observation, the analytics and functional teams can, possibly, undertake a one-time project, but the analytics team cannot set up an analytics process and models that undertake a continual observation and sustained improvement process.

As analytics professionals, we need to coach the executives, sponsors, and subject matter experts to understand and to have the business professionals communicate their vision and thinking about their perceived view of the value of data and analytics. The analytics team needs to ask, is this a one-time project that is only needed now, or is it a periodic project that is needed on a periodic basis, or is it an analytic process that is continuous and on-going? Each scenario – one-time project, a series of related project, a series of interdependent projects, or an environment that monitors, manages, and improves operations – can be accomplished if designed for and worked toward. It all starts with the data.

Data – internal and external sources

Internal data sources will provide insight, value, and a starting point for analyzing activity, but if the organization wants to model and predict the future, more than likely, external data will be needed.

Internal data sources will enable the team to analyze activity and profile patients, customers, users, suppliers, and other entities of interest. Internal data will not enable the team to find new patients, customers, website visitors, or other entities that the business may want to understand or interact with.

External data extends the ability of the organization to project their view and understanding of customers and patients forward in time and into the market. We have discussed the value of employing an ensemble or collection of data rather than looking at a single facet of the market or customers. All analytics beyond descriptive statistics will in most cases increase in value when external data is added into the project.

Typically, valuable external data is expensive and given the wide range of data that can be purchased and used, the funding of these purchasing is usually sourced from the business unit that is benefiting from the analytics project(s). In some organizations, finding the funding for external data is easy and part of the normal operations of the company; in other firms, buying external data is new and the value will have to be explained and justified.

If the company or business unit is looking to expand its reach, impact on new markets, customers, partners, and patients, you will, in all likelihood, need external data.

If you and your organization are new to utilizing external data, start with an open mind and business objective. The options and offerings for external, syndicated, third-party data have expanded dramatically in the previous three decades.

Data – alternatives and workarounds

It is often the case, and has been the case numerous times in my career, that when undertaking an analytics project, you and the analytics team cannot find data that provides direct observation of the phenomena that you want to measure. The data either does not exist, or an organization owns the data, but does not want to share it, or sell it, or license it.

In a recent project, we were interested in when the local Whole Foods store had opened. We wanted to know this for all zip codes in the US going back to when the first Whole Foods store opened. We looked and looked, but this data is owned by Whole Foods and they have no interest in making it available to the public.

The analytics team thought about it and one of the team members suggested that we search for and use the date of the first online review for each store as a proxy for the opening date. The analytics team talked about it, and we realized that we didn't need the actual opening date; we just needed to know when a Whole Foods was operational in the local area. Problem solved.

There are numerous situations where you, the analytics team, and the functional teams will not be able to afford, access, or use the actual data that you want. Do not worry: in most cases, you can find a free alternative that provides almost all of the descriptive or predictive power you need for the model you are building or the analytics task at hand.

Data – harmonizing the relevant elements

Given the plethora of systems, online entities, organizations, governments, academic institutions, and individuals that are creating data and data streams, it would seem nearly impossible that you, the analytics team, and the functional teams cannot find a set of data that does not relate, even in a tangential way, to the processes, people, or products that you want to analyze and understand.

There are cases where even a proxy dataset is not exactly what you want or need. We have talked about analyzing an ensemble or collection of internal and external datasets. We have not explicitly talked about the need to integrate those datasets. Let's be very clear: you, the analytics team, or the information management team needs to integrate and harmonize these disparate datasets. You need the subjects in the data to mean the same thing.

As an example, when I was analyzing sales data for a consumer-packaged goods company using three external datasets and an internal data source, all of them defined Chicago very differently.

To ensure that the analytics that we would produce would be valid, the analytics team had to go through each data source, examine their definition of Chicago and then transform the individual definitions in each data source to match the definition of Chicago that the team had selected, and then the analytics team had to transform the sales data from each source to be the projected Chicago sales volume that matched the new definition of Chicago. The analytics team needs to harmonize and integrate all the datasets so you are comparing apples to apples.

Now that we have a clear understanding of how to harmonize and integrate the relevant data elements, let's return to our discussion of synthesizing data.

As we discussed earlier, you may not be able to find data that directly relates to the people, products, or processes that you seek to analyze. The next course of action is to find an indirect dataset, a proxy dataset, which provides insight into the activity you seek to understand. Failing that, you can then start to look at second order data, and probably, multiple datasets that can be integrated and used to discern the signal you seek to analyze.

Of course, the further down the path described above you and your team travel, the more the cost and effort required increases. At some point, the cost and effort involved in creating the signal outweighs the value derived from creating it.

Data – ethics

The rules and regulations relating to using data and the ethics of employing data has been a topic of great and growing interest over the past several years.

Approximately a year ago, I began writing a book about the ethics of using data and analytics and I stopped working on that idea to write this book.

Not because the topic of ethics is not interesting to me or to the business community or society at large, but because so many books had recently been written about the ethics of data and analytics. The number of academic and business practitioners who are experts on the topic, teaching university-level courses, speaking at conferences, events, and symposiums, and contributing to federal and state legislation is large.

Of course, analytics teams need to be in touch with their internal legal teams and possibly with external counsel to ensure that the acquisition, storage, management, protection, and use of internal and external data aligns with all relevant legislation and ethical guidelines from all governmental, regulatory, advisory, and advocacy groups.

In the European Union, the **General Data Protection Regulation (GDPR)**, and in California, the **California Consumer Privacy Act (CCPA)** and numerous other legislative acts and regulations, outline the duties and responsibilities of firms when they are utilizing data relating to citizens who live in the relevant jurisdictions.

When teams that I lead use data, we make sure to comply with all relevant rules and regulations. When the analytics team is considering buying, obtaining, and using a new dataset, we look at the following considerations:

1. Is there **Personal Identifiable Information (PII)** included? If so, we ask the external provider to strip out the PII or we have the internal information technology team split the data into two datasets; one dataset is the original and complete data, and the other is the new dataset without the PII subset of data. We ask the information technology team to provide the non-PII dataset to the analytics team, and to not allow the analytics team to not have access to the original complete dataset.

2. Is there **Personal Health Information (PHI)** included? If so, we handle the data in the same manner as above.

3. Are there other data elements that are sensitive that we need to segregate? If so, we continue to remove or split datasets until we have removed all sensitive data that may allow the identification and linking of sensitive material to an individual.

4. Are there other data elements that are sensitive that we need to mask? If so, we mathematically change or hash the sensitive data that may allow the identification and linking of sensitive material to an individual.

5. Once we are confident that all PII, PHI, and other sensitive data that can be used to link back to an individual is removed, then we can begin the process of analyzing and modeling the data.

Of course, you must ask yourself, the analytics team, and the business team, "Why are we analyzing the data?" If the purpose is ethical, moral, legal, and for the benefit of all involved, then you are in a good position to move forward. If the use of the data, and the analytics produced, contravenes any of the relevant regulations, government acts, or harms anyone involved in the analytics or as a result of the analytics, then you must stop and reexamine what you are doing or planning.

As noted, there are numerous current and relevant books, government and academic studies, proposed legislative acts and regulations, events, conferences, symposia, and experts on the topic of data, analytics, and ethics. This is just a small section of this book and does not profess to give the topic of ethics a full treatment and deep consideration that the subject requires and deserves.

Ethics is a topic of great importance and should be of significant interest to you. If you need support in understanding the ethical responsibilities of yourself, the analytics team, and the broader organization, I suggest you start with the internal legal team at your organization. If you are not part of a larger organization, I suggest you start by looking for experts and academics focused on ethics. There is a wealth of data available for your review and use.

Technology – hardware, software, and the cloud

In closing out the discussion of the technical factors to be considered when selecting projects, I want to be clear about technology. For the most part, it is irrelevant.

I am sure that my colleagues and friends who write software, build hardware, and run technology companies will not agree with that previous statement, but in my opinion, it is true. To be clear, you need all of those technology pieces, but the ones you chose is truly irrelevant. Put your data in servers in the cloud or in your data center – doesn't really matter which, as long you understand the relative costs and which environment serves your short- and long-term needs. Have your team used R or Python, or R and Python? Again, it doesn't matter as long as the analytics team can do the work required and that they are productive and can collaborate with their analytics colleagues, external consultants, and subject matter experts.

The bottom line is that most of the technology you and your team review and select will do the job you and your team require.

Don't stress over it. Pick what you need and move on to the real work.

Now, let's move on to the organizational factors to consider when selecting winning projects.

Guidance to end users

When I refer to end users, this is an umbrella term that refers to all people who utilize the analytical models and applications that the analytics team builds and deploys. I am including executives, senior managers, functional managers, subject matter experts, and casual users in this category.

End users tend to overthink how an analytical application might be able to help them and their operational teams. Executives and senior managers will self-edit and cull ideas that could be very useful and valuable in how the analytics team thinks about and approaches solving an analytical challenge.

My guidance to end users is this: if you have an idea for how data and analytics can help you and your team, call me or e-mail me immediately. Don't design the solution, don't agonize about the profusion of data or the lack of data, don't think about the budget implications or how long it might take to build the analytical application – just call me or e-mail me as soon as you have an idea that you want to discuss. I suggest you adopt a similar approach.

When the idea is fresh in someone's mind and they have a wide range of related ideas of how the data and analytical application can make a difference to people, processes, and products, that freshness is valuable and needs to be discussed, encouraged, and fostered.

You may think that you will be overwhelmed with requests for meetings. In the beginning, you will be, but you need to persevere and attend all those meetings. Why? Because you will hear amazing ideas, and a few unworkable ideas too, but that is beside the point. You will build connections across the organization and you will begin to see patterns of where you and your analytics team can make a difference on a global, cross-functional basis.

The ideas, the networking, the new global perspective, and the interesting projects are all reasons why you need to open the flood gates to each and every end user in the organization. Yes, you will have some meetings that are truly useless, but that, in and of itself, is instructive and a learning exercise. It is worth your time and you should try it; you will see the value. One-on-one meetings, town halls, and office hours are all mechanisms whereby you can make the organization aware of what can be done and bring a broader group of people into the discussion of data and analytics.

Beyond you and your team learning about what the end users are thinking, this is an opportunity for you to communicate to the end users what can be accomplished through analytics. You will be surprised at the lack of awareness and the misconceptions that exist in the minds of the people you will meet.

Where is the value in a project?

As I noted at the end of the *Introduction* section of this book, I am endlessly curious about all things – all people, anthropology, psychology, processes, products, history, science, economics, and more. One of the problems with being intrigued by a wide range of topics is that you may allow the analytics team to chase down projects and areas just because they are fun to learn about; this is not a good idea.

Of course, there will be topics and subjects that are tangentially related to the business problems and challenges that you and your colleagues are facing, and running down a few wild ideas never hurt anyone, but if it is a regular occurrence, the productivity of the team, and your credibility, will suffer.

It is always good to place context around analytics and analytics projects in the early stages of a relationship with an executive and business sponsor. They have pet projects and personal interests too. Recently, I was in a meeting with an executive.

The conversation had been about the analytics team communicating the business team the projects that had been completed in the past year and what type of projects might be of interest and value to the end users and the business function. The ranking executive in attendance had become excited and engaged and suggested a project that had personal interest, but almost no relevance to the business or functional group. We all talked about the project for a few minutes and I wrapped the discussion with a remark that the analytics group needed to prioritize projects based on business impact and business need. The executive dropped the line of discussion and we moved on to more pressing business areas and challenges. Engendering excitement among executives, sponsors, and subject matter experts is fun and it is interesting, but it needs to be channeled appropriately, and that is part of your role.

Another part of your role as the leader of the analytics function is to ensure that the advanced analytics team is engaged and enjoying their work. One way that I have been able to ensure that the team is growing and learning and yet staying on track to deliver relevant, successful, and impactful results is to look to large digital-native companies like Instagram, Facebook, Google, and others to see what techniques and tools they are employing to solve technical, data, and business problems. Techniques and technologies from other applications and industries are valuable and useful: using them is a good idea, and you are encouraged to bring in innovations to drive operational results, but always keep in mind that the analytics work being undertaken needs to lead to real results and operational improvement. Leveraging proven innovations from other industries and firms increases the knowledge base of the analytics team, reduces the chance of project failure, and raises the profile of your analytics projects in the minds of the executives, sponsors, and subject matter experts.

Analytics for the fun of it is not why we are building an analytics team and investing the funds of the company. We are building an analytics team and capability to deliver results and to provide compelling return on investment. If you can do this and enjoy yourself in doing so, well, that is a bonus.

Operational considerations

In the next three sections, we will discuss best practices to follow in your day-to-day actions in gaining consensus across the organization and ensuring that you and your team have the confidence of the executives, functional managers, and subject matter experts.

Selling a project – vision, value, or both?

As we have discussed, executives have a number of options to choose from when deciding where to spend the money of the company. Analytics projects, the analytics team, and the support for the overall analytics effort needs to be funded and supported.

What is the best path and method for selling the value of an analytics process and all the projects that are included in the total program to the executive level? My suggestion is that you sell the entire process and program and lay out the various major projects/ phases that will be executed over time.

Executives are looking for impact from investments. It is best to start with the most expansive impact and headline possible. If you are proposing to transform a corporate function, like the supply chain, start with the broadest view that you can apply analytics to. The good thing for us is that you can apply analytics to all aspects of the supply chain, just as you can to most human and machine activities.

You need to find out through research and internal discussions the threshold of impact for an executive to have interest in funding and sponsoring the effort. We discussed in *Chapter 5, Managing Executive Expectations,* that a project being considered did not meet the $20 million impact threshold and was therefore discontinued. One of the positive aspects of analytics projects is that they can be wide ranging and have significant impact and at the same time you can start small, use very little cash and resources, and illustrate success very quickly.

My recommendation on selling the value is:

- Construct an analytics process that delivers multiples of the minimum value or return required. Illustrate and communicate the big picture. Ensure that the messaging includes the appropriate corporate stance – thought leader, fast follower, laggard, etc.

- Frame the analytics process as a defined corporate initiative or program. Make sure that the program connects with a strategic imperative stated by the executive level of the company.

- Define a series of projects that start small, deliver results, and scale over time building increasing value and transformation for the operations of the company.

- Wrap it up with a tiered request for funding and support and you should be off and running with the support of the executives and a series of projects to execute on.

If you follow these steps and this process, gaining buy-in for your project will be much smoother and easier.

Don't make all the decisions

Analytics professionals tend to be an independent lot. We are smart, driven, and can be insular and have a tendency to want to make decisions on our own and move forward quickly. We can see consensus building and group decision making as a hindrance to the speed of change and progress. Sounds like some of my past performance reviews, especially when I have worked at large companies like IBM and others.

In most cases, you and your analytics team members will know the right answers before any other people in the organization. You should: you and your team have been given the data, the resources, and the approval to examine operations, pricing, manufacturing, and more with the express purpose of improving these functional areas.

The challenge is that you and your team do not own the daily operations of those functional areas. Knowing what needs to be done is a prerequisite to action, but it does not predestine action. You and your team can know a great deal, but you cannot drive change in most areas; for that you need executives, sponsors, and subject matter experts to be on board with your findings and recommendations.

Why shouldn't you make all the decisions?

Firstly, as noted above, you can't.

Secondly, change in an organization requires agreement and consensus. To arrive at those positions, you need to have the subject matter experts agree with the work that you and the analytics team have executed. The sponsors or managers need to agree that the analytics results support the effort and cost of making the recommended changes and the executives must support all of this.

Thirdly, the analytics team is not equipped, staffed, or able to make the recommended and required changes to the supply chain, manufacturing operations, or other functional areas.

So, in the end, you and your analytics team need to be part of the decision process, not the only party to the decision. Once you realize this fact and begin to work as part of the whole process, selecting and executing project and affecting change will be easier for all involved.

Do the subject matter experts know what "good" looks like?

For some of you, I'm sure that your reaction to the heading for this section is, "They are subject matter experts, and they *should* know what good looks like!" Well, perhaps not.

Subject matter experts are experts in what should be happening on a daily basis. They know how the plant should run, when the supply chain should deliver something, or when the process will complete. They are not experts in how much improvement can be wrung out of a process by using data and analytics.

There are too many stories to recount where the analytics team has undertaken a project and presented the results to the functional managers and subject matter experts only to have them sit in a meeting and ask, "Is that a good result?" I often say, or want to say, "We are presenting it, so, yes, it is a very good result." Most of the time, I do not say that or something like it, but if the team has a sense of humor, I will.

Like many projects that will drive change or illuminate a possibility of improvement, there is a chance that there will be a defensive reaction. Some people are insecure about how they do their jobs and some managers are looking for ways to assign blame.

It is prudent to take the subject matter experts aside and explain to them what "good" looks like and why the work that the analytics team has completed is good for them. And then you have to do this same process with the functional managers and possibly with the relevant executives.

Never assume that the business team understands what you are showing them until you have explained to each of them separately and then to them as a group.

How does it relate to selecting winning projects? You and the analytics team want to select projects and collaborations with functional teams that are open to change and willing to look at how to improve. It is better to understand how open to change the functional team and their leaders are before you start rather than fighting an uphill battle to try to have them adopt the improvements after the fact.

The project mix – small and large

People have short attention spans. No surprise there, but what does that mean for you? How will you counteract the tendency of people to lose focus? How will you keep stakeholders and sponsors engaged with your team and in the projects you are undertaking?

The project mix has a great deal to do with stakeholder engagement, team satisfaction, and workload consistency. My experience shows that a senior data scientist can work on two major projects and multiple smaller projects, around two or three, all simultaneously.

When I first tried this idea with an analytics team, it was unanimous. The staff all came to me individually and explained that there was too much work and that it could not be done. I suggested to each team member that they try the new system. Also, I suggested that they keep an eye on work-life balance and to not increase their hours to try to accomplish the work more quickly.

The team found that the gating factors were outside their control – functional team members were on vacation, the data was not ready, the business users could not agree on the objectives to be focused on, and more. The analytics team found out that by having a portfolio of work that encompasses five or six projects, they always had work available to them, they did not have lapses where they had nothing to do. They also learned that scheduling is one of the most underrated skills and that by improving their ability to estimate work and plan for unexpected delays that their work portfolio could be much larger and they were not working any harder than they were before, but that they were much more productive and they had a much broader network in the organization and a broader sphere of influence.

Functional team members understand that there will be delays. They understand that the analytics team can do more work if they have small and large projects interleaved together.

So, when selecting projects, look for a mix of small and large projects; be open to one of requests for analytics work that can be accomplished in a day or two. Having a diverse mix of projects helps everyone.

Opportunity and responsibility

We are living in a fantastic time to be responsible and accountable for an advanced analytics and artificial intelligence team.

We can pick and choose the programs, processes, and projects that we want to undertake. We can have influence across all the functional units of an organization on a global basis. We can work with front line employees across all functions of the entire company. We can engage with all levels of management, including executive management of the firm. We have an open invitation to go anywhere in the company and engage in a process or processes to improve operations incrementally or exponentially. This can be a heady position to be in, for sure.

Of course, as analytics professionals and leaders, we must live in the real world and drive improvements in operations and functions of the company. Our teams must be looking for practical improvements and methods and ways to implement and drive real and measurable change.

Summary

We have a duty to teach our colleagues what can and cannot be accomplished with data and analytics. Analytics professionals and leaders need to be at the forefront of the discussion of what is a realistic project and expectations of that project and the teams that we have on staff.

We must explain and place context around our proposed programs, processes, and projects to ensure that our colleagues in the functional business units know what is expected of them – from involving their staff, to the spending of their budgets, to the timing of delivery of interim and final results.

Data is a critical element of all analytic efforts. Analytics professionals, in conjunction with the internal and external legal experts, must be the leading voices explaining and examining the internal and external data sources we will be using, integrating, and leveraging to develop insights into customers, patients, partners, operations, and more.

Analytics, legal, and business professionals must be clear on the objectives, benefits, and defined goals of our efforts to ensure that all legal, moral, and ethical considerations are evaluated. Objections must be resolved, and we must ensure and that we are delivering positive benefits for all directly and indirectly involved.

Bias is a challenge for all analytics professionals. It is critical that we talk about and actively counter bias in our thinking, data, models, and applications. We have been biased in past business practices, in society, and in government programs, and data that results from all of this.

It is our responsibility to actively work to counter bias and to ensure that our models include all relevant data, factors, and phenomena.

As we discussed in the body of the chapter, generating excitement is not challenging, but ensuring that the sense of excitement is tempered and aligned with reality can be a challenge – but it must be done. It must be done to ensure success and satisfaction with the investment, the efforts of the combined team, and the improvement of the operation of the company. Disappointment and disillusionment can be the outcome of our efforts if we do not temper and align the views of the analytics team with that of the executives, managers, and subject matter experts we are working with.

The focus of this chapter has been on selecting winning projects, and we now have seen the many factors that contribute to picking the best projects to ensure success, which include business engagement, analytics team growth and satisfaction, consistent delivery, and a perception and belief by the business executives, sponsors, managers, subject matter experts, and more that the efforts related to data and analytics are compelling, worth investing in, and can make a measurable and timely difference in how the company operates and achieves its goals and objectives. Understanding the corporate, management, data, and talent ecosystem is crucial to selecting winning projects.

Now that we know how to pick projects and succeed, let's talk about how to move from projects to making our models, applications, and systems work in a production environment.

CHAPTER 8

OPERATIONALIZING ANALYTICS – HOW TO MOVE FROM PROJECTS TO PRODUCTION

"No revolution ever happened with the support of the establishment."

—Jennifer H. Woulfe

Advanced analytics and AI projects and efforts can become exceptionally long term and conceptual if not designed, directed, and managed appropriately. I have always had a very pragmatic and practical view of working with data and analytics. Managers and end users are typically impatient when seeking numbers and indications of performance or improvements; it helps to keep their impatience in mind when executing analytics projects.

In this chapter, we will examine the process of moving from a program orientation or a project focus to a production focus. This is where we are moving the results or findings from models, applications, and analytical work products into production systems. This move sounds quite clear cut and simple when described in this manner, but there are several considerations, pitfalls, and challenges to understand and overcome. Transitions from a development process to production systems are difficult from operational and organizational perspectives. We will discuss how to navigate this change successfully.

The change management process

I am of the opinion that we, as analytics professionals, are seeking to drive improvements and changes in operational behavior, processes, and metrics. We are not undertaking data and analytics projects to indulge our intellectual curiosity; we are doing so to drive change and improvement.

When we are talking about driving change in a business operation, academic institution, government agency, or other environment we need to consider the entire process and problem; from the first step of the definition of the challenge to be addressed to the last step taken in proving that the modified functional system(s) and process(es) are operating in an improved and improving manner.

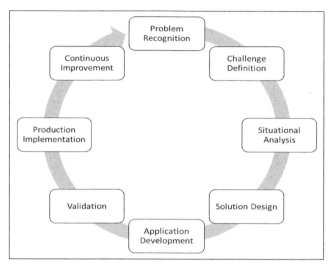

Figure 8.1: A comprehensive view of the change management process

So far in this book, we have discussed a number of salient factors to consider when building an analytics function in an organization, including the relationship between the analytics team and executives. We have discussed the operational factors that play a part in selecting successful projects, considered data and ethics, examined the difference between a focus on projects and programs, and always been focused on and have assumed that the work with data and analytics would produce a result or results. One of the areas that we have not touched on is what we do with those results. How do we make those results actionable? How do we turn those results into top-line or bottom-line results on a one-time or continual basis?

I pointed it out in the *Introduction* section and in *Chapter 5, Managing Executive Expectations,* but it is worth mentioning one last time here: this is the juncture where the majority of analytics project fail. The transition from a development project to a production process is where most analytics professionals assume that the functional leaders and teams will take the lead and immediately see how the results naturally and logically lead to the next step in improving operations.

In the vast majority of cases, functional teams and leaders do not take the lead at this point and they do not see the next step. We as analytics professionals need to remain involved and engaged in the project and drive it forward until the analytics results, models, or applications are embedded into production processes and are empowering data-driven improvements in daily operations on a continual and continuous basis.

Let's outline and discuss the most relevant and important considerations and challenges in moving from analytics projects to production systems.

Getting to know the business

If the business is a complex operation like biopharmaceuticals, the time required for the data scientists to learn the business cannot be underestimated. Also, the time to discover the strategic areas of interest and importance of the business must be uncovered and the intersection between strategic importance and sponsor interest must be discovered as well. This is a multi-layered information and organizational ecosystem that only becomes clear with engagement and personal interaction. Understanding this ecosystem and discovery process takes time to develop, decompose, and internalize.

Change management

An aspect of analytics that is routinely ignored or overlooked is the leveraging of results or insights to deliver an improvement in operations either as a one-time modification to a process or as a permanent change on a continual basis. Implied in any process of improvement is change. One of the hardest things for people to understand, plan for, internalize, accept, and benefit from, is change.

Change of all types presents challenges for managers and for staff members. Leaving the realization that change is a required element of a complete and successful analytics project as an implied aspect of the project rather than making it an explicit agreement within the project framework leaves open the possibility for a significant mismatch in expectations between the analytics team and the functional team. All teams that need to be involved in implementing the many incremental changes required to realize the value of the overall analytics project need to be explicitly aware of the change management process and the need to move analytical models and applications into production systems.

It is often the case that the functional teams do not realize that the results of analytics will require them to change their processes, staffing, and other characteristics of their operations, and this can be a substantial problem. This problem is especially acute in regulated industries and industries that are averse to change.

Required changes for the functional staff can be significant

As an example of how analytical applications can alter the work of a functional team let's examine the impact on a team that had built and managed a spreadsheet-based forecasting tool for a business unit. One of my analytics teams built a new forecasting application at the request of the business unit leader.

The new application could ingest a wide range of internal and external data on an automated and real-time basis. The forecast could be updated and generated on demand by any staff member, and the new forecasting application ran in under a minute.

The labor involved in producing the forecast changed from ~50 people working on a full-time basis to one or two people fact-checking the forecast for validation purposes and a couple of others for ensuring that the data feeds for the new forecasting application were available and completed on time. Those two to four people were only needed until the functional team was comfortable with the new application. At that point, there was no longer a need for any full-time staff to obtain, clean, and integrate the source data into the massive and complex spreadsheet environment or to run the forecast.

Of course, the forecasting team is needed to interpret and utilize the results of the forecast to plan and manage the business operations, but those staff members can now spend the majority of their time analyzing the forecasted data rather than producing it. To be clear, the staff that was required to execute the data management tasks related to the spreadsheet-based forecasting system should be retrained and repurposed to be focused on proactive analysis and becoming involved in analytical work such as scenario planning. Those team members can move from executing work to simply produce a forecast to actively looking for ways to improve the overall business and operations.

The phrase "flipping the script" is apt in this instance. Historically, one of the complaints relating to analytics and analytics projects has been that the time taken to prepare the data and execute the analysis absorbed ~80% of the analytics effort and time, leaving 20% or less of the time to analyze and present the results for action and use. This forecasting application reduced the time to gather the data to zero because the data collection and integration process was automated and the time to produce the forecast was reduced to virtually zero, given that the model run time is less than a minute.

The ability to produce an accurate forecast went from being available four times a year, involving many people and requiring months of lead time, to being available to anyone at the press of a button. The length of the forecast window or results produced was increased by 4X. The previous forecasted results were measured in months and the newly forecasted results are measured in years. A subsequent iteration of the forecasting application produced forecasted results measured in decades. Also, the error term of the forecast improved; the first iteration of the forecast improved the error term by a small margin and each iteration of the forecasting application reduced the error term even further. To sum up the main points – the forecast is faster to produce and is now available on demand, longer in duration by years, requires almost no staff, and is of greater accuracy. I would consider this a winning outcome.

As for the business unit leaders, they are incredibly happy with the forecast and the improvements outlined above without a doubt or reservation. The surprising outcome was that the business unit leaders and their managers were unhappy with the analytics team in that the business unit leaders were not alerted to the change in the work for the forecasting team. The business unit leaders expected the analytics team to provide them with consulting advice on what impact the improvements brought by the new forecasting application would bring to the daily operations of the forecasting team. This was an unanticipated request and expectation. In this respect, the analytics team and leadership were a victim of their own success, and this shows the importance of regular and bi-directional communications guidelines. This is outlined in *Chapter 3, Managing and Growing an Analytics Team*; *Chapter 4, Leadership for Analytics Teams*; and *Chapter 5, Managing Executive Expectations*.

A change in work composition

One of the byproducts of the change outlined above is that the functional team that had been obtaining, cleaning, loading, and managing data in the spreadsheet environment that produced the forecast has now had their workflow and content completely inverted. What are the practical implications of this reversal of work focus?

The forecasting team spent 80% of their time waiting for and working with source data. They do not have to do this any longer. The skills, competencies, and work steps that they had become accustomed to have now been substantially reduced or eliminated. The points in the process where they could reliably expect a half-day or two-day delay in the data acquisition process are gone. This change alone is hard for people accept. People like the lulls inherent in their current jobs and the processes that feed them their inputs and information; these delays give them time to do other things or to distract their attention to other activities.

The forecasting team now has up to 80% of their working hours to dedicate to analyzing the data and forecast. They can now spend time considering scenarios and plans that provide the ability to examine business operations and engage in discussions with their peers and managers about predicted and projected shortfalls or company programs that have positively impacted operations, or competitive activity that needs a response, or world events that will have a positive or negative impact on operations in the coming days, weeks, or months.

From an analytics team perspective, this sounds great, a much-improved focus of the forecasting work to drill in on proactive management of business performance. But we must keep in mind that perhaps the forecasting team was comfortable with the previous work composition and focus. Perhaps their skills are in data management and spreadsheet construction and not in business analytics, forecasting, and proactive scenario management.

Perhaps this change is stressing the forecasting team in that the functional managers will now have higher expectations of the team in areas where they are not comfortable and do not have the skills needed to perform at the previous level of effectiveness and efficiency.

The need for change must be made overt

Once the new forecast application was validated and provided to the functional team, there was a period of disbelief and slight rejection of the application. After a month of examining the results, the application, the automation, and the overall approach, the functional team declared their belief in the application and their acceptance of it. This process was led by the business unit manager, who was being directed by his manager to vet the new application thoroughly and if the application was accurate, then adopt it and change the forecasting process and workflow to leverage the benefits of the new application.

The change management process would have been much smoother if the analytics team had communicated to the functional team that the labor needed to produce the forecast would change significantly after the adoption of the new forecasting application. I am not suggesting that the analytics team should have positioned the project as eliminating 40 jobs, because the functional team would have rejected such a suggestion, but from the beginning of the project, the final phase of the project needed to be focused on change management rather than model delivery.

This is a common error that analytics teams make. It is often the case that the analytics team focuses on building a new and better way to deliver an outcome, in this case, a forecast. The analytics team believed that once a clearly improved model, result, or application was provided to the functional team, the functional team would immediately adopt the new tool and reorganize the team, function, and process to take advantage of the innovation. This has been proven to be a false assumption time and time again.

It is possible that if your analytics team is an artisanal team and is small in number, you may employ another group that is focused on change management to help work as a third party with the analytics team and the functional team to design and implement the organizational changes required to realize the full benefits of the analytics project.

The point to be considered here is that change will be required, and in some cases significant change, to leverage the results of analytics projects, and it is better to overtly communicate to, and plan with, the functional teams rather than to wait for them to realize that change is needed and that the change can and will be beneficial.

Never assume that the functional team or the management of the functional team understands the full breadth and depth of the analytics that you and your team are building and the full impact and benefit of the changes that will be required from them and their organization and operation. Be overt and be clear about all the changes that you, your team, and the third-party change management group can see and anticipate.

Even if you and the analytics team cannot accurately outline the scope and scale of the changes, it will benefit you, the analytics team, the functional team, and the functional team leadership if all your analytics projects are positioned as concluding with a transformation or change process. The overt goal of that change or transformation process is to adopt and leverage the analytics work and to show the organization and leadership the benefits being obtained, and the change being driven, by undertaking a data- and analytics-oriented approach.

We now know that change will be required, and we have discussed how to anticipate it, plan for it, and talk about it. Now let's turn our view to a topic that is rarely considered, but it is critical to our success: how creativity and discovery are a part of the analytics process.

Analytics and discovery

When you are building an analytics team or capability in an organization that has little to no experience with data and analytics, the expectation from many people, including executive management, will be that the analytics team will discover new insights about the business; this is not an unreasonable expectation.

Given the fact that you and your analytics team will be given the chance to look across much, if not all, of the organization, you will have access to nearly all the data available internally and externally, and you will have the goodwill and collaboration of a substantial number of sponsors and subject matter experts, as well as external partners and vendors, you and your team should be able to discover new insights.

This type of discovery-oriented analytical work is typically driven by the art of the possible. You can plan projects, but discoveries rarely show up when planned. Your team may find interesting insights a few days into the work or it may take a year or more to find an insight that is truly game changing for the business.

While most people think that analytics work is the straightforward application of math to data, it is not that simple. You and your team do need data, and need to have a mastery of analytical techniques, but analytics projects have more of a creative element than most people realize. Many of the most talented analytics professionals I have met and worked with possess a unique combination of linear, analytical, left-brain thinking, but also a non-linear, right-brained, creative element to their genius. This fact is part of the reason why managing an analytics team is not the same as managing a technology team. There is a need for data exploration, hypothesizing, testing, and interrogation of ideas, concepts, dead ends, and surprising discoveries.

Often the ideas created and presented by the analytics team as part of the concept generation phase of starting a project or group will be dismissed by the functional teams as being too out there or not practical. These are often the ideas and areas that produce the most impactful models and applications.

The development of analytics and the search for discoveries and new insights is not linear. We discussed linear thinking and thinkers in *Chapter 6, Ensuring Engagement with Business Professionals.* The points made about linear and non-linear thinkers and the conflicts and misunderstandings that can arise are applicable here. The linear thinkers will want to know the date and time when the eureka moment will occur. The process doesn't work that way. Some theories do not pan out, others lead to completely different directions, and others are spot on and take the team forward to new levels of understanding and improved performance.

During the early stages of the analytics process, it is best to not try to limit the scope of investigation too narrowly; it can dampen creativity and lead to suboptimal results. Iterative cycles, not to mention trial and error combined with a bit of patience, is required at this point in the process.

Let's contrast this creative, iterative, unpredictable process of analytics discovery with the environments that are characteristic of operational or production systems.

Production processes and systems

Production systems are planned, built, measured, and controlled in a prescribed manner, and they should be. For manufacturing processes that are producing medicines intended for human consumption, life itself relies on the control of these processes and systems.

Not all processes and systems are mission critical and have a life and death element intertwined with their consistent operation, but many processes and systems are controlled in a way that means making changes to them requires significant discussion, agreement by committees, adherence to standards, action limited to prescribed windows of time, and other restrictions.

Financial systems and processes are one such example. When working with a finance team there will always cyclical pressure to produce results that fit into the monthly, quarterly, or annual reporting cycle. The finance team is imbued with this cadence and they work in this manner as a matter of course. In almost every instance, the finance team will turn to the analytics team and ask if the current project can be completed and ready for a deadline that coincides with the next cycle close. In some cases, the projects do line up with the accounting cycles, but most of the time they do not. In every case where I have explained that the analytics team cannot and will not guarantee the result of a discovery-oriented process for the next month or quarter closing, the finance team and leadership has understood and we, as a joint team, can and do work toward aligning the outcome and results to the next cycle or two if that is possible.

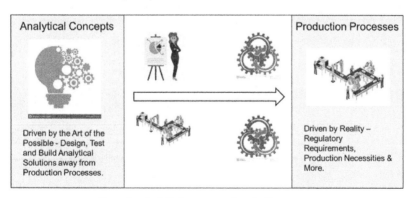

Analytical Concepts		Production Processes
Driven by the Art of the Possible - Design, Test and Build Analytical Solutions away from Production Processes.		Driven by Reality – Regulatory Requirements, Production Necessities & More.

Figure 8.2: Analytical concepts and production systems

We need to keep in mind that we are interfacing a creative/ artistic process with a scheduled, routine, controlled, and mechanistic process. The two paradigms are complementary but must be kept separate. Trying to bring the two together too soon or without the appropriate flexible interface will cause organizational friction and discord.

How do we merge or blend the two disparate cycles and processes together to achieve production processes that are continually improved by data and analytics while serving the needs of the analytics team and the functional teams? Let's discuss an approach and solution next.

Analytical and production cycles and systems – initial projects

In the cases where the analytics team is simply looking to improve a well-known process (that is, a non-discovery oriented improvement process), the analytics team should be able to give the functional team, sponsors, and interested executives a fairly reliable estimate of when the analytics process will start and produce the desired model, application, or result. In the first iteration of approaching a business challenge, we should have a reasonably accurate sense of how long the complete analytical project and cycle will take.

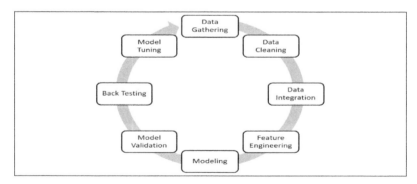

Figure 8.3: The analytics cycle

In contrast, as we discussed above, discovery-oriented processes are different and will take more time, and it is notoriously difficult to estimate and predict when the discovery will be unearthed.

Also, as we discussed in the finance scenario outlined above, we need to be clear with our collaborators from functional teams that their deadlines are of interest to the analytical team, but those deadlines do not drive the analytics team's work cycles or products. The analytics team wants to, and is eager to, collaborate, but the analytics cycle takes time to complete. One element of analytics work that we need to protect is the time to test and validate the results of our models and applications. It is paramount that the analytics team test, retest, and validate that the results are accurate and reliable. Releasing an inaccurate model or application will have far-reaching and negative consequences for all involved.

Once the analytics team has made it clear to the functional teams that the first time through the process will be longer and more involved, we can then provide an estimate of when the analytics team will provide the first analytical model or result.

The first time through the analytics process for each use case or business challenge is a project and as such, it looks very familiar to people who work on other types of projects.

Automating data management

The initial project for each business challenge will develop the infrastructure and systems that provide the automated data acquisition, data cleaning, and data integration capabilities. The building of the automation infrastructure and processes will take time and needs to be planned for. This is a required step and effort that should not be bypassed. There are analytics teams that do not build the time and effort for the construction of the automation infrastructure into their projects, which can lead to problems.

Typically, the analytics team makes this mistake for two reasons: either upper management demands that the analytics projects be cut short and therefore the analytics team and projects cannot afford the time to build the automation infrastructure, or the analytics leadership is not aware of the downstream problems that not building the automation will cause.

If the cause of the shortcut is upper management pressure, then the company management does not value the analytics team and you should start to look for another job, and if the cause is that the analytics leadership is unaware of the need, then you should try to educate the analytics leadership of the value of and need for building this capability into each project.

The tradeoff is to take the time to build the data management automation that provides for the routine execution of the models and applications once as part of the initial project and reap the benefits for all subsequent executions of the predictive cycle, or move more quickly through the initial project cycle and then experience the challenge of maintaining the data feeds manually for each and every model and application on a daily basis.

The data-related tasks outlined above need to run each time a production system executes a cycle. That could be the monthly financial cycle, or it could be a manufacturing process that executes on a millisecond level. To provide automated analytical insights, the data acquisition and data maintenance processes must be fully automated.

The bigger issue is that the data management tasks and related work need to be completed for every model that is built and provided to the business. An analytical application may have numerous models within its framework. Every data maintenance process that is not automated is a set of tasks and work that a data scientist needs to keep track of and ensure that those processes run on time, each time, every time.

It does not take long for every data scientist to become a data management operator with no time to undertake new projects. Automating data management tasks is the only way to keep the data science team from becoming data management operations staff.

There is another pitfall that we should discuss at this point. When less experienced analytics professionals look at *Figure 8.3* in relation to the topic of automation, and automation specifically related to the processes of data management, in most cases they think, "we will automate data management after the Model Tuning step." This never works, or maybe rarely works. Let's discuss why this is a poor approach to accomplishing what may seem like a mundane task, but one that will save the sanity of the analytics team and increase the productivity of the analytics team dramatically.

First, analytics professionals are very smart people, but they are also quite forgetful of the details. They will create and develop very intricate methods of obtaining, cleaning, integrating, and ingesting data, and if they do not document or automate the process while they have it fresh in their minds, there is a good chance that they will forget how they did it, and that will require that they recreate the same results, often through inventing a whole new approach and process. This is a significant waste of time, but often interesting and fun for the data scientist because they learned how to solve a vexing problem in two different ways. So, while forgetting the first approach is mildly irritating, to the data scientist it is a challenge, and in some cases a joy, to create the second approach. Fun for some, but not productive in the eyes of management.

Second, data sources from external organizations change in format or location, and if the source and structure are not documented it may be impossible to find that specific data source again. If the model or application relies on that data, then the model and application will have to be redesigned with new data, if that is even possible.

Third, when each analytics project reaches the point of completion and is ready to be handed off to the team that will put the model into production, that team will not create the automation for the data management processes. The data management automation needs to be completed at that point. The pressure will be on to move the model or application into production without delay and if the data management is not automated, a delay will be incurred.

Fourth, all projects encounter this next dynamic. Pieces of work keep being put off until a later date and all that work seems to build up and needs to be automated, refined, revised, or otherwise finalized at the end of the project, and it is rare that time is allotted or allocated for this type of cleanup, hence more fire drills, hectic effort, and the rush to develop what was not built or fix what was built incorrectly earlier in the project.

Delaying the completion of the data management automation work suffers from all four of these problems. So, in the end, what is the best thing to do?

Build the data management automation as part of the project. Build it, refine it, and revise it in each of the process steps of the analytics process. You, the analytics team, the functional team, the sponsors, subject matter experts, and others will probably not notice that you and your team executed the work in this manner, but they will notice it if you don't.

The data management and the automation of the data management steps encompass the first three steps of the analytics process (see *Figure 8.3*).

Let's move on to discuss the next five steps of the analytics process, how those steps are unique and different in the first project in the development of an analytical application, and the descriptive, predictive, and prescriptive models that operate in the framework of the application.

Analytical models and applications

This first project will also develop and validate the initial models. Again, this project is the first in the life of the analytical application and the initial set of models that operate within that application.

Once the data is cleaned, integrated, and accessible, the data scientists are ready to start exploring the dataset. Descriptive statistics are often employed to understand the size, shape, relationships, density/sparseness, correlations, and other relationships in the data. These early steps lead the analytics team into the feature engineering phase of the analytics process. The data may have all the features required to build highly predictive models, but the data may contain hundreds or thousands of variables. How does the data scientist discern which variables or combinations of variables are the most predictive while not including factors that are confirmatory of the behavior or phenomena that is to be discovered or predicted?

Without delving too deeply into the art and science of feature engineering, much of this portion of the analytics process is guided by data reduction techniques, aided with intuition from the analytics professionals, supported by mathematical experience and expertise, and extended and refined through the utilization of domain knowledge and expertise from the subject matter experts. Does that sound like it is a straightforward process? It can be, but most often it is not. In most cases, it is a few months of trial and error, experimentation, dead ends, and frustrating failures of concepts and hypotheses, followed ultimately by either eventual success or a disappointing realization that the data does not support the theory, or that the data needed to model the phenomena or behavior does not exist or cannot be obtained in the form, volume, or frequency needed to predict the activity of interest.

Again, remaining at a high level, the data scientists now have a clean dataset, they have engineered the required features, and are now ready to determine the model that will be built.

There are a wide ranges of techniques and tools that data scientists have at their disposal, and again they will employ all the elements described in the paragraph above to determine which approach and technique or series of techniques will result in the timely production of results needed to feed into a production environment to drive improved operational results.

We most often hear people talking about neural networks, AI, and machine learning. In reality, these three terms are tightly related and mean similar things but are at different levels of abstraction when talking about modern learning environments.

There are also the techniques of clustering, classification, natural language processing, complex event processing, simulation, optimization, and many more. As we discussed in the early pages of this book, we are keeping with a non-technical discussion for this book. If you want a deeper treatment of any of these techniques, there have been volumes written on each one of them.

After the model has been developed, the data scientist, in conjunction with the collaborators, will iteratively cycle through the next three steps (that is, Model Validation, Back Testing, and Model Tuning) in the analytics process until the model performs in a predictable, performant manner that provides an improvement in the ability to describe or predict the behavior or phenomena of interest.

Once the initial project has delivered, tested, and validated results from the models, time needs to be allotted for the functional team to vet, analyze, understand, and accept the results as valid and an improvement over the previous system. In most cases a month or two is enough time for a functional team to examine the model, the input datasets, and the results in order to feel comfortable in moving forward to replace the old system(s) with the newly developed data and analytics-driven approach and application.

The analytics leadership and the analytics team need to be prepared to spend a significant amount of time with the functional team to answer questions of all types to help the functional team and functional leader to understand the new approach, models, and results.

Now that we are aware of and can talk about the scope, scale, and requirements involved in the initial projects, let's delve into the recurring maintenance of applications and models and how that process differs from the initial projects that we have just examined and discussed.

The care and feeding of analytical models and applications

The world changes on a continuous basis. Some changes are small and slow and are barely recognizable. Other changes are fast, significant, and hard to miss. Both types of change and the many permutations of change between these two end points on a continuum are of interest to the analytics team and need to be captured and understood.

The representation of the world as viewed from an analytical model is derived from the observations and insights in the data that are generated from processes, operational cycles, and selected external data sources. Those datasets and elements are presented to, or fed into, analytical models during the training phase of the analytical modeling process. Training data comes from financial systems, manufacturing control systems, point of sale systems, personal fitness trackers, watches, medical devices, weather stations, seismic monitoring stations, laboratory tests, ocean buoys, the myriad of internet of things monitors and sensors, and more.

As the world, climate, people, business processes, and operations change, the resulting data changes, and the analytical applications and models that were built with data from the previous periods need to be refreshed and updated with data from the current state of the population that we are interested in understanding.

How often do models need to be updated? Such a broad question cannot be answered; a blanket answer is not possible, practical, or helpful. But if we make the question more specific, we can answer the question with a high degree of certainty. An answer can be provided for a model or a class of models that use the same or similar data. To provide a useful answer, the analytics professionals need to understand the data and the environments that produce the data. If the environment that we are modeling, making predictions about, and possibly controlling changes very slowly, then the models can be updated in a corresponding time frame.

For example, let's say that we are interested in the annual financial cycle of a company or an industry, or possibly in the 5-year or 10-year financial cycle of a company or the entire industry. Over the course of a normal business cycle, the performance of the firm or industry does not change quickly or dramatically. The relevant models could be updated annually, and the analytics team and functional users could be assured that the predictions would be accurate and valuable.

Let's look at the other end of the spectrum.

Let's consider the time cycle involved in making consumer credit decisions. Granting loans and lines of credit is dependent on data describing the following factors: availability of funds, creditworthiness of the applicants, the default rates an institution can withstand, default rates of a pool of applicants like the one being evaluated, government guidelines and directives, competitive market offerings and programs, and global, national, and local conditions. All these factors change constantly and are fluid on many levels. One of my previous analytics teams built models for a multinational financial institution to provide real-time predictions of credit worthiness for each applicant. We found that the models performed best when refreshed each night. We were considering refreshing the models multiple times a day.

We had concluded that we should refresh the models continually throughout the day in addition to the scheduled nightly refresh.

There is a wide spectrum of appropriate windows for updating analytical models; certain models are updated almost continuously; others are updated in cycles that are measured in years. Each case is unique and different and needs to be discussed, considered, and managed with the relevant application and data ecosystem in mind.

This is a difficult concept for some executives, functional managers, and a few subject matter experts to grasp and understand. Analytics professionals need to work with functional staff members for them to understand that trained models are products of data that represents a point in time. When the world has moved on from that point in time, the models that describe and predict the characteristics of that phenomenon need to be updated. Those updates could be real-time and continuous, or they could be of a longer refresh cycle. While many people would like an answer that is similar to "all models are refreshed every 26 hours," it just doesn't work like that.

When the data being generated in the current operations has changed and the status of the current environment is different than the data that was used to train the locked models that are currently in a production system, analytical professionals will refer to this as "model drift." This is an interesting and descriptive term that you need to understand clearly so that you can discuss and describe what is happening for our functional colleagues. The term "model drift" is slightly misleading. The models in production are locked and do not change, but the data streaming through the models that is being scored has changed. It would be a more accurate if the term was "data drift" because it is the data that has changed, but we have no control over the industry standard terms that are used. To be clear, model drift is a real phenomenon, but it is caused by changes in the real world. Data coming from source systems has changed, not the models.

We have discussed the need to update and refresh models and how data changes over time. Let's discuss how data and models flow and move between analytics environments and production systems.

The interface between the analytics cycle and production processes

As we have discussed, the initial intermittent projects involved in developing analytical applications and models are different than the ongoing processes employed in the updating of analytical applications and the models contained within those applications. We have discussed the creative and iterative nature of discovery-oriented analytics projects and processes. We have also discussed how production systems are controlled and mechanistic.

Let's now delve into how these two complementary systems—analytics environments and production systems—work in synergistic ways. Let's be clear, the analytic processes and systems and production processes and systems do work together and drive continuous improvement, but these two environments are always separate and share information through defined interfaces and processes. In systems parlance, the two systems are loosely coupled.

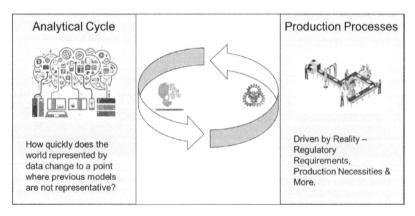

Analytical Cycle	Production Processes
How quickly does the world represented by data change to a point where previous models are not representative?	Driven by Reality – Regulatory Requirements, Production Necessities & More.

Figure 8.4: Analytical and production cycles

Let's start with an overview and delve down to the specifics.

Initial analytics projects develop new analytical applications and models. The analytical applications could have been built with the objective of discovering new insights or opportunities, or those applications could have been built to incrementally improve known processes. Production processes are built, stabilized, and controlled to produce repeatable outputs. Those repeatable outputs could be medicines, gasoline, cars, computers, or ocean liners.

Analytical models are built and trained using data from production systems and other relevant data sources. Once the models are performing as expected, they are locked and exported from the analytical environment. The locked models are then moved to a staging area and are ready to be implemented in the production systems. The team that is responsible for modifying the production systems then takes the locked models and implements them in the production systems and flow.

As an example, let's use the credit risk application that we discussed earlier in this chapter. We said that the credit risk models were updated each night. Once the models were updated and locked, those models were implemented into the logic of the credit risk evaluation system. When a loan officer initiated the process to evaluate a credit application, one of the steps in the process was to run the newly implemented credit risk model. The user interface of the credit loan system was modified to include an indicator of risk for the application. The score underlying that risk indicator came from a predictive model that was updated the night before and refreshed in the credit application system before the day started for the loan officers. Rather than giving the loan officers the number or score from the predictive model, we converted the score into a yes/no indicator. We could have easy displayed the score, but the financial institution wanted a very clear indicator on the screen for the loan officers and the yes/no option was quite clear.

In essence, that is the cycle of refreshing or updating an analytical model and sending an updated, trained, locked model to a production system.

We discussed the fact that analytical models need to be updated with refreshed data from all the sources that are leveraged to train the model. In the example above, we used the transactions from the day before and the relevant external sources of data to train the new model before locking it.

As illustrated in *Figure 8.4*, raw data, transactions, and related data comes from the production system to the analytics environment to train and refresh the analytical models. After training is complete, trained, locked models move from the analytics environment to the production systems. This cycle and process continues for as long as the analytical model provides value.

Synchronizing the needs of the production refresh cycle with the modeling team's ability to deliver is a key to success. Let's move on to examining some of the major variations that you will encounter in interfacing analytical applications and production systems.

Discrete decisions/continual improvements

Teams that I have been responsible for have built a wide range of analytical models and analytical applications. Let's discuss two of the applications that represent two ends of a decision continuum.

There are models that are fed information, and the model produces a score that is used in a discrete decision at a point in time. The example of the credit risk application is such an application and environment.

Another type of model and decision environment is one where data is streamed to the model from a production system or environment and the model continuously streams out predictions about the system or subject being monitored.

An example of a streaming input and output environment is a system that was built to monitor the efficiency and effectiveness of a power plant. The most relevant factor in maintaining the highest level of throughput for energy production was the shape of the flame at the core of the plant. The shape of the flame was monitored and fed into the model and the model made continuous predictions about fuel, oxygen, environmental controls, and other related factors. The plant management staff checked the continuous reading periodically each hour to ensure that the mix was optimal and that the plant would continue to operate at the optimal level.

From a technical perspective, feeding the data into the model is slightly different in each case and the delivery of a stream of predictions is slightly different than delivering a discrete score for each applicant, but for the great majority of data, technical, and operating factors, these models and environments are close enough in composition that from a data science perspective, they are the same.

Management's awareness and support for data and analytics

The common aspirational goal that I hear from executives and managers is that they want to have a purely data-driven, analytically tuned operation; I would be excited by these goals if I felt that the executives making the remarks knew what they were asking for or aspiring to.

Rather than taking these executives at their word, which is dangerous given how little they know about what they are asking for, it is prudent to ask a series of questions to ascertain how serious they are about this goal. If they haven't committed to a multi-year budget allocation with a significant team to execute the vision, then they are just talking and have little to no understanding of what they are asking for. Rather than focusing on this type of situation, all you need to know is that the company that is employing the executive you are talking to is wasting their and your time.

I am not advocating for a large analytics team and I am not postulating that each organization needs to allocate a significant percentage of their budget to data and analytics, but the company does need to commit to a long-term focus on data and analytics. The most significant inhibitor to making progress in becoming a data-driven organization is the on again, off again focus on the objectives and goals.

Having a focus on data and analytics needs to become like sales or manufacturing. You would never hear a corporate executive say we are going to de-emphasize sales for a year, or we will deprioritize manufacturing for the next two quarters.

The analytics process that we have outlined and discussed only works if there is support from executives and management to fund the resources and ongoing support for the efforts and programs.

Summary

As noted at the beginning of this chapter, moving from a project or program perspective to production operations is a critical juncture and transition in every analytics effort. This transition is the point in the analytics process where the majority of projects fail. This level of failure is surprising and disappointing to me personally. I have been vexed by this hurdle and have spent years looking for ways to increase the rate at which analytics projects become successful business projects through skillful navigation of this transition with our functional managers and subject matter expert collaborators.

Analytics professionals need to grasp the importance of successfully completing this transition. This transition is critical to achieving value realization. We, as analytics professionals, need to be aware that our projects, beyond finding interesting insights and information, only deliver value if the models are moved into production and help drive improvements in operations.

Also, the longer our engagements remain as projects and do not transition into production environments, the more the productivity and work throughput of the analytics team is reduced. As much as the analytics team enjoys discovering new insights and sharing interesting pieces of knowledge and discovery, our business sponsors and executives want to see and hear about data-driven change and operational improvements.

The majority of the accountability and responsibility for completing the transition from project status to production operation lies with the analytics team. In the vast majority of instances, the operational or functional teams cannot see or understand the scope of change that is needed in their departments and with their staff members to operationalize and realize the changes required to leverage the new data and models in daily functions and operations. In this chapter, we discussed the need to begin the communication about change and change management early in the process and with executives and sponsors to ensure that they are aware of the need for operational change and support the changes.

I have participated in meetings where I have heard the most incredible rationalizations on why functional teams cannot and will not use the data and insights developed. The most surprising one I heard was where the sales team espoused the view that they could not provide products or services to a broader audience of customers because they were concerned that the manufacturing capability could not provide the products. When asked if the sales team was absolutely certain that the products could not be found in the supply chain or that the manufacturing team had confirmed that the products could not be delivered in order for the sales team to approach and serve this expanded market, the sales team indicated that they had not checked with either the supply chain team or the manufacturing leadership, but that they, the sales team, were certain that serving this newly expanded market was not a good idea. I was stunned.

Do not underestimate the ability of the functional teams to reject good news and analytical findings, but do not allow these hurdles to dim your enthusiasm to drive improvements and change through data and analytics. The need is there, and all industries and businesses will continue to seek out a competitive advantage through data and analytics.

A trend that is moving the market in a favorable direction is evolution in the market. We have discussed the broadening of analytics skills and data literacy across the general workforce. This is a positive development. The more data-literate people we engage with and collaborate with, the more data science will be embraced. Time is our friend in this journey.

After reading this chapter, you now have a greater understanding of how the analytics process differs between initial projects and ongoing model refinement and management. We also outlined the difference between discovery-oriented projects and routine process improvement projects. And we also discussed and described how analytics processes and production processes operate separately yet simultaneously, and how the two cycles feed data and models between themselves to mutually improve and support each other.

In the next chapter, we will move on from understanding the mechanics of the analytical and production ecosystem to discuss some of the challenges in managing the analytics environment as a whole in a corporate setting.

CHAPTER 9

MANAGING THE NEW ANALYTICAL ECOSYSTEM

"Don't worry so much, you'll make yourself sad"

—Danny Elfman

You have a team that is building analytical applications; the analytics staff is engaged with subject matter experts, sponsors, and executives. The ideas are flowing back and forth between the functional team and the analytics team, and the analytics projects are aligning with the corporate strategy. The feedback is that the analytical applications are being adopted and the need to drive change through data and analytics is being recognized and acted upon.

The investments that you and the organization have made in people, technology, processes, and transformation are recognized as being intelligent moves, and promotion for you is starting to be discussed. Looks like it is time for a vacation and a celebratory dinner with your family. Well, maybe it is time for that dinner no matter what part of the story and journey has come to pass.

What am I saying? Even if you have experienced all the success listed above – and I hope that you and your team have achieved the success described above, or more, or that you and your team are on your way to achieving such success – there is more to do.

This chapter will outline the final piece of ongoing operational success needed to build and maintain a healthy internal and external ecosystem that is self-sustaining and grows while maintaining program, project, company, and team health and engagement. Let's start to discuss how this new analytical ecosystem can and should operate.

Stakeholder engagement – your primary purpose

Your primary role and that of your analytics team is to engage with stakeholders, including executives, sponsors, and subject matter experts, to understand their challenges and problems; translate those challenges into analytical applications and models; build those applications and models; prove that the new data-driven approach delivers superior operational results on a reliable and repeatable basis when compared to the previous approach; convince the executives, sponsors, and subject matter experts to adopt the innovations and changes; document and communicate success to sponsors and executives; and then to do it again and again, on repeat. This is the stakeholder engagement process. The stakeholder engagement process is illustrated below in *Figure 9.1*.

The stakeholder engagement cycle/process is at the core of why the executives gave the approval to fund you and your team. You need to know and understand that the execution of this cycle, in an efficient and effective manner, is why you and your team are employed:

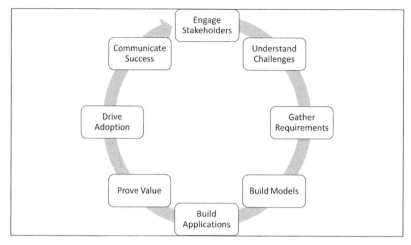

Figure 9.1: Stakeholder engagement cycle/process

Of course, given that you and your analytics team are working inside an organization and that organization is made of a wide range of people with varying backgrounds, ideas, and motivations, it is good for you to be aware of the human dynamics that will be transpiring around you and your team. As you and your team focus on your objectives and goals, you need to know how to take a bit of your time to help ensure that the analytics team assists colleagues in the operational and functional areas to meet their goals and objectives so you and the analytics team can meet your goals and objectives and continue on the mission of improving the organization through the use of data and analytics.

Focus on your mission, but lend a hand when you can

Any distractions that impede the execution of the stakeholder engagement process and cycle, or take focus away from the primary objective of engaging with and transforming operational functions through data and analytics, need to be minimized.

I am not suggesting that you and your team ignore the functional teams when they bring related ideas and requirements to your attention. No, that will cause a wide range of other problems for you and your team. When those related, yet non-core, requirements and requests are brought to your attention, you need to know where to refer those sponsors and subject matter experts to other parts of the organization.

A bit of a side note here to help underscore the importance of the previous point. Other managers and staff members will bring projects to you and your team. First, part of the reason is that you have told them that they should not overthink the problems and just bring the ideas to you. The more ideas you and your team see and examine, the better the grasp you will have on the overall challenges faced by the company. Secondly, some of the simple reporting and dashboarding requirements from the operational or functional teams look like analytics problems to the users and managers, but are really just reports to examine past performance. Thirdly, by now, you and your team will have built a reputation for agility and delivery that the end users and their managers like and would like to see in other groups, but if they can cut the process short and ask you and your team to deliver beyond your remit, then it is easier for them.

What is the main point here? Your colleagues in other functional areas have needs and requirements, and they will bring a wide range of those requirements to you and your team for the reasons outlined above. You and your team need to focus on your mission and primary purpose while providing a valuable service to your colleagues in helping them understand the best organizational units and functions to satisfy the requirements that they have in hand. By being attentive to their needs, even when you cannot serve or resolve those needs, you will be seen as a good colleague while being efficient and effective in your core mission.

It sounds a little trite and perhaps a bit contrived when it is written out in plain terms, but it is important to remember that analytics leadership and staff can sacrifice and ignore the needs of other groups in the service of focus and efficiency. This can be interpreted as indifference and arrogance by the other functional managers in a company.

Take a few moments to recognize the unique position that you and your team inhabit in the organization. Your primary remit is to help by executing your mission and accomplishing your objectives, but you can also help others with your experience and expertise. Employing your goodwill in the latter will go a long way to creating and maintaining a positive perception of you and your team across the organization. And while you may not see this as necessary, it is an illustration of your development and your possession of the emotional intelligence to do so, and to do so magnanimously.

Let's move on to discussing the competing demands that will arise and evolve as part of the normal operation of an analytics team.

First, let's examine the competing demands that will occur within the analytics team and how you, as an analytics leader, need to look ahead to predict and minimize the conflict for resources and to ensure the smooth operation of the analytics team and uninterrupted delivery of value through new analytical applications and revised and refreshed models to the organization.

Balancing analytics work – building versus operating

When you and your group are just beginning your analytics journey in your new organization, all of your projects are novel and most are original work; a statement of the obvious in some respects, but we need to take a moment to ground ourselves and to ensure that we have a common understanding as we begin to discuss the topic of building versus operating the analytics infrastructure.

As you and your team are building analytical applications and models, you need to communicate clearly with the functional teams and managers that the analytics team is building these tools and applications for the functional team, and that when the applications are completed and ready for use, the analytics team will be turning over the running of these applications to the functional team and their staff for use in daily operations. Without this explicit communication and agreed-upon mode of operating, misunderstandings can arise and become problematic.

Let's dig a little deeper into this topic. The organization you are working in may or may not have explicit guidelines about how analytical applications are managed and run. In the majority of my experience, the analytics team builds an analytical application and the analytics team automates the data feeds, builds a useable user interface, and then gives access to the application to the end users in a functional department. The end users interact with the application and consult with the analytics team for new features and to evolve existing functionality to be in alignment with the end users' needs and requirements.

We discussed the operation of the analytical cycle and the corresponding production cycle in *Chapter 8, Operationalizing Analytics – How to Move from Projects to Production. Figure 8.4* provides an overview of the two processes and illustrates how the two cycles interface with each other. Analytics leadership needs to make it clear to the functional team and leadership that the analytics team will take responsibility for the analytics process of building the initial analytical applications and models, and the analytics team will own and be responsible for refreshing the models within the analytical applications, but that the functional teams need to run and own the analytical applications when they are operating as an integral part of the production processes.

In your organization, the process may be the same as described above, but it may not. One common variation of this process is that the analytics team may need to turn the analytical application over to the **Information Technology** (**IT**) team rather than the functional team. The information technology team may host the analytical application in an environment that the IT team controls. The IT team may subject the analytical application, and any subsequent changes to the application and the models within the application, to change control processes operated by the information management team. Ultimately, the IT team may provide access to the analytical application to the functional users. *Figure 9.2* illustrates the involvement of the IT function in the process and interface between the analytics process and the production process:

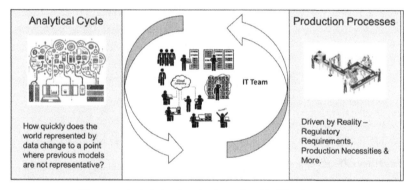

Figure 9.2: Analytical and production cycles with IT involvement

It is of no significant consequence to the analytics team or the end users how the organization manages or governs or does not manage or govern this process. The IT team and the security team will have well-defined processes and procedures to manage and govern this aspect of company operations. The relevant point here is that the analytics team needs to take the responsibility and accountability for understanding the appropriate process within each organization and managing the process, and all the players, to ensure that the process and respective roles are understood and executed appropriately and in a timely manner.

Why is this such an important topic? Because if you, as the analytics leader, are not looking out into the future and ensuring that the end users in the functional departments and the staff of the IT department are ready to undertake the daily running of the analytical applications, the productivity of the analytics team will plummet as you and your team spend more and more time running the analytical applications that you have built rather than executing the stakeholder engagement cycle discussed at the start of this chapter. Being drawn into unnecessary production work that is the responsibility of the functional and IT departments is an avoidable dynamic that you need to proactively manage, plan for, and discuss with the leadership of the functional and IT departments.

Just as you do not want your team operating the applications and models that the team has built, you do not want to be caught off guard by not planning for the work that is required to update each and every model that is built and moved into production. The updating of each individual model and the entire library of models needs to be planned for and scheduled as part of the routine operation of the analytics function. Let's discuss how to do it well.

Balancing analytics work – building versus updating

As time progresses and the analytics team turns over more analytical applications to the information management team for integration into the corporate environment and networks or directly to functional teams for use on a daily basis, there is a continuous accumulation of work needed to manage the update or refresh cycles for the analytical models operating inside the analytical applications that have been built and deployed.

As we have discussed, some models need to be updated nearly continuously and others are updated and refreshed on longer time cycles. No matter what the refresh cycle is for a model or for the company's library of models, it will take time and require work from the analytics team.

Each company needs to implement a method for tracking model performance and executing model movement, in and out of production environments. This is commonly referred to as model management. We are not going to delve into the details of model management theories, systems, and processes here, but we do want to discuss the need to automate, manage, and orchestrate the model management function as much as possible.

One of the requirements of an analytical application environment is that the models are managed and refreshed proactively on a regular, repeatable, and well-understood cycle. As we have discussed, analytical models experience model drift, which is really data drift, and the one implication of this dynamic is that you cannot train models and have them on the shelf ready to go for the next update because the world and the resulting data is continually changing.

Updating models is necessary. The velocity of change in the data or data drift can be understood and measured, and therefore the time frame of the model management process can be anticipated. The updating of models from an analytical team management perspective is more about anticipating, planning, and scheduling than it is about data, technology, or analytics.

The most important aspect of refreshing models is knowing when they need to be refreshed or updated. If the model needs to be refreshed multiple times each day, the decision is easy – the entire process must be automated. Monitoring model performance, model drift, response time, and other factors that trigger the refresh process and model change processes must be automated. No person, or team of people, could execute the process fast enough to keep up with the model refresh/update cycle.

If the models need to be refreshed monthly or annually or at some other longer time cycle, the process is easy to manage. Models must be monitored for the relevant factors outlined above.

When those factors begin to diverge from the optimal targets, or be out of the range of tolerance or acceptability, the new models are created and trained and when the optimal time arrives, meaning either that the old models are out of tolerance and need to be retired or that the new models are performing well and are ready to be implemented, the models are swapped out. The old models are archived and stored for record-keeping purposes and the new models are inserted into the operational systems.

The main point here is that this is important work that is required, and it must be planned for. We discussed how to hire new college graduates and interns in *Chapter 2, Building an Analytics Team,* and *Chapter 3, Managing and Growing an Analytics Team.* Updating models and managing the model management systems and processes is good work for interns and younger staff members to be engaged in. Being involved in the process teaches them the production/operations side of managing an analytics environment. There are routine operations that form the backbone of the analytics process. Most younger staff members are either not aware of this type of work or are disinterested in it. They need an introduction to the work and an educational process that illustrates the value of and the need for the work.

In this section, we have discussed the main tradeoffs in planning and balancing work inside the analytics team. Let's move outside the team to organizational and societal considerations that we need to take into account as we manage and grow the analytics function of your company.

Bias – accounting for it and minimizing it

We briefly discussed bias in *Chapter 6, Ensuring Engagement with Business Professionals,* but bias is a significant issue that we must face when building and managing an active and engaged advanced analytics and AI ecosystem.

Most people think of bias and they immediately talk about the data that is used to train systems. That is one very important part of bias. This is selection bias. We select data that we use to train our systems. Given that many aspects of our world are dominated by limited groups of people, we further institutionalize bias when selecting data from historical or current operational systems. Let's examine a few examples to bring the point to life.

Most C-level executives and board members are men, and more specifically, white men. When we select and use data about this group of people, we are including bias toward and related to white men toward the later stages of their careers. We bias toward men, white men, and older white men. If you are attempting to understand and predict future outcomes from and about C-level executives as a whole, you will need to examine your dataset to ensure that you have included enough examples to capture executives outside the majority.

Most mammogram images are from women. Depending on where the sample comes from, the images may be from certain subpopulations of women – white, black, Asian, Latino, old, young, healthy, smokers, those with hereditary risk factors, etc. But if you are looking for breast cancer, there is a measurable number of men affected by this disease as well. Admittedly, a vastly smaller population, but still a measurable one. If you are looking to model the entire population affected by this disease, you may have to work hard to find mammogram images from men to include in your analytics.

We know that there is bias in the world. We know that bias is represented in the historical data that we want and intend to use. We know that in the current world, there is bias. The relevant questions we need to ask and discuss are explored next.

Bias – should we strive to solve it?

Again, not a trick question. Yes, we should strive to solve it.

We want to represent the world as it is, because we want to predict what will happen with the greatest accuracy possible, but predicting the world as it is today does not preclude us from considering how the world is evolving and including a wide range of possible scenarios.

We can, and should, look at the world as it was in the past, how it is today, and the many scenarios into the future that we can conceive of within time, resource, and data constraints. We can predict "both and," not "either or," and it costs us almost nothing to predict a wide range of future scenarios.

We should execute this as a simulation exercise looking at as many simulated futures as are possible and probable.

Bias – why should we solve it?

As noted above, it costs us almost nothing to simulate and consider highly probable and varied scenarios.

In addition to being nearly free, it is the best way to increase the probability that our models will be successful in considering and predicting the phenomena that we are interested in making money or avoiding cost.

It is the right thing to do. For example, the world is always changing. In the global economy, unemployment is low in the majority of developed countries, the composition of the workforce is modified by necessity. By virtue of low levels of unemployment, the workforce is changing. More people in the 50+ age group are reentering the workforce. Neurodiversity programs are bringing in a wider range of neurodiverse people in organizations in a way that they have never been before. Women are joining the workforce in greater numbers and they are in all levels of the organization in greater numbers.

Bias, whether unconscious or conscious, reduces the accuracy of our work product and increases the error terms in our predictions. We should solve it because it is in our vested interest to do so. And, we should solve it because our role urges us to see the world as it is, not as it was or how some might want to see it. Our work is forward-looking; therefore, we need to not only see the world as it is, but as it will be in the near future.

Bias – how do we solve it?

The thorniest question of them all, in my opinion, is this: we said that we want to solve the problem and we know why we should solve the problem, but how do we go about doing so?

Again, we need to keep in mind that we want to include factors from the real world. Our role is to not create the future or to create a future that we think is just or in our image or a figment of our imagination.

And, again, we can simulate a wide range of scenarios that can exist simultaneously without significant additional cost or any concerns about them interfering with each other.

One of our challenges is finding data that represents the reality of the world we are examining.

Let's use an example to make this discussion more concrete.

Let's say that we are examining data from an e-commerce site in the United States that promotes its products heavily to people residing in Florida, Georgia, Alabama, and Louisiana. Clearly these are southern states that embody many traits of the region and the population that resides there. As in all modeling exercises, we use historical data to train and test our models. Given that our data is limited to the people who are buying via the e-commerce engine, our models will not perform well in predicting the general behaviors of people from Western Europe, Asia, or maybe even other regions of the United States.

Let's now assume that the management of the company decides that there is a global market for the products that have hitherto been sold predominately in the aforementioned U.S. states. How do we go about making our predictive environment useful considering our dramatically broadened remit and selling territory?

We have a few options.

We can do nothing and wait for the selling volume to transpire and we can then use the actual data to expand our models and learn over time. Most management teams do not like or support the "do nothing and wait" approach.

We can create test data to simulate what we think might happen given our marketing and promotional programs, but that is biased in that we are assuming that if we promoting to the same demographic in France as we are in our original market that only that target population will respond. Perhaps the message we are delivering in France will appeal to a completely different demographic in ways that are completely counter to anything that we have ever seen.

As I say to people regularly, we are data scientists, not magicians. Although some of our work does look like magic, it is all based on data, and typically, historical data.

We can and should attempt to create or buy the data that will help us predict the efficiency and effectiveness of the efforts of the organization in its entirety; sometimes our models and efforts will miss the mark in the short term, but they will always be brought back in line with reality as the volume of data increases.

We should always start with the reality that we are seeing today. We then postulate what the future will look like. This is hard because we need to have diverse voices in the discussion. All types of diversity – racial, geographic, gender, age, socioeconomic, disability, and more. Is it practical to have all these voices at the table for every project that you and your team undertake?

No, it is not. You must make judgment calls on which voices are the most relevant and not only which voices are most relevant, but how those voices rank in importance in the analytics that you and your team are building.

Will there be bias? Yes, there will be bias. Will it be unconscious? Let's hope that there will be as little unconscious bias as possible. Will it be conscious? Yes, it will be. Will it be transparent? It better be and it should be. Budgets and time frames demand that choices be made. Like our parents exhorted us, we need to make good choices, we need to make the best choices that we can make, and we need to document and discuss our choices will all interested parties, which in some cases may include the government, academics, regulatory agencies, and more. Be open, be smart and be ready to change.

One of the great underlying fundamentals of data and advanced analytics is that it is always changing, and it is always open to modification and interpretation. I have always seen the world in shades of gray. Some things I know are right and wrong. Society is good about putting bright lines around things that we should not do at all costs, but in business most things are gradations of decisions. We can move back and forth without much effort or consequence. That is a good thing as long as we stay on the right side of morals, ethics, and legal practice. We have great latitude and flexibility in what we do and that makes our work truly enjoyable.

Diminishing bias is a challenge and a challenge that we should relish and engage with enthusiastically, not shrink from. We can start with the world as it is. We can add in our theories and the observations of related businesses, markets, people, and products. We can blend reality and our theories to see how they perform. We can change and modify our approaches to deliver increasing levels of accuracy in our predictions. We can predict multiple scenarios and multiple outcomes without limiting any one of them. We must be transparent about how we are doing it and we must be open to changing, stopping, or evolving our approaches.

Bias will always be there, and we will always be playing catch up to see the world as it truly is and will be in the short and long term. Enjoy the challenge; it is one of the aspects of the role that makes our job exciting.

Now that you have a basic understanding of bias and the framework for thinking about diminishing conscious and unconscious bias in your data and models, let's turn our attention to another critical consideration in analytics: ethics.

Ethics

I am sure that you have noticed by now that I am interested in and a proponent of acting ethically in all things.

Ethics is mentioned in six of the eleven major sections of this book. We have taken the time to discuss the importance of ethics and transparency and focus on the objectives and purposes for why we are using data and building analytic models and applications.

Now, take some time to consider how you will make ethics a topic of discussion with your analytics leadership team, the analytics team itself, and the functional/operational teams. It is worth the time to ensure that each group and all individuals are aware of your position on using data and analytics for ethical, honest, and transparent purposes.

Another element of the corporate environment that is critical to your success is understanding the mindset of your peers and the executives running the company. Let's talk about how deep the understanding of data and analytics is among the executive ranks and how we best engage with executives to have them gain a better understanding of the value of data and analytics.

Executive attention

Throughout the book, I have sprinkled in indications and examples of pitfalls and problems to foresee and avoid. I have tried to write this book in a manner that ensures that the advice and insights are long-lasting. I doubt that it is within my power to write a book that is timeless, but my goal is to write one where the content is relevant and long-lasting.

We are in a time where the majority of executives and sponsors are interested in the field of data and analytics. Over the past three decades, obtaining and holding the interest of this group has been challenging. They have not been interested in data and analytics and seem to be perpetually preoccupied with the crisis of the day.

Exceptional leaders move back and forth putting their attention on matters of importance for the immediate moment, but also being able to move their attention and focus to medium- and long-term investments, projects, and needs as well.

It is a sad state of affairs that only the exceptional leaders can operate in this mode. In your career, you may or may not have the opportunity to work with an exceptional leader. I have been fortunate enough to encounter a handful of these leaders, but you may never encounter someone of this caliber.

Let's assume that you have the opportunity to work with leaders who are competent. By competent, I mean that they can perform their daily jobs reasonably well, are not too preoccupied with politics, and are somewhat supportive of their teams.

Managers of this caliber for the most part have a difficult time understanding analytics. It is a fact; most managers and executives are not literate when it comes to data and analytics. You cannot and should not assume that they understand even the basics of what you are proposing to do; even if they say that they understand, it is more than likely that they do not.

Keep meeting and communicating with them and explaining the scope, scale, purpose, investment, and outcomes expected. A primary element of your job as the analytics leader is to connect with your peers, sponsors, and executives to maintain funding and support for you, your team, and the infrastructure needed to execute on your mission. Keep bringing the messages back to simple, business-oriented concepts – more revenue, less cost, better delivery times, etc.

We are living and operating in a great time for leveraging data and analytics. Even if the interest in the work and topic is superficial, we can still convert this interest into engagement to drive change and transformation through data and analytics.

Now that we have a better understanding of the executive mindset and attention span, let's move on to discussing how the analytics leadership and team can improve the communications between the analytics team and the functional teams and their leadership.

The translation process

Analytics professionals must be aware that to improve the adoption rates of their applications and models, they need to translate and communicate their analytical findings, results, and suggested operational changes and improvements into the language of the functional teams. Often analytics professionals are comfortable about talking in the terms of their models, curves, and other mathematically oriented terms. In general, this is confusing and off-putting for the functional teams.

Functional teams are grounded in their operational areas. The language and thinking of the functional teams reflect their orientation toward their past experience and expertise and their current roles, goals, and objectives. Their goals and objectives are often described in the following ways – increase revenue, decrease downtime, improve process yields, etc.

The analytics leadership and analytics team need to realize that the transformation or change that is being asked, and, in some cases demanded, of the functional team often induces stress into their systems, minds, and staff. If the functional leadership and team find it challenging to understand the analytics team, the analytical applications being built and delivered, and, ultimately, the analytical results; beginning with confusing and opaque language from the analytics team, the functional team will start to subtly resist the proposed changes.

Often, illustrating that the data and results from the analytics is more accurate and provides better insights will not be enough to convince the functional teams to adopt the analytics system and approach. I am gathering more data on this phenomenon, but the early indications are that data literacy, or the lack thereof, plays a role in this level of hesitation. Do not assume that people with science and technology backgrounds will understand and adopt analytics-based systems. I have seen firsthand where executives and managers with significant education are the most difficult to motivate to move and adopt new analytical applications.

On numerous occasions, when the analytics team changed their approach to describe and justify the adoption of a new analytics system by using simple metrics such as automation time savings, reduced fault rates and improved automated correction capabilities as the primary description of the benefits and the drivers of adoption, we experienced an increased level of success in driving adoption of analytical applications and models.

My theory is that the functional/operational leadership has found, and finds, it difficult to sell the value of proposed change based on analytical results, such as increased accuracy or deeper insights upward to their executive management and downward to their functional teams. The operating executives cannot define and deliver the justification for change up and down in the organization because they either do not understand the case for change, do not believe it, cannot explain the case and justification, or all three.

My recommendation to you as analytics professionals is to communicate the case for implementing and adopting new applications based on simple metrics and language that mirrors the objectives and goals of the functional team, using the metrics that the functional teams use to measure and illustrate success, such as time saved, the ability to redeploy and upskill the team into new and more valuable roles, money saved, new hires deferred.

You, the analytics leadership, and the analytics team will help the operational leadership and team communicate the value and the need for change upward and downward in the organization and you, and the analytics team, will be consultants in the deployment of the new application.

Speaking the language of the functional leadership and team will help move the adoption process forward. Let's examine how we as analytics professionals can improve the probability that the adoption process will be executed smoothly and with a positive outcome.

The adoption process

I am continually surprised by the reticence of people across all levels of an organization to embrace change. From executives to front line workers, the human condition's primary orientation is toward maintaining the status quo. Most people will delay, drag their feet, and continually ask for more positive proof points or data, while working toward ensuring that nothing in their operational area changes.

This is especially true in organizations operating in highly regulated industries – pharmaceuticals, finance, oil and gas, etc. While executives, sponsors, and subject matter experts are curious and interested in data and analytics, actually adopting analytics and making changes based on data and analytics is something that is difficult for them to do.

It is difficult for them to understand the results of the analytical work, models, and applications. As outlined above, the analytical outcomes need to be translated for them into their language. Remember the credit scoring application we discussed in *Chapter 8, Operationalizing Analytics – How to Move from Projects to Production*; the analytical team found it surprising that the output of the model needed to be translated into a Yes/No indication for display in the user interface. The analytics team thought that showing the actual score was better, but the functional leaders told us that displaying a score would confuse the loan officers and slow down the process. A *Yes* displayed in green or a *No* displayed in red was the best form of communication, and they were right: the loan officers could scan the screen, see the indicator, and execute the next step in the process. Simple and effective. Your goal should be to aim for the same level of effectiveness and efficiency.

It is difficult for the functional managers and subject matter experts to envision and understand change as an abstract concept. In the case study we discussed regarding the forecasting application in *Chapter 8, Operationalizing Analytics – How to Move from Projects to Production*, the subject matter experts were convinced that if the forecasting application was adopted and put into production, the only outcome would be that the staff involved in the data management process of feeding and managing the complex and cumbersome spreadsheet would be fired. Who would want to be a proactively engaged collaborator in a process that would, ultimately, lead to the elimination of their livelihood?

Once the analytics and functional leaders realized that the subject matter experts had this concern, we started to weave into our discussions the topics of change management, job security, upskilling, and the plan for the subject matter experts' new roles during and after the forecasting application rollout. Engagement from the team improved and the adoption of the application became a pull process rather than a push process.

The analytics team had a hard time keeping up with the suggestions and recommendations for improvements to the new forecasting application from the subject matter experts. And, luckily for the analytical team, the functional team leaders kept their word and did not fire anyone.

It is in your interest, as an analytics leader, to begin early in the analytics process and project to understand the needs of the functional managers in completing the organizational change element of the adoption process. You need to engage with the executives, the sponsors, and the subject matter experts to determine their motivations in being involved in the project and process. You need to be aware that the motivations may be counter to each other, and you need to be discrete enough to realize that you cannot share the motivations across groups, unless they are all aligned; then, you can talk openly about the shared goals, objectives, and expected outcomes.

The shared or individual motivations will lead and guide how you and the functional manager's plan for the organizational change management process. We have discussed this before, but it is worth reinforcing here: the analytics team will not lead and manage the change management process. There are other organizations, such as project management or human resources, who are skilled and adept at managing the change management process. You and the functional team leader need to bring these supporting organizational entities into the process to help plan for and execute the change management process in relation to the employees, training, process modeling, and more.

As an analytics leader, change management, employee upskilling, and reskilling are probably not in your wheelhouse and probably were not in your consideration set before reading this book, but those elements of organizational change management are gating and mitigating factors that will dampen your success and your ability to succeed. Without adoption, no change and improvement can be realized by the organization, and without realizing value, over time, your team will lose organizational and executive support.

Summary

This chapter has been about discussing and explaining what you will need to do on a daily basis to ensure that you, your analytics team, and your functional team colleagues are successful.

We started the chapter by outlining how the analytical and production processes come together and work in a symbiotic way. These two processes support and engage each other to ensure that we have built, and are operating, an ongoing self-improving process to move the company forward in achieving our goals and objectives.

We are seeking to have a continuous loop of data flowing from operations to analytics and a smooth return flow of data and results to operational systems and to decision makers to support and extend the capabilities of the functional teams and the leaders who manage those teams.

We moved from detailed operational considerations to more conceptual topics.

We explored why you and your analytics team need to be cognizant of how to understand and mitigate bias in data, analytical models, and applications. We talked about the wide range of bias and the need to be looking for ways to model the world of today and the world that will be arriving in the short and long term, while keeping an eye on bias and being aware of where bias can be mitigated when possible.

We revisited two particularly important topics – executive attention and the possibly fraught process of adopting analytical applications.

Executives and managers are, for the most part, not analytics experts, and many of the people who currently inhabit C-level positions have had little to no experience in managing through data and analytics.

Many executives would dispute this assertion given that they look at metrics such as manufacturing yields, financial performance, and investment metrics like net present value and internal rates of return. But, in reality, these are all static and, for the most part, backward-looking metrics.

If these executives could admit that they have little knowledge of and even less experience in managing through predictive, prescriptive metrics, it might be easier to have a meaningful conversation with them, but let's live in the real world.

This leads us to the next topic of the adoption of analytics. Packaging the justification for adopting analytics in the language and frame of reference that makes sense to the executives that need to support the adoption, and the managers who need to drive adoption and gain the buy-in of their functional teams, is the path to success.

Rather than relying on analytical results – which, by the way, need to be overwhelmingly positive – analytics professionals need to translate the results of the analytics into operational results and metrics that can be used across the organization as the driving force to ensure adoption.

Functional managers and executives cannot be expected to understand the analytics results, let alone translate those results into operational metrics that they and their peers have been using as the yardsticks to measure success for years. The analytics leadership and teams need to execute that translation for the functional teams.

We have covered the bulk of what you need to know and understand in your journey to build an analytics capability in the context of a large organization, but the principles outlined in this book can and will apply to any organization, large or small.

You now know what you need to do to be successful to build and manage a high-performance analytics team. This can be the professional journey of your life and career; I hope that you grab the reigns with gusto and enjoy the ride.

Let's move on to what the future holds for data and analytics and see how we can look into the future to ensure that we, and our teams, continue to make smart decisions that will keep us on the leading edge of utilizing data and analytics to drive operational improvements.

CHAPTER 10

THE FUTURE
OF ANALYTICS –
WHAT WILL
WE SEE NEXT?

"The best way to predict the future is to make it."

—Peter Drucker

I have enjoyed meeting people who make a regular practice of mentally living in, and predicting, the future. Two of my favorite people in the world who do this on a regular basis are Larry Smarr and Mark Anderson. Both Larry and Mark are incredibly accurate at seeing what the future state will be; they are, in effect, prescient.

Larry is the founding Director of the **California Institute for Telecommunications and Information Technology (Calit2)** and holds the Harry E. Gruber professorship in **Computer Science and Engineering (CSE)** at UCSD's Jacobs School.

Larry has made a living out of looking forward, seeing the future, and guiding pure scientific innovations, developments in software, hardware, and networking, and has helped guide the forward path for the US government, multiple global academic organizations, and numerous companies to deliver on the promise of the future, as seen through his eyes. We, as a world and society, are better for his vision and contributions.

Mark is the CEO and founder of Strategic News Service and the founding CEO of Pattern Computer and who, without a doubt, produces the most accurate view of the future each week in his **Strategic News Service newsletter** (https://www.stratnews. com/) each year at the **Future in Review (FiRe) Conference** and throughout the year at his numerous global speaking engagements. Each year, Mark predicts what will develop and transpire in the most critical areas of technology, economics, and the interplay between nations at a macro and micro level.

Larry, Mark, and I have known each other for 20 years and I have enjoyed collaborating with them and have learned a significant amount about human behavior, large-scale innovation, analytics, economics, technology adoption, and numerous other topics that I would have never looked at without their guidance and urging.

These two visionaries have overtly, and covertly, helped me begin to stretch my vision of the future and refine my ability to define and communicate an accurate view of what will develop in the areas of data and analytics, all across the world and in specific markets and industries.

My area of expertise and focus is much narrower than Mark and Larry's. I stick close to home in the areas of data and analytics. Given my expertise, experience, and passion for these topics, I am comfortable forecasting and predicting what will happen in data and analytics. I have a framework of understanding that stretches out to the year 2150 for the future of data, analytics, and AI.

I am aware that making predictions for 130 years in the future is a bold assertion. A number of futurists and technology experts have remarked that we, as technologists, typically overestimate what we can achieve in the short term and significantly underestimate what can be accomplished over a longer period of time. Perhaps my estimation skills fall into this category as well. Time will tell!

Let's use this final chapter as a way to discuss the future and how we can best prepare ourselves, our colleagues and co-workers, our children, and our society for a better future by being ready to take advantage of data and analytics for the benefit of ourselves, our families, our organizations, our nations, and the global community and society.

Data

The earliest form of recorded data that exists and is readable and still usable are accounting records from the Sumerians, dating from approximately 3400 B.C. [2] Data has been with us for many thousands of years and will be with us forever.

Single sources of data are useful ensembles of multi-source integrated data that is much more valuable and useful. Data is being generated at a staggering pace. Bernard Marr commented in Forbes:

> *"The amount of data we produce every day is truly mind-boggling. There are 2.5 quintillion bytes of data created each day at our current pace, but that pace is only accelerating with the growth of the Internet of Things (IoT). Over the last 2 years alone, 90 percent of the data in the world was generated." [3]*

If 90% of the world's data was generated in the last 2 years, that means that we have an issue with immediate data overwhelming historical data. Do we need every reading from a light bulb indicating that it is on? Probably not.

We have the ability to store nearly an infinite amount of data. We can compress it, split it up, and store it in sophisticated management systems, but it is likely that we do not need to retain all of this information. We can ascertain patterns and insights from the masses of data that we are creating and store those aggregations of data and then receive just as much value from them as from the raw data.

The value of data

Data is a valuable asset. Doug Laney was the first to write a best-selling book on the theory and science of valuing data. Doug's book, *Infonomics*, [4] lays the groundwork for understanding the value of data, how to account for it in the financial system, and how to think about data as an asset with financial value. Doug does a masterful job in his book of laying out the what, why, where, and how of valuing data. It is common for people to say, "Data is the new oil." There are so many elements and backing beliefs behind that statement that are wrong and misleading. I recommend that you buy or borrow Doug's book to learn more about the true value of data.

Organizations of all types – corporations, governments, academic and research institutions, market research firms, and more – are becoming more and more aware of the value of data. Newly founded service firms are offering valuation services to their client companies to undertake an assessment to determine the book or financial value of internal data assets, as well as to determine if those data assets can be a new source of revenue for the firm that possesses and owns the data. These new service firms are offering a buy and lease back option to their clients. The clients that own and use the data in question to run their business would sell the ownership of their data to a data broker or the new services firm, and then license the rights to use the data in their own business from the data broker. This is an interesting new way to raise cash in the short term.

I have not seen this approach being widely adopted, but I do not doubt that it will be an offer that gains traction. Businesses are moving from data being considered a cost center to a revenue center.

An increasing number of organizations will view their data as an asset, and they will begin exploring methods of monetizing their data by licensing the data themselves or through data brokers. There have been a number of successful businesses built by licensing and leveraging data from specific markets and/or industries.

In the grocery and Consumer Packaged Goods ecosystem, **Nielsen** and **Information Resources, Inc.** (**IRI**) built their entire businesses on the data generated from grocery store point of sale systems. Catalina, SPINS, dunnhumby, Freeosk, and a number of other businesses have been created to generate, gather, and analyze data from this market.

Probably the most extreme example of data being a primary input, output, and value driver is Facebook. If Facebook had to pay for its raw material, that is, the data that all users type and upload into their systems, Facebook would be bankrupt or at least have a dramatically different business model and profit margin.

Historically, businesses like Google and Facebook did not and do not publicly talk about the fact that they rely on their communities and users "donating" their data to the companies, and the companies exploiting that data for their benefit. Google and Facebook have spent billions on lobbying, advertising, and messaging to ensure that the general public does not acknowledge that the widespread use of free data enables these companies to exist and flourish. New businesses like Oura and Kinsa are founded with the importance of data acknowledged and written into the business model and business plan. Those plans and models acknowledge the roles of their users, the value of data, privacy, and fair use and are starting to include the economic value of data.

Within the next 7 to 12 years, all new companies will have these rules, corporate structures, and approaches related to data and the use of data included as an active and acknowledged element of the corporate culture and business operations.

Just because the world wide web and the internet were designed to share data freely, and firms like Google and Facebook were founded to exploit this free sharing of data to the benefit of their corporate operations, management teams, and stockholders, doesn't mean the future needs to remain this way. We can still take back control of our data, and people are working on helping us to do so. Let's delve into the current efforts to take control of our personal data.

Personal control of data

Tim Berners-Lee, the creator of the world wide web, is working on a new company and approach to controlling, monetizing, and managing personal data. His project, **Solid**, is run from the **Massachusetts Institute of Technology** (**MIT**) and aims to enable everyone on the internet and web to own, control, and monetize their own data. [6]

Imagine what would happen to Google and Facebook if they had to pay you, and every person in the world, that shared a piece of data with their systems. You like a post, they pay you. You put in a review of a restaurant, they have to pay you. You complain about your dry cleaning service or a hotel, they pay you. Changes the dynamic, doesn't it? This is the world that Solid is working to bring about.

Think about it – you can protect your children. All their data would be under your and their control. They do not start out by having a profile built about them by other firms unless you allow it. The data that you and your children share is monetized for your benefit, and the money ends up in your account. You and they get paid when you share data.

My children are young adults, but when they were pre-teens, they were playing an online game. The game seemed harmless; they had small, cute characters that collaborated, built houses, furnished the houses, visited each other, and generally were a lovely community. While eating dinner, over the span of a few months, my wife and I inquired about the game, the characters, why the kids enjoyed the game, and the economic model. Both kids said, "there is no economic model, the game is free." Jennifer and I explained that the company, which produced the game, had to make money in some way and even though the children did not contribute money through a subscription fee, they were contributing their data – age, sex, interests, and so on – to the company so that the company could sell the data to firms that were interested in targeting them to sell them toys, food, candy, clothing, movies, and more. The children immediately understood this exchange and business model. We discussed it at length, and both thought that it was unfair for the company to ask for their data without disclosing the extent of its use and purpose.

Beyond protecting children from the beginning, you can decide who you sell your data to. Don't like what certain firms or industries do to society or the environment? Don't sell them access to your data. Alternatively, if you want them to have access, charge them double or triple of what you would charge the other companies. You support what other firms do and their mission, so perhaps you give them access to your purchasing history and browsing data at a reduced rate because you want to support them and their operations.

We, as a global society, need to have every adult and child understand the impact of being aware of the value of data, as well as the impact of controlling our data and monetizing the data for our personal gain.

Control over your data is an incredible concept and one that should have been built into the internet, but none of us were smart enough to see that far out.

Most people say it is too late to provide personal control of data. Data has a shelf life. If all the new data or even a meaningful portion of newly generated data came under personal control, it would make an economic difference.

Remember, most of the people who are saying that personal control of data is not possible and not needed are paid by internet/ media companies. Don't listen to them; it is never too late to enact change, and this is coming within the next decade or so.

Data brokers and intermediaries

Data brokers have tried to be all things to all people by indiscriminately collecting and storing all sorts of free, unrelated data. However, this approach has failed.

The vast majority of people agree that data is valuable, but data needs to be delivered and leveraged in a relevant context. Grocery store point of sale data has limited to no value to an oil and gas company trying to understand the geological formations in an area where they intend to drill for new sources of oil and gas.

In the very near future – almost immediately, as a matter of fact – data will be traded and sold as an asset much more widely than it is today. Data brokers of all types are becoming part of the market economy. The data brokers that will be most successful in the short term will be those that focus on a market, an industry, a process type, an asset class, or an analytical problem.

Data brokers will collect and catalog data and act as a clearing house; these activities will be the base of the data broker's value proposition and business model. As we discussed earlier, AI requires massive amounts of known or labeled data. The base line of this type of clearing house or data brokers will be firms that possess and sell vast libraries of data, images, and video footage. Images – muffins, dogs, school busses, road signs, buildings, mail trucks, and more – will also be cleaned, organized, and labeled for use in training AI models.

Data brokers will move up the value chain by integrating data as a standard offering. They will also integrate data on a custom basis for paying clients, and data brokers will add value by offering analytical services to synthesize and create new metrics and measurements from the integrated data that they manage.

Data is an important ingredient in the analytics equation. Machine learning algorithms perform with increasing accuracy with more high quality, relevant, clean, and integrated data that is fed into them.

Now that we have outlined the framework of data and how data is a critical raw material and input into the analytics process, let's discuss the future of AI. If data is the raw material in the analytics process, then AI is the factory of machinery in the analytics process.

AI today

As we have discussed in this book, mankind has been attempting to build humanoid forms and robots that either mimic or extend human intelligence for thousands of years. The first known recorded instance of the creation and demonstration of a humanoid invention is 976 BC, in the court of King Mu of the Zhou dynasty, in what is now known as China. [5]

The term *artificial intelligence* was coined in 1956 at Dartmouth College. [7] Since the founding of the field, we have seen the inventions progress along a development path of playing checkers, to chess, to Jeopardy!, to Go and AlphaGo, and to selected massive online multiplayer games where AI teams compete with human teams and win.

The field of AI has made impressive leaps and bounds in the last 10 years. I am certain that part of the reason that you are reading this book is due to the unmitigated success and widespread interest within the field.

The field of AI owes much and most of its success to the advancements related to neural networks. There have been numerous books written on the many techniques and technological innovations related to neural networks. I am tempted to start listing the major advancements due to the excitement I feel when I think, write, and talk about those recent inventions and innovations, but I will spare you the pain of wading through a geek out session in the middle of this final chapter.

If you are intrigued by **convolutional neural networks** or the functioning of **Long Short-Term Memory**, or any of the other very interesting developments, then head over to your favorite search engine and find a couple books that will provide you with the technical depth and knowledge that you seek. Then, you can immerse yourself in the world of neural networks.

There is no questioning the advances and successes of AI, but we must recognize that these early applications are limited due to the fact that we, as an industry, have not developed a wide base of technology to broaden our solution approaches to the problems that we can address and solve. Neural networks have expanded with the development of a significant number of supporting and related innovations, but as a field, we have not developed multiple techniques and algorithms to broaden our approach to developing and delivering a diverse set of solutions.

Gary Marcus has been a vocal critic of the narrow focus of AI and its reliance on neural networks. Marcus and his co-author, Ernest Davis, in their book, *Rebooting AI*, outline the steps AI researchers and practitioners must take to achieve a truly robust AI. The authors explain that, "creating an intelligence that rivals or exceeds human levels is far more complicated than we have been led to believe."

Marcus and Davis argue that a computer beating a human in Jeopardy! does not signal that we are on the doorstep of fully autonomous cars or super intelligent machines. The achievements in the field thus far have occurred in closed systems with fixed sets of rules, and these approaches are too narrow to achieve genuine intelligence. However, if we focus on endowing machines with common sense and deep understanding, rather than simply focusing on statistical analysis and gathering ever-larger collections of data, we will be able to create an AI we can trust – "in our homes, our cars, and our doctors' offices." [8]

Neural networks will continue to improve, expand, and deliver value, but AI will truly start to evolve and develop in a meaningful way when researchers, academics, and innovators create new algorithms and mathematical treatments that will enable us to train an ensemble of models to act in concert. This will help provide machines with a deeper understanding of the real world and the nuances that humans take into account in a matter of seconds.

I am a firm believer that we will develop these new technologies and mathematics. I can start to see early stages of these innovations now, but we are years away from those innovations delivering on their promise.

It is clear, to me, that the approach of using a collection or pipeline of an ensemble of models is the future of AI. IBM's Watson and Pattern Computer's software architecture are early implementations of this architectural model. Both of these systems are impressive but in the early stages of fully developing their capabilities.

My view is that the continued and future development of these solutions will automate and expand the ability of these systems to ingest immense amounts of data, clean and prepare the data, and automatically select the path and recursion of the data through a series of mathematical treatments, including reduction, expansion, feature engineering, feature selection, modeling, scoring, and delivering actionable results.

In some cases, results will be delivered in a matter of seconds, in the way that Watson participates in Jeopardy!, while in other use cases, the results will be developed and delivered in hours, or days, depending on the complexity of the data, the answers required, and the need for the ability to examine the logic behind the suggested or predicted answer or data.

As with most innovations in computer science and software engineering, we will look back and be amazed at how many interrelated innovations were required to arrive at autonomous, highly performant, accurate AI that operate in our daily lives to deliver outcomes like fully autonomous driving and optimized energy consumption in homes, factories, and data centers. We will also be amazed at how limited our view was as we traveled along the journey, and we will also find out what unintended consequences will come about due to the delivery of these innovations to the global population.

This type of development is proceeding in an active manner. Every industry can benefit from the innovations and advancements that will be developed in this area, but one that seems imminently promising is analyzing the genetic code of difficult to treat cancers, or even the RNA of novel viruses, and searching the existing pools of known chemicals and drugs that can be used to relieve or eliminate the harmful effects of these diseases in people. The world as a whole possesses and manages an impressive array of drugs that have been developed, but we do not do a very good job of matching those drugs and chemicals to disease-causing genetic codes. If we did a better job of this matching – and we can through AI – we would see an improvement in the quality of life for many people. We will see more advancements in these areas in the next 2 to 5 years.

What are some of the areas of development that need to experience meaningful progress for society to realize the benefits of these technologies and the solutions developed from them?

Training AI models

The current state of AI models, or to be more precise, neural network-based models, requires a tremendous amount of training data and computing resources. As an example, image analysis was, and remains, an early use case for AI. Researchers and practitioners trained and continue to train models to recognize faces, road signs, school buses, animals, landscapes, houses, and more. The models were built to differentiate between categories of, or individual, images. One of the most famous examples was to delineate between a blueberry muffin and a dog that was a pug. When you look at a collection of the two sets of images, you can see why this is a good image recognition challenge.

When training any neural network model, more data is better. In the image analysis examples provided previously, the researchers and practitioners fed millions, and in some cases billions, of labeled datasets into the models. It is challenging to find clean, labeled data in these volumes in the real world. Currently, neural network models need this level of training data to achieve commercially viable levels of accuracy in their predictions. Not only does the access, and rights to obtain and use, these numbers of images, transactions, or other illustrations of real-world phenomena limit the areas of applicability to the organizations and individuals who have access to billions or trillions of images, video feeds, transactions, and more to train the models, but another challenge is paying for the compute time and cycles needed at the scale required to process the data and train the models is a significant hurdle to all but the largest of firms.

A side effect of this activity being executed by numerous companies and governments globally is that the compute cycles needed are on an astronomical scale. It has been estimated that the energy consumption required for training predictive models and the pollution associated with it has a measurable effect on global warming. This has not been proven or systematically studied, but it is logical and makes perfect sense by simply looking at the consumption and usage patterns.

Given that training AI models requires massive amounts of data, costs a significant amount to obtain the access and rights to use the data, the data is required multiple times, the computing resources are substantial and costs, and there is a possibility that the activity contributes in a meaningful way to global pollution, we need to find a better way to train our models.

Paul R. Daugherty, Accenture's chief technology and innovation officer, and his co-authors H. James Wilson and Chase Davenport, assert in a recent article in the *Harvard Business Review* that:

> *"Companies considering how to invest in AI capabilities should first understand that, over the coming 5 years, applications and machines will become less artificial and more intelligent. They will rely less on bottom-up big data and more on top-down reasoning that more closely resembles the way humans approach problems and tasks. This general reasoning ability will enable AI to be more broadly applied than ever, creating opportunities for early adopters even in businesses and activities to which it previously seemed unsuited."* [9]

This is the same or similar argument that Marcus and Davis are making in *Rebooting AI*. We, in the field of computer science, need to make AI less artificial and more intelligent. We need to, and researchers are doing this expand the reasoning capabilities of our software through data modeling, mathematical treatments, and approaches in order to have a more broad-based nuanced approach to developing answers, solutions, and predictions.

Similar to our discussion earlier where we stated that we do not serve our children and students by teaching them through singular methods like rote memorization, we do not develop or deliver broad-based, flexible solutions by relying on narrow, single-track solutions aided or trained in massive amounts of single type data. Our approaches must be, and are, evolving.

As Mr. Daugherty of Accenture and his co-authors assert, we will see the training of AI systems and models move away from the brute-force model of the recent past to a broader, more nuanced approach. It has been interesting to watch, listen, and participate in this movement and discussion.

One area that has been fascinating to observe is the proponents of ethical data use and the demise of personal privacy through the widespread use of massive data to train AI-based models and applications. When the commentators then turn to the researchers and developers of new solutions to discuss their position on using large amounts of data, and the resulting problems we have discussed in this section, for the most part, the collective response from the research community has been "you are right, we need to use less data," and we are moving in that direction. The ethics researchers and press observers need to catch up on this topic in this regard.

While AI is moving in a direction that will mitigate some of the negative side effects we have outlined, there are still core issues that need to be addressed. Beyond the need to use less data, rely less on a narrow field of math and computer science, and to not contribute to global warming, one of the most significant challenges is the opaque nature of neural network operations and predictions.

Let's examine how the ability for people to be able to examine, analyze, understand, and transparently explain how AI arrives at predictions and decisions can be developed, as well as the importance of how and why this needs to be developed and widely available.

Explainable AI

At a very high level, conceptually, neural networks work by ingesting data into the input layer. The input layer passes data elements to a processing or hidden layer. There can be hundreds, thousands, millions, or more processing/hidden layers consisting of hundreds, thousands, millions, and maybe more individual processing nodes.

All of the layers are connected and all of the nodes from within each layer are connected in a forward and backward direction to the layers and nodes to the left and right of it. See *Figure 10.1* for a high-level depiction of a neural network.

All neural networks need to be built and the initial weights need to be associated with each connection between the nodes and layers. These all need to be set with a starting value. This value setting exercise is an art that is evolving, and the industry and leading practitioners are refining this process. There are numerous research papers describing the wide range of value setting strategies that are being developed. If you are curious about this and interested in learning more, I suggest that you engage in a research process to find the theories and models that work with your views on how to initialize the starting state of a neural network.

If the weights are set in a manner that are too far from reality, it will take a significant amount of time for the weights to converge in the training phase. And if the weights are impractically far away from reality, the network may never be able to be trained. If this is the case, the input data will be fed into the initialized network on a continuous basis, but the connection weights will not converge to produce meaningful predictions or results.

As data is fed into the network with layers and nodes, estimates are made from the new input data that is ingested. Those new readings are compared to the estimates and actual readings of the data that the node had read and stored previously. During the training phase, the difference between the previous data and the new data, the error term, is used to adjust the weights so they are more in line with the new and old data. This process is repeated millions to billions of times.

The data is fed into the network in a forward mode called the **feedforward** process. The results can also be fed into the network in a backward mode. This process is referred to as **backpropagation**.

Backpropagation is a process where results are fed into the network in a backward direction to, again, compare the expected results with actual results and adjust the weights to reduce the error term of that connection.

The input data and results can be fed forward and backward as many times as needed (or wanted) to train the network to realistically predict the desired outcome. The desired outcome may be to recognize pre-cancerous cell structures in mammogram images, to predict the level or outcome of a complex production process, the resulting flame in an energy processing plant, or a plethora of other operational activities that can benefit from being accurately predicted from the numerous, fast changing input factors available:

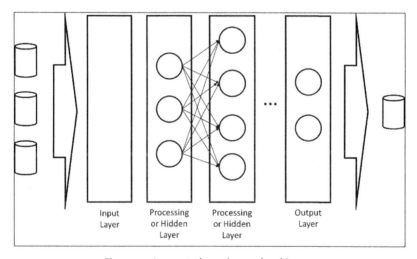

Figure 10.1: A conceptual neural network architecture

As you may have guessed, or intuited, or read, this process of feeding data into the model and results back into the model refines the ability of the model to predict at an increasing rate of accuracy.

However, given the possibly millions, billions, or trillions of adjustments of the weights between the nodes and layers, it is impossible to explain how the network or model composes the aggregate result from the multiplicity of factors that are working in an interrelated manner. This is a problem where decisions need to be explained.

Decisions are required to be explained in a number of cases. Many of them are related to activities that are regulated by governments. Decisions related to granting credit are closely monitored and regulated to ensure that individuals and small businesses are not disadvantaged by restrictive, regressive, or discriminatory practices in granting loans and access to credit.

Decisions that people or firms make about investing their own money – not the money of their customers – where there is no responsibility to reduce the risk of others and that the primary motivation is to optimize growth or obtain the maximum return and where the activity is not illegal or immoral, firms and individuals can use the most accurate and most powerful tools to predict what a market will do at any time, and then use those results and that advice to drive their decisions without concern of intervention from the government. Being able to explain the detailed reasoning and combination of factors that came together to make that decision will be nearly impossible, but in these cases, there is no responsibility or duty to explain the decisions, especially if those decisions result in a positive outcome.

Neural networks, as well as the models built using this approach, are very powerful and very useful in applications as diverse as military campaigns where decisions need to be made in selecting sites for building a new facility. As we have discussed, they are very powerful and quite accurate, but completely opaque in the operation and refinement of how decisions and results are produced. In some cases, this is fine, but increasingly, people and organizations are not willing to blindly accept what a neural network produces as a recommendation or decision.

Work is underway to augment core neural network models with the ability to track when, and how, the weights and internal scores are changed in the training phase of model building and refinement. Tracking these changes and the use of that information can be developed into models and explanatory materials that begin to provide insight into how and why a neural network arrives at decisions and recommendations. These innovations are within the further and continued development of the neural network environment.

There is also work underway with a wide range of researchers contributing to the effort of building supporting models and environments that can examine a neural network, extract information from the network, and analyze the information to produce explanatory materials that provide insight into the operations of the neural network.

Another related effort is to take the neural network and transform the neural network into a derivative structure that is easier to explain and understand. One of these efforts is to transform a neural network into a **decision tree**. Decision trees are easy to read and allow us to understand how decisions and recommendations are made.

There are similar efforts being made to convert neural networks into a set of rules. Rules engines were one of the precursors to neural networks in decision sciences. Rules engines proved to be very successful in the internet boom of the late 90s and early 2000s for producing recommendation engines for companies like Amazon, Netflix, and others. However, rules engines proved to be rigid, hard to scale, and difficult to expand to related areas. However, they were also completely transparent in terms of how decisions were made and recommendations were produced. The combination of the flexibility, power, and ability to scale a neural network combined with the explanatory power of a rules architecture is very attractive to a wide range of industries, markets, and governments.

Why is this important? For a number of reasons, including the following.

Currently, we cannot use AI models in most regulated industries. AI-based models produce the most accurate predictions, but the results cannot be adequately explained. We are losing productivity and profitability because we cannot use the best technology to obtain the optimal result in business operations.

Beyond regulated industries, other firms and markets refuse to use AI-based models, just in case they are asked to transparently explain the decisions that they and their managers took based on AI-based inputs. It is impossible to know how many managers and companies operate in this manner, but I have met many of them in my travels around the world.

In addition, opaque models do not help us in adding to our understanding of the phenomena being analyzed by the AI models. We, as analytics professionals, want to know why the combination of factors come together to deliver a better diagnosis, or why the combination of air, fuel, and environmental factors are optimal for energy production. We want to know why we have arrived at this level of optimization so we can begin to work on delivering the next level of optimization. One of the great things about analytics and math is that the quest for improvement never ends, but it is slowed down when we cannot extract insights from opaque models.

In my view, the efforts outlined here, as well as the efforts that we are unaware of at the current time, will produce commercially and widely available explainable AI in the next 2 to 5 years.

Quantum computing and AI

Quantum computers are fascinating for a number of reasons. These are the three that I think about the most:

- The ability of a machine to calculate and manage an infinite number of states for each elemental unit of measurement, beyond the standard options of 1 and 0, is mind-boggling.

- It is equally mind expanding to think that individual quantum operations or calculations can be deferred in the computing or calculating sequence until later in the process, with intermediate calculations being resolved at the end, or near the end, of the process.

- Also, something that's amazing is that the entire calculation process can, and does, dissolve into the complete loss of the calculation process due to the loss of coherence in the system in the middle of a process.

"Quantum computing began in the early 1980s, when physicist Paul Benioff proposed a quantum mechanical model of the Turing machine. Richard Feynman and Yuri Manin later suggested that a quantum computer had the potential to simulate things that a classical computer could not. Despite ongoing experimental progress since the late 1990s, most researchers believe that fault-tolerant quantum computing [is] still a rather distant dream". [10]

When quantum computing started being discussed, I was fascinated by, and remain to be, with the topic. I have read research papers, scholarly articles, journal submissions, marketing materials, and other sources of information and have had the pleasure of meeting a few of the innovators and inventors involved in making quantum computing a reality.

The use cases for quantum computers include, but are not limited to, cryptography, search, simulation, subsets of optimization, solving linear equations, and a number of other very specialized mathematical problems. [11]

In 2019, a leading firm offered my group time on a quantum computer to solve one of our advanced analytics challenges. Once we learned the class of problems that are best suited for the machine, we did not have any challenges that fit into those categories.

I often hear people talking about when quantum computers will replace traditional computers. That is not the way to think about this exciting, yet evolving, computing architecture. Traditional computers are not going to be replaced by quantum computers.

Traditional computers will be extended with novel chip architectures like **central processing units (CPUs)** that have been augmented by **graphics processing units (GPUs)** and **tensor processing units (TPUs)**. The extension of traditional computing architectures has decades, if not more, to run before it sees any diminishment in applying it productively to our most pressing computational problems and challenges.

In my view, quantum computers will be refined, improved, and extended. The recent paper, *Quantum Supremacy Using a Programmable Superconducting Processor*, published by Google claims quantum supremacy has yet to be proven to be valid. [12] Certainly, IBM took exception to the paper, commenting that Google had done nothing special and that the Summit supercomputer that IBM had installed at the Oak Ridge National Laboratory could produce the same result in 2.5 days. [13]

For all the positive and negative coverage of Google's announcement, one thing is clear to me: the field of quantum computing is alive, well, and moving forward, which, for me, is reason to celebrate.

We are uncertain about the types of problems that quantum computers will ultimately solve and prove to be supreme in solving. We do not know when quantum computers will work in a mode where we can rely on them as part of the global computing infrastructure, providing insights and information that we can rely on to make decisions on vexing questions.

We do know that the scale and scope of potential improvement is game changing. If a quantum computer can provide reliable and repeatable answers to immensely challenging problems in the span of seconds to minutes, rather than the estimated time of 10,000 to 100,00 years on a traditional computer, isn't it worth the time, effort, and cost of a few of our best and brightest computer scientists and researchers to make this a reality? I believe that it is and is fun for the researchers to work on a problem of this magnitude.

In my opinion, we will not see reliable quantum computers operating in commercial environments for enterprise class corporations as part of those corporation's typical computing environments in my lifetime (unless I live to be incredibly old). I expect we are 40 to 50 years away from this kind of widespread implementation of quantum computers for commercial use, either in the data centers of large corporations or as elements of the cloud services offered to large corporations.

I do expect that quantum computers from Google, IBM, D-Wave, and other firms will continue to be used as they are today in attempting to solve very challenging problems. We will see interesting announcements of incremental results and improvements over time, but I do not expect any developments that will increase the level of reliability and widespread use in scientific, research, or commercial applications for at least 10 years.

To be clear, we will hear announcements like the one from Google over the next few years. Announcements will involve theoretical breakthroughs and interesting tests and results that may be difficult to impossible to validate and reproduce. We will see and be excited by these on a regular basis – at least, I hope we will.

Quantum computers will continue to develop, and we will see interesting results immediately. Commercial success and use are in the distant future.

Our final topic is one that garners significant press attention and seems to enthrall every high school class I interact with: **Artificial General Intelligence (AGI)**. When will computers be as smart or smarter than people? Let's delve into this.

Artificial General Intelligence

Humans are simultaneously fascinated and abhorred by the prospect of building human-level intelligence into a non-human creation or innovation. Books, movies, research papers, inventions, and countless hours have been dedicated to creating human-like intelligence. There truly seems to be equal measures of wonder and terror in the idea.

In almost every high school class I have spoken with and to over the past 10 years, this topic is raised. Typically, a student raises the subject and a lively and wide-ranging discussion ensues. The conversation has evolved over that time period, but where we have landed over the past couple years is that the students want to know when AGI can be used to improve live battlefield operations (that is, killer drones), as well as first person shooter games, and another group of students want to know when AGI will be able to lessen the harmful effects of global warming and the problems related to food distribution, leading to global hunger. There you have it. I believe that these two poles of unmodulated teenage interest are instructive.

One of my take-aways from this completely unscientific, uncontrolled market research experiment is that when young, impressionable minds are given unrestricted permission to ask about any aspect of AGI, these are the topics that they care about, think about, and are fascinated by. I find that interesting.

In almost every public speaking engagement, no matter if it is a public event or a closed company meeting with more than 10 participants, the topic that is raised without fail is, if and when, we as the human race, will be beset by something similar to SkyNet from the Terminator movie franchise. Adults truly want to know if computer systems and networks can and will become sentient or self-aware beings. The short answer is no, they will not, and most likely cannot, not as long as people with the level of intelligence we, as a human race, possess at this time, are programming and building the systems in question. It is highly unlikely that we *can* create a self-aware AGI computer system or network.

Someone than typically rebuts my assertion explaining that with the evolution of ubiquitous data, quantum computers, neural networks, brain implants, and other unforeseen developments, how can I be so sure that AGI is not within the grasp of the human race in the next few years.

I further explain that data is ubiquitous but also unorganized, disparate, and rarely integrated, so currently quantum computers can only maintain a state of coherence for subsecond time frames, and neural networks can suggest the next movie we might want to watch, but that is about as far as intelligence goes at this point in time, and calling that intelligence can be debated.

Also, I like to point out to my audiences and attendees that the billionaires who are the most vocal naysayers and Cassandras relating to the topic of AGI are also the most aggressive investors in AI technologies today. Perhaps there is a conflict of interest in their public statements and their investment strategies. I would completely ignore their warnings of doom and gloom and subjugation of the human race by our supposed machine overlords. I also like to point out that these systems are computers and computer networks, so if humans are that concerned about what the computers are doing, we can just shut off the power.

In science fiction movies, the plot typically has a part where the humans try to turn off the power, but the machine is too smart and outwits the hapless humans. This is not realistic by any stretch of the imagination.

Before we move past the movie scenarios and the visions of killer humanoid robots from the future, indulge me in one more diversion. I am always surprised that people want to talk about the possible doomsday brought on by AGI, but no one ever brings up the fact that killer robots can time travel. That is the development that fascinates me, but everyone suspends disbelief on that topic. Again, interesting.

Ok, let's discuss AGI as a future development. I can, and do, feel very comfortable predicting with a high degree of confidence that my descriptions of proposed scenarios, technological developments, and topics related to data and analytics can and will be accurate up to 10 to 20 years into the future.

My view of AGI is that we will see the rudimentary operations of AGI beginning to be exposed in early-stage research and scientific journals, the same way we see the developments of quantum computers today, in the year 2150. Given that this book will be published in the year 2020, that is 130 years from now. Two and half generations from now, AGI will be just getting off the ground and out of the lab.

This timeline is hugely disappointing for some, and most of them will reject this idea, given that it does not align with their hopes and dreams of a benevolent AGI environment. For others, they are greatly comforted that they and their children, as well as their children, will not be running from the tyrannical and destructive reign of the robots.

People have great capacity for imagination. That is one of the incredible strengths of the human race and one of the reasons why we will not go lightly into the AGI debate and development cycle.

Students ask me how long it will take to develop Jarvis, the AI support system from the Iron Man and Avengers movies. I explain that it has taken years to develop Siri and Alexa, and all they do is look things up. Taking complex voice input in very chaotic environments related to fast moving, integrated systems, and then developing a coherent response while reconfiguring complex systems with infallible accuracy... that is going to take some time. I always reply that it will not happen in their lifetime. Universally, this is a disappointing answer for the high school students.

AGI will come, but it's likely that we won't be here to see it.

Today, we are failing

In the US, we need to change the way we teach **Science, Technology, Engineering, and Math** (**STEM**). We are failing our children. I know, because the system failed me or I failed to perform in the system – either way, the result is the same.

When I was 12, my father died. He died in front of me. It was him and me, alone. I ran and got help, but it was too late. That was a tough day.

I was stressed, and my schoolwork suffered. I lost my way in math and never recovered. I struggled with math in academic settings from then on. Eventually, I made it through high school, undergraduate school, and through trigonometry in graduate school. I passed all my exams and classes, but it was always an anxiety-producing experience.

From high school, I could never catch up. I couldn't understand what the teachers were talking about, but I could see how to arrive at the answers. I developed my own intuitive approach to every math class. I arrived at the right point in the end, but most of the time, I took a different route to get there. I cannot even explain it well to this day, but I can look at problems and derive the correct or nearly correct answer most of the time.

This approach was not well received or well graded by some teachers. In the moment, it continued to cause me stress and anxiety, but in the end, I decided that I didn't care what those teachers thought or how they graded my work. I learned how to arrive at the required answer and figured out how to use those answers for practical purposes.

This is a great deal of work and stress for one person to undertake; most children and young adults will not persevere through this. I had to; I had no other options that I could see or access, but why should they? It is the responsibility of parents and teachers to teach children and young adults, not torture them to gather an understanding of a topic.

The way we teach STEM courses from primary school to graduate schools needs to change. We need families; governments at the local, state, and the federal level; teachers; academic administrators; and business leaders to work together to design and implement this change. There are few challenges that are more important and that will have the same or similar long-term positive effect on our world and society as a whole.

Last night, I spent an hour debugging code with my daughter. She was frustrated and was coming up to a deadline. It seemed like I did little, but shortly after that hour, she found the two remaining errors and her code worked flawlessly. She submitted her programs on time and with complete functionality required in the assignment.

It would have been easier for me to grab dinner, sit down, and watch television and hope that she figured it out, but even though I have not actively coded for decades, I know how to think critically and support her efforts in combing through the code looking for logic and syntax errors. In the end, we laughed, tried silly ideas, and had fun while sitting shoulder to shoulder looking at her programs. Not only did I help, but I had a great time with my adult daughter.

I have been working on this issue for over 20 years and expect I will continue to do so the rest of my life. We need everyone to join in this movement. Volunteer at the local high school, attend school board meetings, meet with your elected officials, be a tutor, work with universities.

All your efforts, large and small, will have an impact. Jump into the game today. You will be glad that you did. You will enjoy it and have a sense of wellbeing for your efforts. And beyond all the good feelings, you will be helping our children have a better, more fulfilling life, and at a larger level, you will be part of building a better, more well-adjusted, intelligent society.

Whatever distraction that you think you want to engage in rather than actively making a difference can wait. The recording of your favorite television program will still be there later, or you can stream it at any time. The time to help is now.

Teaching children to love numbers, patterns, and math

I met Dean Kamen in Chicago when he came to speak at an event. I remember him talking about one of his organizations, **For Inspiration and Recognition of Science and Technology** (**FIRST**). [1] Dean spoke about how he wanted to see the United States inspiring children to aspire to be scientists and researchers the way we inspire children to throw, bounce, or shoot a ball.

His position and remarks made, and make, so much sense to me. I never did, and do not, understand the obsession with sports figures and other celebrities. The time and interest on the part of the general public for celebrities and sporting events always seemed misguided and a waste of time and effort. We spend significantly more time watching reality television programs and sporting events than we do helping our children succeed in school. In what world does that make sense?

In the US, we have such a pervasive view that the majority of the population does not like math and is not good at math. This is not true. We teach math in a way that alienates most people. I am not an instructional designer, but I have taught classes at the undergraduate level, I have guest lectured at the graduate level, and I have volunteered at the high school level to talk about STEM-related topics and education for over 10 years. I can guarantee that if we focused on the issue, we can change the math curriculum in a way that makes learning math fun and engaging for all children from preschool to graduate school.

We need to start with families. Parents need access to the resources, skills, and support so they feel comfortable and empowered to guide their children to enroll in elective STEM classes. We also need to make those same parents feel confident enough that if they cannot support their children through their own skills and abilities, they can find and afford the outside resources to support the skills development process of their children.

As our children progressed through high school, my wife, Jennifer, and I encouraged them to take Advanced Placement math classes, knowing that if they wanted to attend top universities in engineering and/or computer science, which both did, they would need a solid, functional, and comprehensive base understanding of advanced math. They worked hard, spent time with their teachers after classes, did their homework, took practice tests, leveraged tutors, and learned the required math skills. I am certain that there were times where both of them wanted to drop out of those classes, but that was not an option. Our children knew that we, as their parents, expected them to succeed and complete these classes, and they rose to the occasion and performed brilliantly.

As a society, all of our children need to be literate in math, science, technology, and data. These are "meets minimum" skills for people who want to succeed in the future. Yes, even for our artistically oriented children, a basic understanding of math through algebra, the core sciences of chemistry, biology, and earth sciences, if not mandated by the school system, should be required by parents. One of the primary roles of a parent is to prepare children to be functioning adults. Core knowledge is power, and we need our children to possess and master this knowledge. We all need to step up and play that role.

I have worked with, for over 10 years, and I am actively working with our local high school – New Trier, University of Michigan, University of Illinois – and a handful of other universities to improve the curriculum, teaching methods, and approaches to engaging students at all levels to instill a curiosity and passion for learning STEM-related material and topics. This is not an issue that can be left to the schools to improve. This is a societal issue that we all need to engage in.

If you are a parent, grandparent, uncle, aunt, or a friend of people with children who are in the academic system, find ways and opportunities to talk about education. Talk to the children and young adults about their course work. Ask them about STEM classes, provide a positive view on these classes, the skills being taught, and the reasons why these skills are relevant to life today and tomorrow. You don't need to be dogmatic and you don't want to be overbearing, but instead of saying something like, "Math is hard. Everyone hates math," you can say, "Math is interesting. I use it every day. I found math challenging in school, but I am so glad that I stuck it out and learned skills that I use every day."

Our words are powerful. Children watch, learn, and internalize everything that they hear. Let's help them embrace the powers of critical thinking and subjects like math that will help them develop these core faculties.

Blending rote memorization with critical thinking as a teaching paradigm

In fifth grade, I recall the teacher barking multiplication problems at the class and expecting us to write down answers at a rate of about one answer every 5 to 7 seconds. I did not enjoy this, and I am quite sure this is where I started to fall away from math as a subject of interest. I remember looking at Mr. Pabst and really disliking him, his crew cut, and his drug store aftershave.

Teaching children to memorize things is not the same as learning. I understand that there are base elements of all subjects that are useful to memorize, and the multiplication tables may be one of those useful bits of data, but memorization cannot be the end goal of teaching a subject. Well, it can be, but our children are not well served by this approach and method.

Even as I was failing to learn symbolic math and traditional mathematics, I was working diligently to hone my logic, reasoning, and critical thinking skills. It is intriguing to think that I was inept at higher level math but I excelled at programming and coding.

Ferris State University, my undergraduate alma mater, had a path through the Computer Science program that emphasized logic and critical thinking in place of traditional mathematics. I am certain that without this alternate path, I would have flunked out of college.

Not everyone is a math acolyte, no one is a well-rounded person for memorizing tables of numbers, but all people can memorize what they need, and they can find and be taught to reason, think, and decide among a multitude of options.

My main point is that we are all individuals, we all learn in a wide range of styles, and we can all excel in left and right brain activities. However, to do so, we need an educational system and a parental view for each and every person to learn and reach their potential. Not an easy task, but it is obtainable.

It is obtainable, but the federal, state, and local governments, parents, academic administrators, teachers, professors, and students all need to be active participants in making our society function at a higher level of producing more engaged and enlightened citizens. Isn't that what we want?

I am sure that you have gotten the point. Our educational systems and methods need to change, expand, and improve, and we need to be part of that change.

Let's move on from what we need to do today to have a brighter and better future to what the future will hold for us in the areas of data, analytics, AI, technology, computing, and more.

Summary

First of all, let me say thank you. Thank you for investing your time, energy, and interest in reading this book.

Before I started writing this book, I had multiple people tell me that this book might not be a book that someone would sit down and read cover to cover in a short period of time.

The first time I was told this, my heart sank because I translated the feedback into a subtle way of saying that there would be little to no interest in the book, but as I asked further questions and the dialog developed, people were saying that they felt that the book would be read in parts as people had areas of interest in creating an analytics function in a corporate environment, and that the readers would use the book more as a reference guide over time to gain knowledge of how to approach a task or challenge. The readers would then keep the book on their bookshelf to refer to over time. That feedback raised my level of excitement and engagement in writing this book. I do hope that you have found this book instructive and useful. As I remarked earlier in this book, one of my goals was to write a book that has endurance and longevity and that the guidance and advice offered was and is applicable for decades to come.

I do believe that we are entering an era where data and analytics will be increasing in importance in all human endeavors. Certainly, corporate use of data and analytics will increase in importance, hence the focus of this book. However, beyond corporations, the active and engaged use of data and analytics will increase in importance and daily use in managing multiple aspects, including people's personal lives, academic pursuits, governmental policy, military operations, humanitarian aid, tailoring of products and services, building of roads, towns, and cities, planning of traffic patterns, provisioning of local federal and state services, intergovernmental relationships, and more. There will not be an element of human endeavor that will not be touched and changed by data and analytics.

Software, computers, computing networking, human/computer interfaces, user experience design, and all related fields are burgeoning in their need for diverse talent. Not only do we need core programmers and developers, but we need creative people who can – and will – design all aspects of the modeling, engagement, and interactions with this new data and analytically driven environments.

We will need unforeseen numbers of people to work on building these globally connected systems. As these systems recede into the background like our utility and telecommunication infrastructures have in the past, we will need more and more people working on extending and improving the computing services infrastructure, to the point of where the computing services is thought of in the same way as electricity and gas services are today – they will be taken for granted by future generations.

It takes a substantial amount of talent to build and maintain mission-critical infrastructure that the world's population relies upon on a daily basis. In this respect, I see no slack in the demand for new talent. If you want to be employed and want your children to be employed, expose them to the world of data and analytics.

Data and analytic systems have been thought of as a thing or system that needs to be built to provide backward-looking indicators of how we executed and measure the objective performance of our activities. This was the past. I am grateful for that view; it has provided me with a fulfilling and interesting start to my career. However, that view is of the past and it is fading away. Don't get me wrong, it is not fading that fast. Careers will still be made in developing a wide range of data and analytics systems, and those will be enjoyable and fulfilling, but the future demand will be for systems that predict, simulate, optimize, and facilitate a proactive forward-looking view of how to proceed in our endeavors.

Data and analytic-driven systems will automate and improve repetitive and rote operations. That is part of why it is important to not teach our children through these types of approaches, because these type of tasks and routines will be the domain of machines. To be clear, memorization as a tool is fine, but it should not be the cornerstone of how we teach any subject or curriculum.

People are very good at higher-level thinking and designing sophisticated environments that engage and enable humans to do more and see more. This is the domain of people.

We will use data and analytics to support and extend the ability of people to focus on our unique value-added abilities and capabilities.

I hope that you can see that we are just starting to scratch the surface of what can be done. Just scratching the surface presents some daunting challenges. This includes challenges in the areas of technology, executive management, seeing the larger vision, management of data, hiring and managing high performance analytics teams, and more.

If I had a chance to do it all over again, I would have either become an astronaut or I would have done the same thing that I did this time around. I love data and analytics and I cannot think of a better career path for me. As we discussed, I am endlessly fascinated by almost everything in the world, and I want to learn about each and every process that is out there. The best way to indulge that craving to learn is to engage with people who want to describe and explain their vision of how that part of their world can be improved through data and analytics. My voyeurism is fed by data and analytics, as well as my drive to build new systems that help people achieve their goals and objectives. This was facilitated by the process of utilizing data and analytics.

Recently, my wife, Jennifer, asked me to write down all the industries that I have worked in over the past 3 decades. The final list was 20 industries. I extended this list to include all the major analytical applications that I have had a hand in building and deploying. The extension of the original list exceeded 60 applications. What other career could anyone have a significant role in influencing 20 industries? Government or management consulting, maybe. I have dabbled in both – perhaps I will try one of those in the next lifetime.

For me, writing this book has been a pure joy. I have reveled in almost every minute of being at the keyboard and sharing my thoughts and ideas with you.

My sincere hope is that you find this book useful today as you embark on building an analytics function in your organization, as well as hiring and managing your own high-performance analytics team. I hope you also find this useful as a reference guide when you are facing challenges along your journey.

My best wishes to you for a safe, productive, and enjoyable journey into the world of data and analytics. I look forward to meeting you along the way.

Chapter 10 footnotes

1. *FIRSTL,* https://www.firstinspires.org/

2. *9 Things You May Not Know About the Ancient Sumerians, Evan Andrews, Updated*: Feb 5, 2019, Original: Dec 16, 2015: https://www.history.com/news/9-things-you-may-not-know-about-the-ancient-sumerians

3. *How Much Data Do We Create Every Day? The Mind-Blowing Stats Everyone Should Read, Bernard Marr, May 21, 2018*: https://www.forbes.com/sites/bernardmarr/2018/05/21/how-much-data-do-we-create-every-day-the-mind-blowing-stats-everyone-should-read/#598b0a1e60ba

4. *Infonomics: How to Monetize, Manage, and Measure Information as an Asset for Competitive Advantage, 1st Edition*: https://www.amazon.com/Infonomics-Monetize-Information-Competitive-Advantage/dp/1138090387

5. *King Mu of Zhou*: https://en.wikipedia.org/wiki/King_Mu_of_Zhou

6. *Solid,* https://solid.mit.edu/

7. *Dartmouth workshop:* `https://en.wikipedia.org/wiki/Dartmouth_workshop`

    (Solomonoff, R.J., *The Time Scale of Artificial Intelligence; Reflections on Social Effects, Human Systems Management, Vol 5 1985, Pp 149-153*, Moor, J., *The Dartmouth College Artificial Intelligence Conference: The Next Fifty years, AI Magazine, Vol 27, No., 4, Pp. 87-9, 2006*, Kline, Ronald R., *Cybernetics, Automata Studies and the Dartmouth Conference on Artificial Intelligence, IEEE Annals of the History of Computing, October–December, 2011, IEEE Computer Society*)

8. *Rebooting AI*, Gary Marcus and Ernest Davis: `https://www.penguinrandomhouse.com/books/603982/rebooting-ai-by-gary-marcus-and-ernest-davis/`

9. *The Future of AI Will Be About Less Data, Not More*, H. James Wilson, Paul R. Daugherty and Chase Davenport, January 14, 2019: `https://hbr.org/2019/01/the-future-of-ai-will-be-about-less-data-not-more`

10. *Quantum computing*, `https://en.wikipedia.org/wiki/Quantum_computing`

11. Ibid: `https://en.wikipedia.org/wiki/Quantum_computing`

12. *Quantum Supremacy Using a Programmable Superconducting Processor*, John Martinis, Chief Scientist Quantum Hardware and Sergio Boixo, Chief Scientist Quantum Computing Theory, Google AI Quantum, Wednesday, October 23, 2019: `https://ai.googleblog.com/2019/10/quantum-supremacy-using-programmable.html`

13. *Why Google's Quantum Supremacy Milestone Matters, Dr. Scott Aaronson*, Founding director of the Quantum Information Center at the University of Texas at Austin, October 30, 2019: `https://www.nytimes.com/2019/10/30/opinion/google-quantum-computer-sycamore.html`

OTHER BOOKS
YOU MAY ENJOY

If you enjoyed this book, you may be interested in this book by Packt:

The Successful Software Manager

Herman Fung

ISBN: 978-1-78961-553-1

- Decide if moving to management is right for you
- Develop the skills required for management
- Lead and manage successful software development projects
- Understand the various roles in a technical team and how to manage them

- Motivate and mentor your team

- Deliver successful training and presentations

- Lead the design process with storyboards and personas, and validate your solution

Artificial Intelligence with Python

Alberto Artasanchez

ISBN: 978-1-83921-953-5

- Understand what artificial intelligence, machine learning, and data science are
- Explore the most common artificial intelligence use cases
- Learn how to build a machine learning pipeline
- Assimilate the basics of feature selection and feature engineering
- Identify the differences between supervised and unsupervised learning
- Discover the most recent advances and tools offered for AI development in the cloud
- Develop automatic speech recognition systems and chatbots
- Apply AI algorithms to time series data

Leave a review - let other readers know what you think

Please share your thoughts on this book with others by leaving a review on the site that you bought it from. If you purchased the book from Amazon, please leave us an honest review on this book's Amazon page. This is vital so that other potential readers can see and use your unbiased opinion to make purchasing decisions, we can understand what our customers think about our products, and our authors can see your feedback on the title that they have worked with Packt to create. It will only take a few minutes of your time, but is valuable to other potential customers, our authors, and Packt. Thank you!

Index

W

Printed in Great Britain
by Amazon